Colin Wilson was born in Leicester in 1931. He left school at sixteen and spent several years working in a wool warehouse, a laboratory, a plastics factory and a coffee bar before *The Outsider* was published in 1956 to oustanding critical acclaim. Since then he has written many books on philosophy, the occult, crime and sexual deviance, plus a number of successful novels. His work includes *The Mammoth Book of True Crime*, *The Mammoth Book of the Supernatural*, *The Mind Parasites*, *New Pathways in Psychology*, and *The Occult*. Mr. Wilson is well known as a lecturer and radio and television personality. He lives in Cornwall.

Colin Wilson's True Crime File

MURDER

in the 1930s

Edited by Colin Wilson

Carroll & Graf Publishers Inc
New York

First published in Great Britain 1992
First Carroll & Graf edition 1992

Carroll & Graf Publishers, Inc.
260 Fifth Avenue
New York
NY 10001

ISBN: 0–88184-855-7

Printed in Great Britain.

10 9 8 7 6 5 4 3 2 1

Contents

Acknowledgements

The publishers would like to extend their grateful thanks to the following authors, publishers and others for kindly granting them permission to reproduce the copyrighted material included in this book. Every effort has been made to secure and clear copyrights and the publishers trust that their apologies will be accepted for any errors or omissions.

'Misapplied Ingenuity of a Bigamist: The Rouse Case' by F. A. Beaumont. Originally published in *The Fifty Most Amazing Crimes of the Last 100 Years*, Odhams, 1936.

'Man Hunters: The German Rouse Case' by F. A. Beaumont. Originally published in *The Fifty Most Amazing Crimes of the Last 100 years*, Odhams, 1936.

'The Otterburn Mystery' by Val Gielgud. Originally published in *Great Unsolved Crimes*, Hutchinson, n.d. Reprinted by permission of the author's estate.

'The Murder of Julia Wallace' by Dorothy L. Sayers. Originally published in *Great Unsolved Crimes*, Hutchinson, n.d. Reprinted by permission of David Higham Associates and Lloyds Bank PLC.

'The Vera Page Case' by George Cornish. Originally published in *Great Unsolved Crimes*, Hutchinson, n.d.

'Winnie Ruth Judd' by Geoffrey Homes. Originally published in *Los Angeles Murders*, Duell, Sloan and Pearce, 1947. Reprinted by permission of John Hawkins & Associates Inc.

Introduction

From our age of sex crime and serial murder, we look back with something like nostalgia on the less complicated crimes of the 1930s. Some crimes – like Wallace, Rouse and Ruxton – have become gruesome classics; others – like Winnie Judd, Frau Marek and Georges Sarret – have hardly achieved the celebrity they deserve. One of the aims of this collection is to restore the balance.

Let us try to place the decade in some kind of criminological perspective. One of the most interesting things about the 1930s is that crime detection was becoming so efficient that the period has rather less than its fair share of famous cases. In earlier decades, the careful criminal had a far better chance of getting away with murder. In fact, even as late as the 1880s, there was virtually nothing that could be called a science of crime detection. When Conan Doyle created Sherlock Holmes in *A Study in Scarlet*, which appeared in *Beeton's Christmas Annual* in 1887, real crime detection was a hit-and miss affair; detectives did not crawl on the floor with magnifying glasses, or even sprinkle fine dust on polished surfaces to reveal fingerprints – for although the uniqueness of fingerprints had been known for about ten years, no one had yet discovered how to classify them, and it would be another ten years before the police learned to make practical use of them.

But by the early years of the 20th century, fingerprinting, ballistics (the study of guns), blood-grouping and the use of the microscope were turning crime detection into a formidable science. Poison, the favourite method of murderers since Roman times, was now as dangerous to the killer as to the victim. In 1910, Crippen was sentenced for the murder of his wife on the evidence of the hyoscine found in her body, and on Bernard Spilsbury's identification of the mutilated remains – largely through an operation scar on the stomach. In 1917, Louis Voisin was convicted of murdering and dismembering his mistress, again largely on the evidence derived from Spilsbury's painstaking forensic study. In 1923, two professional burglars named Klauss and Doelitzsch were found guilty of the murder of an Alexandrian merchant because of an ingenious chain of deduction on the part of forensic expert Sidney Smith. Even the famous "St. Valentine's Day massacre" of 1929 was solved by a ballistics expert – Calvin Goddard – who was able to identify the tommy guns used to shoot down seven men in a Chicago garage.

So by 1930, murder had become a highly dangerous method for the solving of personal problems. Sidney Harry Fox learned this the hard way after strangling his mother in a hotel room in Margate, Kent, and then setting the room on fire top make it look like an accident. Doctors decided that her death was due to asphyxiation and shock, and a death certificate was issued without question. But the insurance company who had to pay Sidney Fox £6,000 was suspicious. Examination of the hotel room revealed that although the blaze was supposed to have originated in the gas fire, there was a six inch patch of unburnt carpet between the fender and Mrs. Fox's burnt chair, which was directly in front of the fire. And when charred fragments of paper were discovered in the room, and a bottle containing petrol, Fox was arrested (on a fraud charge – he and his mother had never been known to pay their hotel bills), and Mrs. Fox's body was exhumed. Again, it was Spilsbury who discovered that she had been dead before the fire began – proved by absence of smoke in the lungs – while a bruise on the throat pointed to strangulation (although the hyoid bone was unbroken.) But it was finally Fox's own damaging admission that led to his conviction. He described going into the room and finding it full of smoke, then rushing out again and closing the door. Asked why he had closed the door, he explained that he did not want the smoke to spread into the hotel. In short, said the prosecution, he preferred to allow his mother to suffocate rather than let smoke into the hotel . . . Fox was hanged on April 8, 1930.

It might seem that the Fox case would have made an ideal opening chapter for this book. But then, it was necessary to choose carefully, in order to achieve the right balance between well-known and lesser known cases, and for me the deciding factor was that I could find no account of the case that seemed a good anthology piece. I felt equal regret in having to exclude one of America's most famous murder trials of the 'thirties – the case of Albert Fish. Born in 1870, Fish was one of the worst, as well as one of the earliest, serial killers of the 20th century. A sado-masochist who loved to drive needles into his scrotum, he also had an obsessive need to castrate boys and kill – and eat – girls. It was in 1928 that this mild-looking old man persuaded a New York family named Budd to allow him to take their ten year old daughter Grace to a birthday party. When they failed to return, the Budds discovered that the address of "Frank Howard's" sister was non-existent. A long and exhaustive police search produced no result. But in November 1934, Fish wrote a letter to Grace's parents, admitting that he had strangled her in an abandoned cottage, then cooked and eaten parts of her body. The envelope carried a set of printed initials that had been blacked out; a spectroscope revealed them to be the initials of a Chauffeurs' Benevolent Association. Detective Will King questioned employees at the Association, and finally persuaded one of them to admit that he had occasionally borrowed envelopes for his correspondence. He went to the boarding house where the chauffeur recalled leaving some of the envelopes in a cupboard, and described Grace Budd's kidnapper to the landlady. "That sounds like Mr. Fish." Albert Fish had occupied Room 7 after the chauffeur. After keeping a watch on the place for three weeks, King was finally able to arrest Fish – although the little man tried to attack him with a razor in both hands.

Fish subsequently claimed to have committed 400 child murders over the years. Although clearly insane, he was sentenced to death and electrocuted in January 1936. At least his masochism made him look forward to his execution as "the greatest thrill of my life".

These, then, are the two main omissions. Otherwise, I trust that this first volume of famous crimes of the decade will be regarded as reasonably complete.

Colin Wilson

Misapplied Ingenuity of a Bigamist: the Rouse Case

The Rouse case has always held a special interest for me because it is possible that, had things turned out differently, Alfred Rouse might have become my father. In 1930, my mother – then a nineteen year old named Hattie Jones – was working for a garment firm called Rudkin and Laundon in St. Saviours Road, Leicester. Rouse, a commercial traveller in braces and garters, visited the factory periodically. One day, my mother was looking in the window of a shop that sold coats when Rouse came and spoke to her. He had seen her in the factory and asked her if she would like to go for a meal. My mother had already eaten, and said that in any case, her father would probably object. When she told him her father was on the telephone, Rouse rang him and asked if he could take her out, promising to bring her straight home.

It seems to have been an odd "date", for my mother said she would prefer to wait in the car while he had a meal. He brought her a box of chocolates, and she ate some of them as she waited. After this, Rouse took her for a short drive and then, as he promised, drove her home. I asked her to repeat the story just before writing these words – she is now 81 – and she confirmed that Rouse behaved like a gentleman and took her home as promised. She never saw him again. From this I deduce that the episode took place not long before the murder (her memory on the subject is now poor). That he behaved "like a gentleman" is probably one of the reasons of his remarkable success with women. For seducers of the Rouse type, the pursuit is just as enjoyable as the capture; they enjoy the courtship procedure. If Rouse's life had been less complicated, he would probably have taken her out again next time he came to Leicester, and in due course, my mother might have succumbed to his charm. (I was, in fact, conceived about a month before Rouse murdered the unknown tramp.)

I first read about the case some ten years after it happened, in a book called *The Fifty Most Amazing Crimes of the Last Hundred Years*, published by Odhams Press in 1936. This volume was, as far as I can recall, my first encounter with the subject of true-life crime – my reading had so far been confined to boys' weeklies and tales like Ballantyne's *Coral Island* – and no doubt it was this early introduction that explains why I continued to be interested in the subject twenty years later when, together with Pat Pitman, I produced the first encyclopedia of murder that had ever appeared. But although I wrote an account of the case in the *Encyclopedia*, and have written about it several times since then, I have preferred to use here the account by F. A. Beaumont from *The Fifty Most Amazing Crimes of the Past Hundred Years*.

A n aeroplane burst into flames, hung poised, before crumpling and diving earthwards through a spiral of black smoke. The blaze in the sky held the eyes of Private Alfred Arthur Rouse during the moment in which he waited for six inches of cold steel to plunge into his belly. He was in a bayonet mêlée in Northern France in 1915, and had just missed his man . . .

Then there was a terrific explosion, and everything went black. A shell had burst near Rouse, stunning him into merciful oblivion. He was severely wounded in the head and thigh, and was immediately evacuated to England. And he did not regain consciousness until the train conveying him to hospital was passing through the station of Bedford, where he was to be executed fifteen years later.

After the wound in his temple healed, the medical reports on its condition and effects were "scar irritable . . . patient unable to wear a hat of any kind . . . memory very defective . . . sleeps badly . . . easily excited . . . talks and laughs immoderately at times."

Sweating with terror, Rouse would often awaken in the small hours waiting for that bayonet thrust, seeing again the blaze in the sky that was as the angel of death to him.

Eventually Rouse was discharged with "capacity reduced three-quarters." Anxious to regain his health by an outdoor job, he became a commercial traveller for a Leicester firm, motoring up and down the country. Cars fascinated him, and he bought one after the other, quickly becoming not only a superb driver, but a highly skilled mechanic. With his "gift of the gab" and his cheery manner, it was not long before he had built up a wide and lucrative connection.

He was also very popular in the neighbourhood of his little home in Buxted Road, Finchley, which he was buying through a building society. He could tell a good story, and shone on the local tennis courts. His easy ways, lack of "side," good looks and charm made him well known and popular in the neighbourhood, but there seemed no reason why the world at large should hear anything more of him.

Until one night in 1930, when he fled from another blazing horror . . .

William Bailey and Alfred Thomas Brown, two young cousins, were returning at 2 a.m. from a Bonfire Night dance at Northampton, to their homes in the little village of Hardingstone. They had to walk along the main road from Northampton to London and then turn to the left down Hardingstone Lane.

Just as they reached the corner, a motor-car flashed by them on the main road to London. It had scarcely passed when a man scrambled from a ditch. At first he did not seem aware of the cousins, who had indeed been momentarily hidden behind the advancing car.

It was a bright moonlight night, and they had a clear view of the stranger. He was bareheaded, agitated and breathless. He wore a light mackintosh and carried an attaché-case in his hand. The cousins wondered first why a respectably dressed man should be without a hat in winter, and then why he should be jumping out of a ditch at two in the morning.

They looked past him and saw a bright red glow about two hundred yards down Hardingstone Lane.

"What is the blaze?" Bailey asked his cousin.

Hurrying away from them, the hatless man gasped over his shoulder, as if he thought the question had been addressed to him. "It looks as if some one has had a bonfire."

The cousins began to walk swiftly towards the glare. They had to pass it in any case on their way home, but by now their curiosity was awakened. Once or twice they glanced back in the direction of the hatless man. He was still behaving queerly. He took a few steps towards Northampton, then turned towards London, and finally stood hesitating, as if undecided which way to go. The last the cousins saw of him was that he was watching them as they broke into a run towards the huge bonfire.

Through flames that were leaping fifteen feet high from a furnace so dense that scarcely anything else could be seen, they glimpsed the outlines of a motor-car. They ran on into the village. Bailey called out his father, the village constable, and he brought with him Police Constable Copping.

By this time the flames had dropped to a height of five or six feet, and they could go nearer. With the aid of Brown's torch, a black "ball" could be seen, and as the

4

flames lowered it was realised that this was the head of a huddled, shapeless body.

Twelve minutes later the fire had been extinguished with buckets of water. The car was almost completely burnt out. And slumping face downwards in it, like some horrible effigy that had been left behind by the revellers of the night before, was a charred and shrivelled corpse. Its trunk was lying across the passenger's seat and its face was in the driver's seat. The right arm was burnt off at the elbow, but it appeared to be stretched as if over the passenger's seat towards a petrol can in the rear, burst in on one of its seams, and with handle and screw missing.

The left arm could not be seen until the body was taken from the car. The left leg was doubled up underneath the trunk. The right leg was burnt off below the knee, but it was extended where the running-board had been, and was sticking out eight inches from the remains of the chassis.

Near the running-board was found a charred boot heel, and fourteen yards in front of the car a mallet with three or four hairs adhering to it, one of them human . . .

Wrapped in sacking, the corpse was removed to Northampton General Hospital. At first it was thought to be that of a woman, for every external evidence of sex had been destroyed by fire. Police inquiries were made in Northampton, including visits to every hotel and inn, but no woman in the town was reported missing.

The car was a Morris Minor, and its registered number, MU 1468, enabled the police to trace it to the home of Alfred Arthur Rouse, in Buxted Road, Finchley. Two plain clothes officers called on Mrs. Rouse during the afternoon of November 6th, 1930, and requested her to go to Northampton. There she was shown "brace buckles and pieces of clothing" which she thought might have belonged to her husband, though she was not allowed to view the charred body. Later it was discovered that Rouse had taken out an insurance for £1000, to be paid in the event of the accidental death of the owner-driver of the car.

Impressed by the information given by Brown and Bailey about the mysterious stranger they had encountered, the police circulated a statement that they were anxious to get into touch with a man aged between thirty and thirty-five, height five feet ten inches to six feet, with a small round face and curly black hair, wearing a light mackintosh, dark trousers, no hat, and carrying an attaché-case.

Tongues began to wag. It was hinted that the body found in the car was that of an unknown man, murdered by Rouse, and intended to be mistaken for himself, in order that Rouse could start life afresh under a new name.

On the face of it, such a suspicion appeared wildly absurd to every thinking person – in the early days of the case. Rouse had an excellent job, a comfortable home, and plenty of friends. If he disappeared, he would become a destitute vagrant, liable to be recognised at any moment and charged with murder. No man in his senses would even contemplate such a step. But the tangled forces of character and circumstances can impel towards strange hells . . .

Rouse was born on April 6th, 1894. There was discord in his home, and when young Rouse was only six years old, the children were separated from their mother, and committed by their father to the care of his sister.

Arthur Rouse was educated at a local Council school, and was remembered there as a keen, bright lad, fond of athletics. When he left he attended evening classes, and learnt to play the violin, piano and mandoline. His first job was as office boy to an estate agent. Then he worked for five years in a soft-furnishing house in the West End. During this time he became a sacristan at a church in Stoke Newington.

Only four days after the declaration of war in 1914, he enlisted as a private in the 24th Queen's (Territorial) Regiment. And before being drafted to France, he married on November 29th of that year, Lily May Watkins, a young woman clerk, at St. Saviour's, St. Albans. He was twenty then, and she three years older.

After his discharge from the army, Rouse found during his roving life as a commercial traveller that his really good looks, ingratiating air and plausible tongue appealed irresistibly to many women. He began to "pick up" attractive girls – waitresses, shop assistants, probationer nurses, and others – and take them for a ride.

In 1920 he met a fourteen-year-old Edinburgh girl. By the time she was fifteen she was in a home for unmarried mothers. The child died when only five weeks old. Rouse posed to the girl-mother as a single man, and in 1924 persuaded her to go through a ceremony of marriage, which she believed to be valid, at St. Mary's Church, Islington. A second child was born to her, and later it was arranged, after a meeting with Mrs. Rouse, that the boy should be reared in the Rouse home.

A young domestic servant, aged seventeen, and living in Hendon, met Rouse in 1925. She believed he was a single man with rooms in Victoria. Soon he was taking her with him on his journeys, and promising to marry her "when trade improved." A girl was born to her in 1928, and she obtained a maintenance order against Rouse.

A week before the fatal Bonfire Night of 1930, she gave birth to a second girl child by Rouse at the City of London Maternity Hospital, London. She did not know that at that time another young girl was lying very ill in her parents' home in Gellygaer, where she was expecting a child by Rouse.

This girl in distant Monmouthshire believed she was already married to Rouse. He had visited the home as her husband, and persuaded the family that he had paid £1,250 for a house at Kingston, which he had furnished sumptuously for the bride. Her sister was to stay with them during their first three months in their Kingston home.

But for once Rouse realised he had gone too far. The girl

he betrayed had a devoted father and brother. If Rouse failed to keep his promises he would have to answer to them. During these ominous days before November 5th, he racked his brains in vain to discover some way out of the net of lies and intrigues in which he had snared himself.

He was earning about £10 a week. He was paying £1 12s. a week on his car, and £1 7s. 6d. to the building society. He gave his wife £2 a week for housekeeping, and another 10s. when the Edinburgh girl's boy was with them. His outgoings and expenses in connection with various women throughout the country were ruining him. There was a child in Paris, and another in an English county . . . And strong grounds exist for believing that Rouse, bragging of his conquests on the road, was also being bled white by blackmailers. Finally there was the nightmare dilemma of Gellygaer.

If he could only vanish away from it all, start life again in some place where he was unknown! If every one thought, for instance, *he had died in a car accident*?

And out of the morass of his worry and despair rose a hellborn inspiration. A few days before, outside The Swan and Pyramid public-house in the Whetstone High Road, an unemployed man had accosted him. Rouse stood him a drink. The man told him he had been to Peterborough, Norwich, Hull and other places trying to get work, obtaining lifts on the road from passing motorists. "*I have no relations*," he added. And as he said so, Rouse suddenly perceived that the man was about his own height and build, and looked fairly respectable.

On the evening of November 5th, Rouse was sitting with the domestic servant previously mentioned. She noticed that he was very depressed and preoccupied. He seemed annoyed on hearing how soon she was leaving the maternity home, as if he feared he might have to find accommodation for her earlier than he had expected.

"Are you meeting any one?" she asked, noticing that

8

he kept an anxious eye on the clock all the time he was with her.

He stared at her vacantly and said, "No." Then he left, muttering that he had so many things to pay that he hardly knew where to turn.

Shortly after eight o'clock Rouse met the unemployed stranger by appointment outside The Swan and Pyramid. It had been arranged that Rouse should give him a lift as far as Leicester. Rouse was a strict teetotaller, but he bought a bottle of whisky for his passenger to drink on the journey. Near St. Albans, the stranger switched out the lights by mistake, and a policeman spoke to Rouse. The rest of the journey is best told in the grim confession he made just before his execution.

"He was the sort of man no one would miss, and I thought he would suit the plan I had in mind.

"He drank the whisky neat from the bottle and was getting quite fuzzled. We talked a lot, but he did not tell me who he actually was. I did not care.

"I turned into Hardingstone Lane because it was quiet and near a main road, where I could get a lift from a lorry afterwards. I pulled the car up.

"The man was half-dozing – the effect of the whisky. I looked at him and gripped him by the throat with my right hand. I pressed his head against the back of the seat. He slid down, his hat falling off. I saw he had a bald patch on the crown of his head.

"He just gurgled. I pressed his throat hard. The man did not realise what was happening. I pushed his face back. After making a peculiar noise, the man was silent.

"Then I got out of the car, taking my attaché-case, the can of petrol and the mallet with me. I walked about ten yards in front of the car, and opened the can, using the mallet to do so. I threw the mallet away and made a trail of petrol to the car.

"Also, I poured petrol over the man and loosened the petrol union joint and took the top off the carburettor. I put the petrol can in the back of the car.

"I ran to the beginning of the petrol trail and put a match to it. The flame rushed to the car, which caught fire at once.

"Petrol was leaking from the bottom of the car. That was the petrol I had poured over the man and the petrol that was dripping from the union joint and carburettor.

"The fire was very quick, and the whole thing was a mass of flames in a few seconds. I ran away."

No murder in the annals of British crime was more fiendish and callous. And certainly none was ever planned with such ingenuity to defeat even the finest scientific methods of detection.

Rouse was infinitely more cunning than Sidney Fox, for example, who murdered his mother and then lit the fire that he thought would perfectly explain her death. The postmortem examination of Mrs. Fox conducted by Sir Bernard Spilsbury, however, showed that she had not breathed in smoke or carbon monoxide gas, and proved, therefore, that she must have been dead when the fire broke out.

But Rouse left his victim unconscious. He was actually burnt to death. Spectroscopic tests of his blood, and microscopic examination of the lining of his air passages revealed beyond all doubt that the man had been alive when the car burst into flames.

Nor could it be proved that the origin of the fire had not been accidental, even though the loosened petrol union joint and the open carburettor might afterwards arouse suspicion.

Petrol union joints are often left slack by careless garage mechanics, and, in the opinion of many experts, are nearly always found loose after a car has been burnt very badly. And the carburettor top might easily have been blown off during the fire.

The body of the unconscious man had been placed with such devilish skill that its identity was bound to be destroyed. The left leg was doubled up in such a position that the continuous drip from the leaking petrol union joint would fall on it just at the knee, feeding an intense flame which would rise from the floor of the car to shrivel the features of the face, turned downwards to meet it. The soaked cuff of the right arm reached backwards to the petrol can in the rear, so that another source of flame would travel from the can up the arm and shoulder to the face.

Rouse had planned it as a flawless murder. And if he had kept his head after the crime, probably all the legal, medical and engineering evidence in the world would not have sufficed to convict him. But at the sight of that roaring inferno, something must have snapped in his brain. Perhaps the flare of the aeroplane at Givenchy was before his eyes again, reviving that awful second when he awaited death.

His nerve broke and he stumbled down Hardingstone Lane in a panic to get away, anywhere, from that blazing, snarling horror. Once, he saw through a gap in the left hedge "a ploughed field," rushed towards it, then, with terrified animal cunning, thought of the footprints he would leave, and kept to the road. It was a meadow he could have crossed to safety without leaving a trace!

Nevertheless, he still had a million to one chance of "getting away with it." Yet that one chance defeated him. Rouse had almost as much reason to believe he would be struck by lightning as that two people should meet him just at that very moment in a quiet country lane during the small hours of the morning. If ever the hand of Fate caught a murderer, it was when the lighthearted young cousins stepped from behind the motor-car at the corner of Hardingstone Lane. Yet Rouse could still have saved his skin, in all probability, if a shred of reason had remained to persuade him to go back with them, and help to put out the fire.

Instead, the ruin of his original plan left him baffled and helpless. As he watched the two young men run towards the blazing car, he realised, too, the awful plight in which the encounter with them, and his impulsive remark about a bonfire, had placed him. And like a bewildered, hunted creature, he made instinctively for home.

He got a lift on a passing lorry, arrived at his house in Finchley at about 6.20 in the morning, and stayed there nearly half an hour. He ate nothing and did not even change his clothes. His own explanation was that he wanted "to tell my wife not to be worried," though actually he did not tell her anything. Mrs. Rouse said afterwards she thought he had returned at 2 a.m. – a mistake in time easy to make on a dark November morning – and that she thought the fire had occurred after his departure.

Rouse now behaved as if his mind had been shocked by another shell explosion. The cool, implacable murderer was once again the garrulous case who had been invalided home from Givenchy. He made no attempt to disappear, or to reason a way out of his predicament.

In his pocket was a telegram urgently summoning him to the bedside of the girl in Gellygaer. He went to a motor-coach company near the Strand and booked a seat to South Wales, joking with the agent, and telling him, quite unnecessarily, that his car had been stolen on the Great North Road while he was drinking coffee at a drivers' stall. On the journey he sat beside the driver, and told him that his car had been stolen near St. Albans, and that he was going to see his wife, who lived near Cardiff.

He opened a newspaper at Gellygaer, and saw *a full account of the car tragedy, a description of himself, and a report of the police visit to Mrs. Rouse and her visit to*

Northampton. It was a terrific blow to the murderer. He had expected at the most a line or two about a burnt-out car, and later perhaps a paragraph about an inquest. He was not a journalist or he would have realised before the crime the immense news value of such a discovery as that of a man burnt to death in a car.

After seeing the girl who had summoned him so urgently to her bedside, he went downstairs to supper. A Mr. Reakes called in with a newspaper displaying the car story, showed it to Rouse, and remarked, "Is this your car?"

Rouse answered, "It is not my car," and said nothing more about it that night.

Realising now the danger that the girl's family would see the paragraph about his wife, Rouse resolved to leave for London next morning. But before he left, the girl's sister showed him a paper with a photograph of the burnt-out car, with his name and registration number, and a statement that the Northampton police wished to interview the man seen near it at the time of the fire. Rouse put the paper in his pocket.

A Mr. Brownhill gave him a lift to Cardiff, asking him on the way if he had reported the loss of the car to the police. Rouse replied that he had done so, and also informed the insurance company. Mr. Brownhill asked how the accident had happened, and Rouse said that the matter was too long and complicated to go into.

They stopped for a few minutes at The Cooper's Arms Hotel, and Rouse told the proprietor, Mr. Morris, that his car had vanished after he had gone into a restaurant in London for a meal. A butcher's assistant entered and said that the body of a woman had been found in the burnt car.

"Oh, dear, dear," exclaimed Rouse, "I cannot bear to hear about it."

Then he went to a coach depôt and booked a seat for London.

The coach was met at Hammersmith by Detective-Sergeant

Skelly of the Metropolitan Police, at 9.20 p.m., on November 7th, and Rouse said to him:

"I am glad it is all over. I was going to Scotland Yard about it. I was responsible. I am very glad it is over. I have had no sleep."

At the Hammersmith police station, Skelly informed him that the Northampton police wished to interview him, and Rouse at once began a rambling statement.

"I suppose they wish to see me about it. I don't know what happened exactly. I picked the man up on the Great North Road; he asked me for a lift.

"He seemed a respectable man, and said he was going to the Midlands. I gave him a lift; it was just this side of St. Albans. He got in and I drove off, and after going some distance, I lost my way. A policeman spoke to me about my lights.

"I did not know anything about the man, and I thought I saw his hand on my case, which was in the back of the car. I later became sleepy and could hardly keep awake. The engine started to spit, and I thought I was running out of petrol. I pulled into the side of the road. I wanted to relieve myself, and said to the man, 'There is some petrol in the can; you can empty it into the tank while I am gone,' and lifted up the bonnet and showed him where to put it in.

"He said, 'What about a smoke?' I said, 'I have given you all my cigarettes as it is.' I then went some distance along the road, and had just got my trousers down when I noticed a big flame from behind. I pulled my trousers up quickly and ran towards the car, which was in flames. I saw the man was inside, and I tried to open the door, but I could not, as the car was then a mass of flames. I then began to

tremble violently. I was all of a shake. I did
not know what to do, and I ran as hard as
I could along the road where I saw the two
men. I felt I was responsible for what had happened. I lost my head, and I didn't know what
to do, and really don't know what I have done
since."

Skelly asked him if he had rescued the attaché-case he then
had with him and Rouse explained that he had seen the
man's hand on it when it was in the back of the car, so he
took it with him when he got out.

The Northampton police officers arrived at one in the
morning, Rouse was cautioned, and gave a statement sub-
stantially the same, except that now he said he met the
man half a mile past Tally Ho Corner, in Finchley, and
added:

"I thought his breath smelt of drink."

Then he mentioned a wooden mallet which he carried
for beating out dents in mudguards, and was "practically
certain" that when he last saw it it was in the well of the
car. He was asked to explain how a human hair had got on
the mallet, and replied:

"I cannot account for the fact in any way whatever,
excepting that I may have rubbed it over my own hair."

"Can you explain how the car caught fire?" asked Inspector
Lawrence, of the Northampton police.

Rouse answered: "First of all, I gave the man a cigar,
which he would naturally light in some way or other. I
presume he would have a match. Presuming he filled up
the tank, he would put the petrol can back in the car, and
he might not have put the cap on, and may have upset some
petrol in the car, and then if he had lit his cigar the car would
have caught fire."

Rouse was then taken to Northampton. And in Inspector
Lawrence's office, he made an observation which, when
published later by the press, was enough to condemn him,

whether murderer or not, in the eyes of millions of respectable citizens.

> "She is really too good for me," he said. "I like
> a woman who will make a fuss of me. I don't
> ever remember my wife sitting on my knee, but
> otherwise she is a good wife. I am very friendly
> with several women, but it is an expensive game.
> I was on my way to Leicester on Wednesday when
> this happened, to hand in my slip on Thursday
> morning to draw some money from my firm. I was
> then going to Wales for the week-end. My harem
> takes me to several places, and I am not at home a
> great deal, but my wife doesn't ask questions now.
> I was arranging to sell my house and furniture. I
> was then going to make an allowance to my wife.
> I think I should clear between £100 and £150 from
> the sale."

"The man is easily excited and talkative," stated a medical report on Rouse in September, 1918. If Rouse could
only have kept his mouth shut, he might have been alive
to-day.

After further sensational evidence about his private life
given before the County of Northampton Bench, Rouse
was committed for trial and brought up at Northampton
Assizes on January 26th, 1931, before Mr. Justice Talbot.
Mr. Norman Birkett, K.C., M.P., and Mr. Richard Elwes
were Counsel for the Crown, Mr. D. L. Finnemore and
Mr. A. P. Marshall, Counsel for the Defence.

Rouse recovered some of his old composure during the
trial. He knew that his case was a strong one. The story he
had told was one that would convince the average motorist.
He had been in a hurry to relieve himself, and it takes more
than a few seconds to fill a petrol tank from a two-gallon can.
And nearly every motorist had met the type of passenger who
does not realise the danger of smoking when handling petrol.
Besides, this man was in a stupor of drink and drowsiness.

So it was with a jaunty and self-assured air that he made answer to the deadly cross-examination of Mr. Birkett. His smile suggested to more than one observer that he knew a cleverer way of arranging a murder than that suggested by the prosecution.

For instance, Mr. Birkett suggested at one point that Rouse had thrown the man in an unconscious position, face forward, into the car that he was to light.

"Most decidedly not," answered Rouse. "I should not throw a man. If I did a thing like that, I should not throw him down face forward. *I should think where I put him, I imagine.*"

"You would imagine what? – Hardly that I would throw him down like nothing. That is absurd.

"If you rendered him unconscious, would you have a delicacy about his posture? – No, but I think if I had been going to do as you suggest, I should do a little more than that.

"Would you? – *I think I have a little more brains than that.*"

When Colonel Buckle, an expert on car fires, and a leading witness for the prosecution, was giving evidence, he watched Rouse closely, and noticed that he seemed unperturbed, and even amused, when Colonel Buckle assumed that the carburettor top had "melted" or "fallen off." After Colonel Buckle left the box, this carefree reaction of Rouse led Buckle to wonder if Rouse had deliberately removed the top.

And suddenly, without any warning, at a later stage of the trial the actual carburettor from the burnt car was placed in Rouse's hands. Every one noticed that, while he had remained unmoved by the evidence about the loosened petrol union joint, he now blanched visibly. He tried to mask his nervousness by a show of technical knowledge that produced exactly the opposite impression to the one he intended. He knew too much, he was far too clever, in the eyes of the now intent Court.

"If the cap of that (carburettor) is wrenched off by hand as it could be—? Yes, it could be. *It is not a wrench*; *I think you simply turn a clip*."

And again: "The petrol from the carburettor could be lit from a person standing in the road? – Yes, but you would get a flash in any case, and a very bad flash with the amount of petrol in there . . . I have never lit a quantity of petrol. *When I light the blowlamp, I always do it with a rag.*" (Rouse had a blowlamp at home.)

The most damning clue against Rouse was that brought forward by Sir Bernard Spilsbury and Dr. Eric Shaw, a Northampton pathologist. The body of the victim had been burnt almost to a cinder, but strangely enough one tiny piece of cloth in the fork of his trousers had not been burnt. The doubling up of the left leg against the trunk had prevented air and fire from getting to it.

When this fragment of cloth was examined, it was found to be soaked in petrol, showing that Rouse, as he afterwards confessed, had emptied petrol over the man. But even this evidence was challenged by another witness, who declared that it was quite possible that the man, lurching drunkenly as he handled the petrol can, had spilt some of the petrol over himself.

Stolidly the jury listened to one great expert after another. It is doubtful if their findings, either for or against Rouse, were sufficient in themselves to sway them. One bucket of water fetched by Rouse, even one word of sympathy – "that poor man in my car," for instance – would have probably counted more with them than all the technical evidence in the world.

They might even have forgiven his flight from the fire, his lies to every one he met. People do queer things when they are panicstricken. What they could not forgive or forget was that Rouse never for one moment showed afterwards the slightest concern about the unknown wretch who had perished in his car. "He was the sort of man no one would miss," said Rouse. But this fiend had yet to learn that the awful might of British justice will protect and avenge even the humblest and lowest in the land.

On January 31st, 1931, Mr. Justice Talbot sentenced Alfred Arthur Rouse to death. His appeal against this judgment was dismissed on February 23rd. And on March 10th, 1931, Rouse was hanged at Bedford. Thus ended the career of one of the most loathsome murderers of modern times.

F. A. Beaumont

Man Hunters: The German Rouse Cases

In Germany at the same period there were two cases in which a random victim was burnt to solve the financial problems of the murderer. The first of these took place five weeks before the beginning of the 1930s, but since it inspired the second case – and possibly the crime of Alfred Rouse – I feel that it should be allowed inclusion in a book of cases of the thirties. It is also from *The Fifty Most Amazing Crimes of the Last Hundred Years*.

A week after Alfred Arthur Rouse was hanged at Bedford, another young commercial traveller, Kurt Erich Tetzner, stood in the dock at Ratisbon, Germany, while the Public Prosecutor accused him of burning to death in his car an unknown tramp whose body he had tried to pass off as his own.

But Tetzner had been arrested nearly a year before Rouse was taken to Hammersmith police station. Indeed, the Public Prosecutor at Ratisbon referred to Rouse as "just a pupil of Tetzner." But he paid a tribute to the efficiency of British law by emphasising that Rouse had been tried, found guilty, and executed only five months after the murder, whereas it had taken the Germans fourteen months to bring Tetzner to trial, after his arrest at Strasbourg on December 5th, 1929.

Tetzner's car had been found burnt out near the village of Ettershausen, Bavaria, on November 25th, 1929. A charred body was at the wheel. The police of Leipzig, where Tetzner lived, were notified, and Frau Tetzner was sent for. She identified the body as that of her husband.

The corpse was buried with great pomp, and Frau Tetzner, in deepest mourning, wept copiously as she followed the coffin. But the insurance companies with whom Tetzner had insured his life for 145,000 marks (£7250) were not convinced so easily. They got in touch with the Leipzig police, who began to shadow Frau Tetzner.

She had no telephone in her flat. Twice in the next few days she was summoned to the flat of a neighbour to answer calls from a Herr Stranelli, ringing up from Strasbourg, Alsace. The Leipzig police telephoned the French police at Strasbourg, giving them a detailed description of Tetzner, and asking them to take a good look at Stranelli. A Leipzig detective-officer set off by plane to Strasbourg. When he arrived, the French police had already arrested Stranelli, who was soon identified as Tetzner.

And now Kurt Tetzner, thick-set, with a fat white unhealthy face, and small beady eyes, stood in the dock, and licked his dry lips nervously as the Public Prosecutor thundered at him.

"First of all, after your arrest by the police, you confessed that you had murdered your passenger, then burnt his body in your motor-car in order to lead insurance companies, with whom you had insured your life, to believe you had been killed in a motoring accident. Later, you withdrew this confession and made, instead, a fresh statement, in which you declared the man whose body was found burnt in your car was a pedestrian, whom you had accidentally run over, and who had then died in the car. You said you had burned the body later in order to commit the fraud on the insurance companies. Which of these two statements," demanded the Prosecutor, "do you wish to put before the court to-day?"

Tetzner hesitated.

"The second," he replied, almost inaudibly.

The Prosecutor then referred to the death of the prisoner's

mother-in-law a few months before the burnt car was found. Tetzner had first dissuaded her from undergoing an operation for cancer. Then he had recommended it, after insuring her life for 10,000 marks (£500). She died three days after the operation.

"The ease with which you obtained those ten thousand marks was your undoing, was it not?" asked the Prosecutor.

Tetzner refused to be drawn.

"It was a great misfortune," he answered.

"Is it true your wife suggested to you that you should dig up a newly-buried body from the cemetery instead of murdering a man, and that you said to her, 'Don't be a fool. There must be blood about'?"

"I may have said something of the sort," replied the prisoner.

Tetzner then described two attempts he had made to lure a victim into his car. At first he advertised for a travelling companion, but a young man who got in touch with him grew suspicious and refused at the last moment. Then one day, while driving along the highway near Ingolstadt, he met a motor mechanic called Alois Ortner, who was seeking work, and who wanted a lift to Munich.

"I at once realised," Tetzner went on, "that this young man would be ideal to leave in the car. Passing through the town of Hof, I gave him some money, and told him to get a shave and buy himself a collar. I wanted him to look as respectable and as much like me as possible.

"Later, I asked Ortner to crawl under the car and look at the oil valve. While he was under the car, I seized a hammer and a pad of ether. When he emerged I fell on him, but he fought back powerfully and succeeded in escaping into the forest.

"On my return I told my wife of a new plan I had formed. I now intended to pick up a man in my car, blind him by throwing pepper in his face, then burn him alive while he was helpless."

22

The Public Prosecutor interrupted him with a gesture of loathing:

"What a fiendish idea!" he cried. "Don't you realise this is the most cruel form of death a man can devise?"

Tetzner stared at him blankly.

"It didn't seem so bad to me at the time," he muttered.

Then he went on with his grim story.

"On the night of November 25th, 1929, I ran over a man shortly after passing Bayreuth. I placed him on the seat beside me and drove on until he died. Then I put him in the dickey.

"While having supper in an inn, it occurred to me that here was an opportunity to carry out my scheme without murdering anybody. I drove on, and, shortly before reaching Ratisbon, I ran the car into a tree to make it appear as though an accident had happened. Then I sprinkled the car with petrol and set it on fire."

The Prosecutor riddled this account with sarcasm.

"How do you explain, Tetzner," he snapped, "that a man of your intelligence could for many months accuse himself to the police in his own statements (Tetzner had at first made a confession, then, after five months in prison, repudiated it) of a terrible murder in order to cover up a case of manslaughter?"

But Tetzner could not explain.

Alois Ortner was called into the witness-box. He told a horrified court how he had staggered from the car, with his face streaming with blood, and had collapsed a few moments after Tetzner had driven on. Later, in hospital, he could not remember the number of the car. The Ingolstadt police would not believe his story, said it was fantastic, and suspected him of an unsuccessful attempt to rob a passing motorist.

The chief witness for the defence was Dr. Kockel, post-mortem expert of Leipzig University. He was convinced Tetzner was telling the truth when he said he had run over a man, killing him, and then burnt him in his car. The internal organs of the corpse, he argued, bore no traces of smoke or soot, as they would have done if the man had been alive when he was burnt. There were injuries to the body which showed that it had been violently maltreated, in a manner that suggested it had been run over by a car. Dr. Molitoris, of Erlangen University, another post-mortem expert, gave counter-evidence on behalf of the prosecution, and a long and wordy duel ensued between these leading witnesses.

Tetzner was condemned to death. Before he was executed at Regensburg, on May 2nd, 1931, he made a full confession. On the night of November 25th, 1929, he had given a lift to a travelling journeyman, aged twenty-one, whose name he did not know. The thinly-clad youth complained of the cold. Tetzner wrapped him in a heavy rug, pinioning his arms to his body. Then he strangled him with a piece of rope. Outside Ettershausen he crashed the car into a tree, opened the petrol tank, laid a petrol trail from the tank over the mudguard and right footboard to the back of the car, which he then set on fire.

"Gentlemen of the jury, think of my terrible position. I was leading a double life. At home I had to appear cheerful and contented, while my heart was breaking. At night I was forced to go out hunting for men to murder." And Fritz Saffran, fighting for his life in the Court of Bartenstein, East Prussia, spread out his hands with an appealing gesture, in an attempt to convince his hearers that he had played an unwilling part in one of the strangest crime dramas of the century.

Six months earlier, few men were so popular as Fritz Saffran in the little town of Rastenburg, only thirty miles away from the court in which he was to face his trial on the capital charge. He was young, good-looking and successful. Business men admired the acumen of this thirty-year-old manager of the Platz Furniture Store, who had made it a flourishing concern during the worst years of the depression.

His keen grey eyes and tight, determined lips impressed them with the feeling that here was a "warm" man. Customers thronged the store, enjoyed chatting with the affable young manager, who was never too busy to advise them regarding the choice of furniture, and always easy-going and ready to waive a clause or two in the hire purchase agreements. There was something about his confident smile and high intellectual forehead (he was formerly a schoolmaster) that made them trust him instinctively.

Herr Platz, the owner of the store, could never speak too highly of the brilliant young fellow who had enabled him to retire a few years before, leaving the direction of the business entirely in Saffran's hands. And when Fritz respectfully asked him for the hand of his daughter in marriage, the old man readily consented. Many a woman in Rastenburg envied Frau Saffran her handsome and distinguished young husband, whose devotion to his wife was a byword in the town.

On the evening of September 15th, 1930, a terrific explosion shook the store, and it burst almost instantly into a mass of flames. Thirty people were at work inside the inferno, and it was afterwards regarded as a miracle that every one of them managed to escape from it alive. The fire brigade arrived within a few minutes of the outbreak, but so fierce was the blaze that nothing could be done, and the firemen could only stand by helpless while the building was razed to the ground.

Wild-eyed, Erich Kipnik, chief clerk of the store, rushed into the home of Herr Platz and stammered hysterically that Saffran had perished in the fire. He and Saffran had spent the evening in a café, he said, and on their way home they had noticed a glow in the sky coming from the direction of the store. Saffran broke into a run, and when he saw that the store was indeed ablaze he had shouted to Kipnik that he was going inside to rescue the ledgers.

"Without a second's hesitation," sobbed Kipnik, "he dashed into the heart of the burning building. I have never seen anything so brave in my life."

And only a few hours later searchers among the ruins found the charred remains of a body, round which the tatters of a suit identified as Saffran's were still clinging. On the fingers of the corpse were rings belonging to Saffran, and in the waistcoat pocket was discovered his monogrammed silver watch.

Saffran had always been well liked by all his employees, but one in particular, Ella Augustin, grieved so much over his death that two days after the fire she collapsed sobbing in the street. She was not a pretty girl, but her vivacity and unruliness had already earned her a reputation as a "character" in the firm. Her resolute mouth and strongly marked eyebrows suggested that here was a woman who usually got what she wanted.

But a great disappointment had clouded her life. It was no secret that ever since she came to the firm, six years ago, Ella had fallen madly in love with the handsome young manager. Every one in the firm knew that she had been throwing herself at him ever since. What did she care if he were already married? She loved him, and that was all that mattered. Sooner or later she would make him respond to her passion.

Saffran tolerated for a time her open and unashamed advances with an air of pleasant good-humour. But soon he realised that her conduct was arousing comment among people who came to shop in the store, besides undermining the respect of his employees. She must stop this nonsense. And one day when he found she had made an error in her books, he seized the opportunity to upbraid her severely before the rest of the clerical staff. She cried with shame and humiliation, and Saffran almost regretted his unusual sternness. But afterwards, when he saw her going about her work with a subdued and chastened air, he decided that the lesson had been worth while. She would cause him no more embarrassment.

Two days after the fire Ella Augustin called at several garages in Rastenburg. Her mother was seriously ill, she explained, and she wanted to hire a car to take her to Königsberg. Eventually a chauffeur named Reck offered his services. By arrangement with Ella, he called at the Augustin home at three the next morning. To his surprise, instead of the ailing mother a man came out of the house and stepped into the car. Reck recognised him instantly as Saffran.

The chauffeur drove Saffran as far as the village of Gerdauen, then refused to go farther. Saffran walked off towards the village, and Reck turned back towards Rastenburg. The chauffeur was often employed by the Platz firm. Later the police charged him with aiding and abetting. It was never proved that he was a member of the conspiracy. What is certain is that he opened his mouth to some one about that mysterious night ride, for the very next day the police began to make inquiries.

They discovered by persistent examination of reluctant clerks formerly employed in the Platz store that the firm, which every one thought so prosperous, had been since 1928 in serious difficulties. The customers whom Saffran had so easily persuaded to hire furniture were not paying their instalments. Unknown to Platz, Saffran had begun to obtain large credits at high interest, and soon the firm was staggering under a huge load of debt. Then Saffran raised money by submitting the same hire purchase contracts to two different financing houses, one in Berlin, the other in Königsberg. As the struggle to keep the firm afloat became more and more arduous, the desperate young manager forged nearly four hundred sale contracts, and raised money on these in Berlin and Königsberg. Finally he had been forced to falsify the balance sheets. The assets on the firm's books were stated to be 285,000 marks, when actually there was a bare 25,000. The police also learnt that Ella Augustin had been carrying on a liaison with Saffran, and had helped him to falsify the ledgers.

Ella was arrested and put in prison. She tried to smuggle out a note to Saffran. It was intercepted, but it told the police little more than that Saffran was staying with one of her relations at an unknown address, somewhere in Berlin.

This man was a poor carpenter in the Lausitzer Strasse. Saffron hid for seven weeks in his tiny lodging, never daring to stir out until after dark. When he left Rastenburg, he had only three hundred marks with him. He was tired of living like a hunted beast, his money was ebbing fast, and he decided that his only hope of escape was to get out of the country. With the carpenter's identity papers, which he did not hesitate to steal, he thought he could make his way to Hamburg and there take a boat to Brazil.

Saffran bought a ticket to Hamburg at a Berlin travel bureau. But he was too clever to risk capture at the terminus station in Berlin, which he knew would be watched day and night. Instead, he went by the town railway to the suburb of Spandau, and there, at one o'clock in the morning of November 7th, he boarded the train for Hamburg. And had it not been for a stroke of almost incredible bad luck he would soon afterwards have been safe at sea.

Kipnik swore that Saffran had murdered the man whose body was found in the store. But it was not until Saffran addressed the court, and vainly tried to save his skin by denouncing his associates, that the full amazing story of their desperate crime came to light.

"When I realised that the store would soon be engulfed by a flood of unredeemable obligations," he began, "I insured my life for 140,000 marks (£7000). It was my intention to commit suicide, so that my wife would be provided for, but Ella dissuaded me from taking this step. I asked Kipnik for his advice, and he said we ought to get a body from somewhere and burn it in the store.

"At first it was our intention to obtain a corpse from a graveyard. But later we decided this would not be good enough for our purpose. So we established a murder camp in the Nikolai Forest. The girl stayed behind in the camp while Kipnik and I, each in his own car, roved the countryside for miles around, looking for a likely victim, then reported to the camp at evening. After a time we all three began to go out on these man-hunts. During one of these drives, after passing the village of Sorquitten, we overtook a man and asked him if he would like a lift.

"He got in the car, and I drove off at a furious pace. Then suddenly I jammed on the brake, while Kipnik struck the man three blows on the head with his life preserver. Ella lost her nerve, however, and held Kipnik back, so that the man escaped. We then decided it was no good murdering a man and burning him in the car afterwards. Instead we decided we would take the body to the store to burn. In this way it was to appear as if I had committed suicide.

"On the night of September 12th, 1930, between eleven and midnight, Kipnik and I drove out in the car once more. In the dickey we had put a carpet in which to wrap the man whom we murdered. When we got to the village of Loetzen my courage failed me, and I said to Kipnik, 'Let us drive home.' Kipnik, however, declared that the crime had to be carried out that night or never.

"Near Luisenhof we met a pedestrian. Kipnik got out of the car, and I drove on at a furious speed for about one and a half miles, hoping against hope that Kipnik would not succeed in killing the man. When I returned Kipnik stopped me, tore open the dickey, pulled out the carpet, and said to me, 'I have got him down there in the ditch.' I was paralysed with horror. I remembered nothing more until I heard Kipnik shout to me, 'Now, drive for your life!'

"Something heavy seemed to bump into the back of the car as I pressed the accelerator and we got away. We took the body to the store, dressed it in my clothes, put my rings on its fingers and my watch in the waistcoat pocket. Then we poured twenty-five gallons of petrol over the floor of the store and set fire to it. There was a big explosion."

Whether Saffran or Kipnik shot the man will never be known, as each carried pistols. Saffran's story was not in accord with some of the established facts. For instance, he referred to the victim as a pedestrian, whereas he was actually a cyclist. He also stated that the body was dressed in one of Saffran's suits. Frau Dahl, on the other hand, identified the clothing as similar to that worn by her husband. Though most of the truth came to light in the combined accounts given by the accused, not much reliance can be placed on each separate statement, since each was trying to win the clemency of the court by a version that was obviously distorted in his or her own favour.

Saffran fell on his knees and cried like a child when Frau Dahl, the widow of the victim, a frail little woman wearing a heavy black veil, entered the witness-box.

"Frau Dahl, I share the responsibility for the death of your husband," he sobbed. "I beg you, I beseech you on my bended knees to forgive me for what we have done. And if you cannot grant me your forgiveness to-day, perhaps at some time in the future you will be able to sympathise with me."

Kipnik, too, made a great show of repentance, shouting to Frau Dahl, "It is terrible to me when I think of my own poor wife and our boy, and imagine what they would have suffered if what we did to your husband had happened to me."

But the public prosecutor cut short his display of remorse by snapping:

"Enough of this play-acting!"

Kipnik revealed under cross-examination that one night the three man-hunters got a pedestrian in their car and had decided to murder him when the man told them that he had six children. Moved by compassion, he added, they let him go. He also mentioned another occasion when the three of them were scouring the roads around Sensberg in their car and saw a man walking along a lane. Saffran shouted to him, but either the man did not hear, or was afraid, for he paid no attention and went on his way.

Night after night, continued Kipnik, they lurked in wait for their prey. Sometimes they would leave the car in a wood and hide behind a nearby hedge, watching for a man to come along the road. But it was Saffran who actually killed Dahl, protested Kipnik, with three shots fired through the head. They hid his cycle and leather bag afterwards in the forest bordering the highway. Kipnik admitted he had wrapped the body in the carpet they had brought with them. When they arrived in Rastenburg, he added, they carried the bundle into the Platz store, and Saffran said, "Now it can burn." It was Saffran, too, according to Kipnik, who forced his rings on the dead man's fingers, and also put his own gold collar studs into the man's shirt.

But the court put no more trust in the terse quiet statements of the cool and contemptuous chief clerk than they had in the hysterical blabbings of Saffran. Kipnik began to lose his nerve, made wild and incoherent charges against his accomplices, and finally, raising his hands in appeal, shouted a supreme protest:

"Saffran has ruined my life! I place my fate in the hands of the court. I wish I could prove to them that I am really a decent man!"

A scream rang out through the densely-packed courtroom. The astonished spectators turned to see Ella Augustin on her feet, her eyes blazing, her face livid with rage as she pointed an accusing finger at Kipnik.

"And yet you are the murderer!" she yelled.

Saffran and Kipnik were condemned to death. Later, however, the Prussian Government commuted their sentences to penal servitude for life. Ella Augustin was sentenced to five years' penal servitude. Such was the end of the man-hunters, inspired by modern greed, not ancient superstition, for this strange murder drama seems to belong more fittingly to those far-gone days when bands of savage priests roved the countrysides of primitive Europe in search of a human sacrifice to offer up on their altars.

F. A. Beaumont

The Otterburn Mystery

The theme of death by fire continues in the next case, the unsolved murder of Evelyn Foster – if, indeed, it was a murder. The story is to be found in a collection called Great Unsolved Crimes, *published by Hutchinsons in the 1930s (the volume bears no date.) The idea was to ask various policemen and writers of mystery stories for their accounts of various unsolved crimes, and for their suggestions for solutions. It is a classic compilation, with writers like Mrs. Belloc Lowndes, A. J. Cronin, G. B. Stern and J. D. Beresford – all names, I suspect, that have been totally forgotten by the present generation, but who, in their day, formed part of England's literary establishment. (I see that I picked up my own copy for four shillings; I saw one in a bookseller's catalogue the other day for £30.) Val Gielgud, the author of the present piece, was the elder brother of actor John Gielgud, and known to a generation of radio listeners during the Second World War as head of BBC sound drama.*

In spite of the book's title, the case is certainly not one of the great unsolved mysteries; yet it is oddly puzzling and disturbing. After I read this present account in the 1960s, it stuck in my mind, until I exorcised it by putting it into a novel called Lingard *(in England,* The Killer*) more than ten years later.*

To a writer of sensational fiction there can be few cases more fascinating than the story of what came to be called "The Otterburn Mystery."

Both as regards its environment and its circumstances, the story might so easily be judged to have sprung from the slightly morbid imagination of the novelist, rather than from cruelly hard fact. But once again fact proved stranger than fiction.

About half-past nine during a night in January of 1931, a bus belonging to a garage proprietor of Otterburn, Northumberland, was returning along the road from Otterburn to Newcastle, driven by a Mr. Johnson.

At a desolate spot on the moors, known as Wolf's Neck – the name of the place immediately brings to mind some chapter heading – he saw a motor-car about seventy yards away from the road. The car had been on fire and was still smouldering.

On investigation, Mr. Johnson and his conductor were amazed to find that the car belonged to the firm by which they were employed – that is to say, by Mr. Foster, the garage proprietor, of Otterburn. Not far from the car they made a hideous discovery.

Miss Evelyn Foster, Mr. Foster's twenty-seven-year-old daughter, was lying moaning on the grass, crying out for water. Below the waist all her clothes had been burned off, her hands were black from the effects of a hard frost; her face was severely discoloured.

Mr. Johnson wrapped the girl in his overcoat and took her home as quickly as possible. Most of the way she kept on muttering about "that awful man – that awful man." During intermittent periods of consciousness she told a long and detailed story of the incidents that had preceded and accompanied the tragedy, and shortly afterwards she died.

Her story in brief was this:

Miss Foster was in the habit of driving cars about the country for her father, and on the previous day she had driven three passengers to Rochester, a village in the neighbourhood. At Ellishaw, a village two miles away from Otterburn, she was accosted by a stranger, who told her that he wished to go to Ponteland in order to catch a bus to Newcastle.

About 7.30 in the evening she picked him up on the bridge just below the hotel at Ellishaw and drove him as far as Belsay. It must remembered that when she made her statement Miss Foster was in great pain, and was, in fact, dying.

But of what happened at Belsay no satisfactory account emerged. In reply to the urgent questionings of her mother, Miss Foster's words seemed to imply that her passenger made advances to her; when she resisted him he struck her in the eye; that she lost consciousness, and that the man finally drove the car away with Miss Foster inside along the road to Otterburn as far as the Wolf's Neck.

At that point her car was turned off the road and run down a 3-ft. bank on to the moor for 70 yards or so.

She described her assailant as rather a small man, wearing a bowler hat and a dark coat and speaking like a gentleman, although he had a Tyneside accent.

As to what happened at Wolf's Neck Miss Foster was unhappily, though not unnaturally, vaguer still. According to her story she recovered consciousness owing to the jerking and jolting of the car as it passed on to the moorland. The passenger then got out, took something from his pocket and applied a light to it.

There followed a small explosion and a blaze. Miss Foster, in horrible agony and feeling that she must be suffocated, struggled to get the door of the car open. This she finally succeeded in doing, and she crawled out and fell on to the grass where she was found. She seemed to remember seeing the man go back to the road, hearing another car coming along the road, hearing a whispered colloquy, and the other car drive away.

The only other significant item that the victim could add was the fact that the man had told her that he had been picked up at Jedburgh by a party of motorists on their way to Hexham, and had had tea with them – the party consisting of three men speaking with a Scottish accent in a saloon car, probably an Essex.

The B.B.C. broadcast a police message containing a

description of this party. The men were found and interviewed by the police, but said they gave no lift to anyone answering to the description of the wanted man.

The inquest on Miss Foster was opened by the Coroner, Mr. P. M. Dodds, on Thursday, January 8, at the Otterburn Memorial Hall.

Formal evidence of identification was given by the dead girl's father, and the inquest was adjourned until February 2. In the interval Professor Stuart Macdonald, a well-known pathologist of the College of Medicine at Newcastle, had been called in to consult with the doctor who made the post-mortem examination. It was not until February 5 that Professor Macdonald's evidence was given.

According to him, no external marks suggesting injury other than burning were found on any part of the body. He gave the cause of death as the result of shock caused by severe external burning.

He said that the distribution of the burned areas suggested that Miss Foster was sitting during some period of the burning, and he added that there was absolutely no trace or evidence of bruising of the face. There was also no evidence of outrage.

The next witness, Mr. W. Jennings, a motor engineer of Morpeth, said that it would have been very difficult for anybody to have driven the car from the position in which Miss Foster said that her assailant had driven it after taking the wheel from her, always supposing that she had offered any resistance.

And the Coroner put the whole problem flatly when he pointed out to the jury that the two main points before them were:

(a)   Was the girl murdered?
(b)   Did she set fire to the car, and in doing so obtain the burns accidentally?

If the latter, was her object to obtain money from the insurance on the car?

The jury, after a retirement of two hours, returned the verdict that Miss Foster had been murdered by some person or persons unknown.

Of course, the unfounded suggestion that Miss Foster had met her death by means self-inflicted in the course of carrying out a criminal fraud was hotly resented by her family, and Miss Foster's father wrote a letter on the subject to the Home Secretary.

"There was no title of evidence," he said, "to support such shameful theories," and he resented most strongly the fact that though the jury's verdict had vindicated his daughter's honour, the Chief Constable of Northumberland had stated in an interview with a newspaper reporter that the verdict was against the weight of evidence.

"The police," Mr. Foster continued, "were defending themselves in a case in which they had failed by attacking his dead daughter." And it transpired that, though there were two insurance policies – one for £450 and the other for £700 – in existence, Miss Foster left estate valued at £1400.

It must be remembered on behalf of the police that the description of Miss Foster's assailant was comparatively comprehensive; that he must almost certainly have had a good knowledge of the locality to have been able so effectively to disappear without leaving trace behind him; and yet that no one answering to his description was ever traced.

It is true that during the night of February 13, a seaman walked into the Newcastle police station and said that he wished to give himself up for the Otterburn murder. But after being interviewed, he was removed to hospital for observation and was presumably suffering from delusions, or an insane desire for notoriety.

The problem was infinitely complicated by Miss Foster's condition both of mind and body when she made her statement, combined with the very understandable confusion which seems to have emerged from some of the facts given by her mother.

The Coroner asked Dr. McEachran, of Bellingham, who was called in to Miss Foster when she was brought home injured, if he recollected the mother asking Miss Foster if she had been interfered with – using that or a similar expression. To which the doctor replied that there had been a question of that nature, and apparently the girl's reply was to the effect that she had been interfered with.

This fact seems to have been put in parallel with the medical report, which stated that there was no evidence of outrage.

And this, combined with the fact that no corroborative evidence could be found of the existence of the assailant, and no trace of anything inflammable except petrol had been found on the girl's clothes, led the Coroner to the summing-up which read distinctly adverse to the verdict as ultimately given by the jury.

What of the possibilities of accident? The car had left the road at not more than ten miles an hour. It had not overturned in crossing the embankment. It seems to have been definitely under control before it stopped. It had suffered no damage which could have caused it to ignite.

The valves, the ignition and carburettor were all in perfect order, and there was no trace of abnormal heat below the line of the float chamber. In the back of the car was a burned-out tin of petrol – but it was customary always to keep a full two-gallon tin in the car for emergencies. The cap of the petrol tin had been removed before the fire started.

It seems, therefore, quite definite that this tragedy cannot be put down to any misadventure, however singular. Nor, unless Miss Foster's is to be categorised as a most extraordinary case of mental instability, can the theory hold water – and it was only very tentatively put forward – that she might have been one of those persons obsessed with the idea of achieving notoriety.

We are left, therefore, with the alternatives of murder or suicide by mistake.

The Coroner himself, though evidently inclined to believe

the greater part of Miss Foster's statement to be unreliable owing to her condition at the time it was made, pointed out that the suggested motive of obtaining insurance money was inadequate. There remains that "Wilful Murder by a Person or Persons Unknown" which the jury gave finally as their considered opinion.

The murder has been described as motiveless. Miss Foster's money was in her bag and her personal ornaments were untouched. But, disagreeable though it may be to accept such a conclusion, the facts as they stand point, in my view, quite clearly in one direction.

There are three significant sentences in Miss Foster's statement which form strong links in this chain. First of all was her repetition of the phrase "that awful man," while she was being driven home by Mr. Johnson.

Next we find her first reply in answer to her mother's questioning as to what had happened to her: "It was a man. He hit me and burned me."

And thirdly her story that when the car stopped on the top of the hill by Wolf's Neck, the man offered her a cigarette, and when she refused it, made the remark: "Well, you are an independent young woman!"

Perhaps it should be added at this point that in reply to the Coroner's questions, Mrs. Foster insisted that her daughter's condition was perfectly lucid and sane while she was telling her story, and Dr. McEachran said he saw no reason to think that she had any idea that she was going to die.

It does not seem to me that this statement combined with the facts admits of more than one explanation. It remains, of course, questionable whether the assailant was a sexual maniac, who deliberately hailed Miss Foster because she was a girl driving alone, or whether his revolting purpose arose only with the incidence of opportunity.

It was, as a matter of fact, quite exceptional that Miss Foster should have been unaccompanied on such trips, and it had been suggested by her sister that she should take a man with her, but she had not done so.

But whatever his original motive, the lateness of the hour and the darkness of the moors provoked in the unknown an attitude to which Miss Foster objected, and in this connection his remark about the cigarette is by no means without significance.

Finding that his overtures were not welcomed – probably they were actively repulsed – the man must have lost both his head and his temper, with results catastrophic in an individual almost certainly pathologically abnormal. He then struck Miss Foster in the eye.

It seems likely that this first attack was comparatively slight, and that the girl was completely terrified, which in the circumstances is not an unlikely supposition. This would account for the absence of bruising on the face, which provoked the comment in the medical evidence.

He then bundled her into the back of the car, drove to the desolate neighbourhood of Wolf's Neck, and deliberately turned the car off the road. At that point, roused to frenzy by Miss Foster's continued resistance, he wrenched the cap off the spare tin of petrol, drenched her with it and, with a brutality almost unbelievable set her on fire.

That done, he disappeared over the moors into the darkness.

It is perhaps worth making a point in this connection that in pouring petrol from a petrol tin it flows in a stream and not with a splash, which would account for the comparatively localised nature of the burns. That the victim in this awful condition of physical and mental torment – that is to say, after the burning – should have believed that a casual car stopped on the road, and going on again, should have picked up her assailant, although, in fact, it had done nothing of the kind, is surely not stretching the issue to any great extent.

And it emerged that a motor salesman of Hawick, named Beatty, passed Wolf's Neck between half-past nine and ten that night, saw a blaze on the right-hand side of the road and put on his brakes. He saw that it was a car, but it appeared to him to be completely burned out and he saw no movement, so he imagined that it had been abandoned and drove on.

The only other clues that were discovered near the burned-out car were a single footprint, a glove and a cap. They were all systematically examined. They all led to nothing.

Mr. Foster was not alone in taking exception to the fact that the Northumberland police had shown the very minimum of inclination to call in the experience of Scotland Yard to help them towards the solution of one of the most remarkable unsolved crimes of modern days.

Val Gielgud

The Murder of Julia Wallace

The classic murder mystery of the 1930s was the Wallace case. In fact, as we shall see in the aftermath, the mystery is now almost certainly solved, due to the detective work of crime writer Jonathan Goodman and radio journalist Roger Wilkes. That is a recent development. But in the intervening years, there have been several full-length books about the case, and a dozen or so chapters devoted to it in books about famous murders.

The detective writer Dorothy L. Sayers wrote about it on two occasions, the longer of the two being "The Murder of Julia Wallace", in *The Anatomy of Murder*, (1936) an anthology of pieces by members of the Detection Club. Dorothy Leigh Sayers, born in Oxford in 1893, was primarily interested in religion, but began to write detective stories – about Lord Peter Wimsey – to support an illegitimate son she bore in 1924. As soon as she could afford to, she stopped writing detective fiction and returned to more serious interests, with a series of radio plays about Jesus, *The Man Born to be King*, and a translation of Dante. Her shorter account of the Wallace murder – from *Great Unsolved Crimes* – remains as excellent a presentation of the case as any in existence.

Perhaps the most remarkable thing about the murder of Julia Wallace is that from the beginning to end there

was no important conflict of evidence. That is what makes
it such a fascinating puzzle.

Except for the usual polite medical squabble over *rigor
mortis* and a trifling uncertainty about the precise moment
of a milkboy's visit, the essential facts were never in dispute.
There they were, and you could make what you liked of
them. The judge made one thing, the jury made another, the
Court of Appeal decided that nothing could be made of them,
and so set the prisoner free at the very gallows' foot.

The case has been compared to a detective story; but in
fiction the author always supplies one key-incident which
cannot possibly be interpreted in more than one way. In
the Wallace case everything that the accused said or did
might be construed as the behaviour either of an innocent
man caught in a trap or of a guilty man pretending to be
innocently caught in a trap. It is like a web of shot silk,
looking red from one angle and green from another.

William Herbert Wallace was an agent employed to collect
payments for the Prudential Assurance Company. He was
fifty-two years old and of frail physique, had been married
for eighteen years to a wife of about his own age.

For sixteen years they had lived together at 29 Wolverton
Street, Liverpool, apparently in perfect harmony. Music,
chess and science were the husband's inoffensive pursuits;
Marcus Aurelius, the gentle stoic, his favourite philosopher.

The wife, delicate and retiring, played the piano, painted in
water-colours, and listened with interest while he expounded
as best he could, the new theory of atomic physics and the
great riddles of the universe.

They took their few quiet outings together and enjoyed
an ideal companionship. There was no other man; no other
woman. No one ever heard a harsh word pass between this
happily married, middle-aged couple.

At about 7.15 in the evening of Monday, January 19,
1931, Wallace left his house to play a competition game
at a meeting of the chess club, held at the City Café, about

half an hour away. About the same time a telephone call was put through to the café from a public kiosk just off Wolverton Street, and was answered by the club captain, Mr. Beattie.

The caller, who gave the unusual name of "Qualtrough," asked whether Wallace had arrived, said he was too busy to ring up again, and left a message asking Wallace to call on him next day at 7.30 p.m., at "25 Menlove Gardens East," about "something in the matter of his business."

At 7.45 Wallace reached the café and was given the message.

"Who's Qualtrough? I don't know the chap. Where is Menlove Gardens East? Is it Menlove Avenue?"

He entered the address in his note-book and went on to play and win his game of chess. Some time after ten he left the café with a friend, observing that he did not know whether he should keep this odd appointment or not.

On the Tuesday the Wallaces had an early supper at home, and between 6.30 and 6.45 Mrs. Wallace took in the milk from the milk-boy. *This was the last time she was seen alive*.

At 6.45, according to his own statement, Wallace set out to visit Qualtrough, and between 7.6 and 7.10 he was certainly boarding a tram about twenty minutes' ride from Wolverton Street. A few minutes later he changed trams again, making repeated and detailed inquiries of both conductors for "Menlove Gardens East."

He was put down at Menlove Gardens West and told that it would probably be somewhere in that direction. He replied: "Thank you; I am a complete stranger about here."

Now, in a sense, that was not quite true. Two years previously he had visited a Mr. Crewe, living in that neighbourhood, on five occasions. But since he had always gone there in the dark of the winter evenings it was scarcely surprising that he should not be familiar with all the adjacent streets.

After three and a half years' residence Mr. Crewe himself

had no idea whether there was or was not a Menlove Gardens East. Actually, having inquired at a house of a passer-by and of a police constable, Wallace was told by all three that, though there was a Menlove Gardens North, South and West, and also a Menlove Avenue (all of which he tried), Menlove Gardens East did not exist.

Unwilling, however, to lose the chance of a useful commission, he asked the constable where he could consult a directory, adding: "It is not eight o'clock." The constable agreed that it was only 7.45, and told him where to find a newsagent's shop still open. Here Wallace again searched, and asked for Menlove Gardens East, and was told for the fourth time that there was no such place.

It was now getting on for 8.20, and Wallace, remembering that there had been one or two burglaries of late in his own street, began, as he said, to feel uneasy. He took the next tram home.

A little before 8.45 Wallace's next-door neighbours, a Mr. and Mrs. Johnston, heard knocking at the back door of No. 29. The residents in Wolverton Street made frequent use of their back doors, which all led out into a long entry, running parallel to the street itself.

Going out themselves by the back at a quarter to nine they met Wallace coming down the entry towards his own back door. He greeted them with the rather surprising question: "Have you heard anything unusual to-night?" They said: "No; what has happened?"

He said: "I have tried the back door and gone round to the front, and they are both locked against me." Mr. Johnston suggested that he should try the back door again. He did so; called out: "It opens now," and went in.

The Johnstons, standing in the yard, saw him turn up the gas in the two upstairs back rooms and heard him calling as though to his wife. After about three minutes he came hurriedly out, saying: "Come and see; she has been killed."

Then they all went in, by way of the scullery and kitchen, and in the front sitting-room they saw Mrs. Wallace lying dead on the floor near the unlit gas-fire. Her head had been brutally battered in, and the wall and furniture was splashed with blood. In the kitchen a cabinet had been broken open and a cash-box emptied of its contents (about £4) and replaced on the shelf.

This box was where Wallace kept the insurance money each week, till Wednesday, when he paid it in. On most Tuesdays it would have amounted to £20 or £30, but that week he had paid out about £14 in benefits.

Wallace then ran upstairs to see if anything else had been stolen. He returned almost at once, saying: "There is £5 in a vase; they have not taken that." Mr. Johnston then went for the police.

Wallace and Mrs. Johnston returned to the sitting-room, where they looked round in vain for the weapon. They then noticed that a mackintosh, which Wallace at once identified as his own, was lying rolled up against the shoulder of the corpse, "as though," to quote a police witness, "the body was a living person and you were trying to make it comfortable."

They touched nothing, but went back to the kitchen, relit the fire, which was almost out, and waited. During this time Wallace, who till then had shown astonishing self-control, twice broke down and sobbed. When the police examined the mackintosh it was found to be heavily splashed and smeared with blood all over and also partially burnt. Mrs. Wallace's skirt was stained and burnt also. Upstairs, the bedclothes in the front room, which had not been used for a fortnight, were pushed off the bed and flung about the floor, though no cupboards or drawers seemed to have been disturbed or opened.

One clot of blood was found in the bathroom, but there were no damp towels. A small smear of blood was also found on one of the currency notes in the vase in the back bedroom. There were no finger-prints on the cash-box and no signs of forcible entry into the house. The locks on both doors, front and back, were discovered to be defective, so that they were rather awkward to open.

Wallace said he "thought" the front door had been bolted before he opened it to admit the police, but this point was never quite cleared up.

The police surgeon arrived at ten o'clock and asserted that Mrs. Wallace had by then been dead four hours. Actually, we know she was alive at least as late as 6.30; but *rigor mortis* is always a very uncertain indication, in spite of the dogmatic pronouncements of doctors in detective fiction. It seems unlikely, however, that she was alive much after seven.

Eleven ferocious blows had been struck, and it seemed clear that the murderer must have been heavily spattered with blood. Wallace, now once more "cool and collected," and smoking cigarettes, said he had no suspicion of anybody, and, after making a statement, was sent to sleep, if he could, at his brother's house.

Next day the charwoman who occasionally worked for the Wallaces, reported that two things were missing from the house since her last visit on January 7: a small kitchen poker and an iron bar used for cleaning under the gas-fire in the sitting-room.

A minute search of the drains and waste ground in the district failed to disclose these, or any other, weapons. On the 22nd Wallace furnished the police with a list of friends and acquaintances whom his wife might have admitted to the house during his absence.

He was also foolish enough to question Mr. Beattie closely about the exact time of "Qualtrough's" telephone call, remarking: "The police have cleared me." When asked why he had said this, he replied: "I had an idea; we all have ideas; it was indiscreet of me."

It was, indeed; and this explanation did not improve matters. On February 2, Wallace was arrested and charged with the murder of his wife.

The trial opened on April 22, and the prosecution put forward their reconstruction of the crime. Having (for no ascertainable reason) determined to murder his wife, Wallace had himself telephoned to the café in the name of Qualtrough, to prepare himself an alibi for the next day. The voice had been quite unlike his, but he could have disguised it.

On Tuesday evening he suggested a music practice, and asked his wife to light the gas-fire in the sitting-room, which was used only for music and receiving visitors.

Meanwhile, he went upstairs, took off all his clothes (to avoid bloodstains), put on his old mackintosh (to receive bloodstains), came down armed with the iron bar (or poker, or both), savagely killed the poor woman, made a futile attempt to burn the incriminating mackintosh, broke open the cabinet and cash-box to suggest burglary, went up and flung bedclothes about for the same purpose, washed his bloodstained hands and legs, dressed, and rushed away to catch his tram.

After drawing ostentatious attention to himself and his errand, by way of confirming the alibi, he returned, pretended to be unable to get in till he had secured the Johnstons as witnesses, and then "discovered" the body, preserving all the time a callous demeanour, except for a few crocodile tears in the kitchen.

Now, this story has a good many holes in it, the most obvious being the complete lack of motive. Mrs. Wallace was insured for £20 and had £90 in the Post Office; but her husband had his own bank-balance of over £150, and all his affairs were in perfect order.

There was no evidence of any quarrel. The police surgeon said that the number and violence of the blows pointed to homicidal frenzy. True, Wallace had always seemed eminently sane before and since the murder. "The mind," said the good doctor, "is very peculiar."

But a frenzy carefully prepared for by an alibi twenty-four hours in advance is almost too peculiar for belief.

Then the alibi itself fails in the very first duty of an alibi: it makes no pretence of covering the time of the murder. Wallace never attempted to suggest that he left the house before the milk-boy's visit, though nobody saw him go, and he might have said what he liked.

He made, in fact, no effort to fix the time till 7.45 – ludicrously too late to establish the alibi. Then, why his own mackintosh? Why not some garment of his wife's? Or a new mackintosh? Why any garment at all? And why the imbecile attempt to destroy the mackintosh on the sitting-room floor, when there was an open fire in the kitchen?

What did he do with the pokers? They were not thrown away anywhere along his route, and he had no time to carry them far. Why take them away at all? He had only to wipe off his finger-prints and leave them at home if he wanted to support the burglary theory.

As for his having washed himself in the bathroom, there is no real evidence that the murderer ever went upstairs at all, for it turned out that the blood-clot in the bathroom and the smear on the £1 note were quite likely carried there by one of the dozen or so policemen who hovered about the house all night, while the unconvincing disorder in the bedroom might well be explained otherwise.

But, indeed, every incident in the case might have two explanations, each as plausible as the other.

For example:

Question: How is it that "Qualtrough's" telephone-call was put in at a point about three minutes from Wallace's house about three minutes after Wallace left home? *Answer*: (*a*) Because Wallace put it in himself; (*b*) Because the murderer watched Wallace out of the house and then telephoned at once from the nearest point.

Question: Why did Wallace make so many inquiries for "Menlove Gardens East" after being told that it did not exist? *Answer*: (*a*) Because he wanted as many witnesses as possible to his alibi; (*b*) Because he was too careful a man to believe any statement he had not verified, and it was quite possible that Mr. Beattie had taken the address down wrong.

Question: Why did Wallace not display more emotion when the body was found? *Answer*: (*a*) Because he was a heartless brute; (*b*) Because, as a disciple of the Stoic philosopher he, in his own words, "tried to be as calm and as cool as possible."

And so on, at every point.

You pay your money you see, and take your choice. The judge summed up for an acquittal, calling the prisoner's account of the matter "wonderfully lucid and consistent," and warning the jury, "it is no use applying tests to evidence if none of them really excludes the possibility of the prisoner's innocence."

The jury, after an hour's retirement, found Wallace guilty. Two weeks later, the Appeal judges, "looking very grave," quashed the verdict, on the ground that the prosecution had not proved their case – a decision which made criminal history.

Who, then, murdered Julia Wallace? I think that if a detective novelist had to make a story to cover the facts it would run something like this:

There was a man – let us call him by his own assumed name of "Qualtrough" – who had got himself into financial difficulties through a dishonesty which, perhaps, Wallace had himself helped to expose. At any rate, he knew Wallace well – knew his habits with regard to the insurance money – knew that if the Wallaces went out together they took the money with them, but that if Wallace went out alone he left it at home in his wife's care.

He was also a frequenter of the City Café, and so could see by the list of club fixtures that always hung there which night Wallace was due to play chess. This man determined to rob Wallace's cash-box and throw the guilt on Wallace.

On the Monday night, Qualtrough hid at a point near the end of Wolverton Street which Wallace was bound to pass – by whichever door he went out – on the way to the café. As soon as he saw the little man go past he hurried to put in the bogus telephone-call before Wallace could be there to receive it and recognise his voice.

He may then have taken a taxi or motor-car to the café, arriving in time to hear whether Wallace got the message and meant to keep the appointment. In any case, he would again be in his hiding-place on the Tuesday night, and when he saw Wallace pass he would know that the bait had been taken. Even if Wallace went and returned immediately, Qualtrough had a good forty minutes in hand.

In the meantime, Mrs. Wallace, before sitting down to a quiet evening by the kitchen fire, bethought herself, like a careful housewife, that this would be a good moment to shake out the bedding in the disused front room, to prevent it from getting damp.

It was a January night, and she had a cold; so, on her way up, she took her husband's mackintosh from the hall-stand and slipped it on. While she is stripping the bed the bell rings. She runs down to answer it. The piled-up bedclothes topple over, as is their way, and fall on the floor.

There is a man on the doorstep. Perhaps he gives his own name. Perhaps, if she does not appear to recognise him, he says he is Qualtrough, detained by some accident, unable to get home in time for his appointment, hoping to catch Wallace before he starts. In any case, she asks him to come in and wait.

She takes him into the sitting-room, lights the gas-fire, strips off the mackintosh with an apology and lays it down. Now comes the crucial moment. Perhaps not intending murder (for in that case he would have brought his own weapon), Qualtrough snatches up the handy mackintosh and flings it over her head. But she resists – and in that moment recognises him – calls him by his own name.

That will never do. At all costs she must be silenced for ever! He catches up the iron bar from the fireplace and beats her down. In his terror and rage, he strikes her again and again.

She falls against the gas-fire, burning her skirt, and as he stoops over her the mackintosh swings out and catches fire also. Smoke – smell – fire – the neighbours alarmed – that must not happen! He turns out the gas-fire and stamps out the burning stuff on the hearthrug.

But the coat has been a good friend to him; it has taken nearly all the bloodstains, and now he uses it to wipe his boots and trouser-legs. Has he really killed her?

With a vague hope – a dim remorse – with God knows what confused idea in his mind, he rolls the mackintosh up and thrusts it under her shoulder. But she is dead; and now he must carry out his plan and get away. He goes into the kitchen and breaks open the cabinet with the kitchen poker.

Nothing there. Where, then –? Ah, the cash-box! That will be the thing! He opens it. Four pounds! Four pounds only as the price of murder! Automatically he takes the money out, automatically rubs his finger-prints from the box and replaces it on the shelf.

Finger-prints! How about the pokers? He forces himself to return to the horrible sitting-room, collects the iron bar, and then I think something – a passing footstep, a voice in the street – startles him. He extinguishes the light and creeps out the back way, taking the pokers with him.

The two pokers are a difficulty in any solution of the mystery. Somebody took them; and in Wallace to do so would have been madness. Qualtrough could remove them with less danger, especially if he had his own car waiting. Possibly they were taken purposely in order to incriminate their owner.

After the appeal Wallace returned to his employment with the insurance company, who believed wholeheartedly in his innocence. But in Liverpool he was a pariah. He removed to a little house in Cheshire and sought comfort in his garden, his scientific studies, and the fortifying counsels of Marcus Aurelius.

In a diary, which seems to be absolutely sincere, he has recorded his bitter and unceasing sorrow for the loss of his wife. "Julia, Julia, how can I do without you?" "I seem to miss her more and more."

Sept. 14, 1931. Just as I was going to dinner—

stopped me and said he wanted to talk to me . . .
He must realise I suspect him . . . I fear I put him
on his guard . . . I wonder if it is any good putting
a private detective on to his track?

Oct. 6, 1931. I am dreadfully nervous about
entering the house after dark.

In a newspaper article written in April, 1932:
I know the murderer. . . . He is capable of, and
has reason for, attempting to remove me before
I place him in the dock where I stood . . .

But "that fell sergeant Death is strict in his arrest"; and
before Wallace could accomplish this, the "only mission left
him in life," he was once more condemned to die, and by
this time by a court from whose sentence there is no appeal.
When Qualtrough learned of Wallace's death on February
26, 1933, he must have thought himself a lucky man.

And by the way, why "Qualtrough"? If we could know
what list, what book, what association of ideas suggested
that curious name, we might know to whose mind it was
suggested.

Dorothy L. Sayers

AFTERWORD

In 1960, I collaborated with Patricia Pitman on *An
Encyclopaedia of Murder*. Mrs. Pitman was convinced of
Wallace's guilt, I – in spite of misgivings about his character
– of his innocence. He simply had no reason to kill Julia.
Two or three years later, she surprised me by telling me that
she was now convinced of Wallace's innocence. It seemed
that she had been talking to one of Britain's leading crime
experts, J. H. H. Gaute, a director of Harraps publishers,
and he had told her the real identity of the murderer. I

hastened to contact Joe Gaute, with whom I had had much friendly correspondence about murder. It was from him that I first heard the name of the man he was certain was the killer of Julia Wallace: Gordon Parry. Wallace himself, it seemed, had believed that Parry murdered his wife, and after his retirement had made a public statement to the effect that he had had an alarm button installed inside his front door.

After the murder, Wallace had been asked by the police what callers might have been admitted to the house by his wife; he named fifteen people (including his sister-in-law Amy). Asked if he suspected any of them Wallace hesitated, then admitted that he was suspicious of a young man named Gordon Parry. This man had called at his house on business, and was trusted by Julia. But he had a criminal record. And he knew where Wallace kept his collection money. At the time of the murder, Parry was heavily in debt. Questioned by the police, Parry alleged that he had been with "friends" on the evening of the murder, and the friends corroborated this; however, two years later, Parry admitted that it had been "a mistake".

Crime writer Jonathan Goodman, who was writing a book on the Wallace case, decided to try to track down Gordon Parry. It was a long and complicated task, which began in Liverpool, but which eventually led him to an address in south London. Together with another crime writer, Richard Whittington-Egan, Goodman went to call on Parry.

Parry, a powerfully built little man with sleeked-back grey hair and a military moustache, received them with the "bogus bonhomie of a car salesman", and talked to them on his doorstep. They decided that "his manner masks . . . considerable firmness, even ruthlessness. He would be a nasty man to cross". Parry hinted that he could reveal much about Wallace, and described him as "a very strange man" and "sexually odd". He seemed to know what had become of everybody involved in the case, as if he had been carefully following its aftermath over the years. And when he finally dismissed Goodman and Whittington-Egan, they both had the feeling that he was thinking that he had fooled better people than they were . . . In his book *The Killing of Julia Wallace*, Goodman refers to Parry as "Mr. X", and it is fairly clear that he regards him as the chief suspect.

In 1980, a news editor in Liverpool's Radio City, Roger Wilkes, became interested in the Wallace case, and started researching it for a programme. He contacted Jonathan Goodman, who at first was understandably cagey about revealing Parry's identity, in case he found himself involved in a libel suit. But through Wallace's solicitor, Hector Munro, Wilkes tracked down Parry's record. At the time of the murder, Parry was twenty-two. The son of well-to-do parents, he had worked for the Prudential for a while, but had failed to pay in various premiums he had received – his parents had paid the money. Parry had been charged at various times with theft, embezzlement and indecent assault – at his trial a medical expert had described him as "a sexual pervert".

Wilkes persisted, but when he finally tracked down Parry to North Wales, he discovered that he had died a few weeks before, in April 1980. Nevertheless, he continued with his investigation. Who were the "friends" who had given Parry his alibi for the night of the murder? The answer that emerged was that it was not friends but *a* friend – a Miss Lily Lloyd, to whom Parry was engaged. And from Jonathan Goodman he learned that when Parry had jilted her two years later, Miss Lloyd had gone to Wallace's solicitor and offered to swear an *affidavit* saying that the alibi she had given Parry for the night of the crime was untrue. Wilkes then managed to track down Miss Lloyd, who had played a piano in a cinema in the 1930s. If the police had taken the trouble to check *her* alibi, they would have learned that she could not have been with Parry at the time of the murder – she was working in the cinema.

Finally, Wilkes uncovered the clinching piece of evidence. At the time of the murder, a young garage mechanic named John Parkes had been working near Parry's home. He knew

Parry as a "wide boy" – in fact, had been to school with him. On the night of the murder, Parry had called at the garage in an agitated state, and washed down his car with a high pressure hose. Parkes saw a glove in the car, and pulled it out to prevent it getting wet. It was soaked with wet blood.

Wilkes had finally tracked down the murderer of Julia Wallace, but half a century too late.

C.W.

1931

The Vera Page Case

Like the Wallace case, the sex murder of 10-year-old Vera Page in the Notting Hill area of London is still officially unsolved. Ex-superintentendent George Cornish, who wrote an account of the case, had good legal reasons for not telling the full story – as well, I think, as embarrassment at the mistake that almost certainly prevented the murderer being brought to justice. First, then, Cornish's own account from Great Unsolved Mysteries.

The wanton murder of a child is always horrible, and I think that the death of Vera Page was the most terrible case which I had to deal with during my career as a detective.

Late in the evening of Monday, December 14, 1931, Mr. Charles Page, of Notting Hill Gate, went to the local police station to report that his little daughter Vera was missing.

She had, he told the police, returned home from school as usual about half-past four that afternoon. Tea was at half-past five, and the child had gone out again to visit her aunt who lived a short distance away.

She reached her aunt's home safely and left again at a quarter to five, carrying her school swimming certificates with her. She never returned home, and although he made inquiries from friends and relations to whom she might have gone, no one had seen her.

The police made all the usual routine inquiries. The newspapers published her photograph and other details, and on Tuesday an SOS was broadcast. Still there was no news.

Early on Wednesday morning a milk roundsman discovered the body of a little girl lying in a patch of shrubbery in the front garden of a house in Addison Road, Notting Hill. Vera Page had been found.

When we arrived I suspected that we were confronted with one of the most difficult problems which a detective has to face, that unknown and variable quantity, the criminal maniac whose insanity is intermittent. Before I continue with the story of what followed it is important that something should be understood of the pathological side of this type of man.

In the first place, unless we could obtain definite evidence to the contrary, there was no real reason to suppose that he knew the dead child. He might very well be a stranger not only to her, but also to the neighbourhood.

Perhaps he was a Londoner, but he could equally well have come from some other place. He might have been staying in the neighbourhood, or merely passing through it. If he was suddenly seized with his mania he would probably accost the first woman or girl he came across.

Once the mania had passed, it was quite possible that he would have no recollection of what had occurred. It was not improbable that to his family, relations and friends he appeared a normal man.

It was very likely that somewhere, not necessarily in London at all, there was a man going about his usual everyday occupation with no knowledge that he had recently committed murder. He would read the details of the crime in the newspapers, but he would not know that they had anything to do with him, and therefore he would not do or say anything that might arouse suspicion in the minds of other people.

Our work was to try to find out whether this man had

been seen, where he had murdered the child, and whether he had left any clue which could assist us to discover his identity. From the evidence we obtained the following facts emerged.

Vera Page had last been seen alive between five and six o'clock on Monday evening. A school friend had spoken to her outside a chemist's shop not far from her home. The little girl wanted to buy some soap dominoes, which were being shown in the window, for a Christmas present, and she had probably gone to look at them.

We could discover no one who had seen her near, or with a man, but about that time some man must have spoken to her. The question at once arises as to whether she was in the habit of speaking to strangers.

We were told that she never talked to people she didn't know, but this would probably depend very much on how the strangers spoke to her. If, for instance, he had asked her where she was going, and she had told him "home," he might well have said that "Mummy had asked him to go with her," and she would have gone without hesitation.

Approximately forty hours had elapsed between the time when the child was last seen alive and the time when her body was found. Where had she been during that time?

Medical evidence gave us the information that she had been dead at least twenty-four hours, and probably longer. The body was not rigid; therefore she must have been in a fairly warm place, for it was cold December weather.

It had rained from 3 p.m. on Tuesday until 9 p.m. that evening and Wednesday morning was damp and misty. The child's clothes had absorbed very little moisture, and I formed the opinion that she could not have been lying in the garden for more than two hours before she was found.

This was confirmed by other evidence which showed that if the body had been there before eight o'clock, it would have been seen.

An examination of the clothes gave us little assistance except that there were traces of coal dust and one or two spots of candle grease. Her swimming certificates, which were printed on white paper, and the red beret which she was wearing on Monday evening had disappeared.

We must now set to work on this theory. Between, say, seven o'clock on Monday evening and about the same time on Wednesday morning the child had been somewhere dry and comparatively warm. It was possibly a coal shed or cellar which had been lit by a candle.

The beret and certificates might be there, or the murderer might have carried them away with him, or thrown them away. To find the place where the murder took place, even if it was in the immediate neighbourhood, was no easy task. But we set to work to make exhaustive inquiries, and hoped that some piece of useful information might come in as a result of the widespread public interest in the case.

We then had to try to solve another series of problems. How had the murderer brought the body to the garden from the place where it had been "hidden?" Had he carried it in his arms, brought it in a car, or perhaps on a coster's barrow or even in a perambulator? Had anyone seen him?

Although it was still dark, there were plenty of people about in the streets between seven and eight o'clock in the morning. Why had he chosen that particular place?

There was no attempt at concealment. The body had been laid gently down where the first person who walked along the path by the patch or shrubbery would see it.

To the first two questions we could obtain no answer. No one had seen or heard anything suspicious. To the third question the answer must lie in the psychology of the murderer. He had no reason for choosing that particular road or garden, he made no attempt at concealment either in bringing the body there or when he left it.

All he wanted was to put it away somewhere, and he put it gently down in the first place that seemed suitable. Probably the fact that he might be seen never occurred to him, nor that it would matter if he were.

As far as we could discover he was completely unobserved. But for this chance we might have discovered his identity.

On Thursday evening, December 17, a woman living in the Notting Hill Gate neighbourhood, not far from the garden in Addison Road, brought a red beret to us. This, she told us, she had found, soaking wet, in her area.

Near it were some torn pieces of paper and a bit of candle. The candle end she had used up, the bits of paper she had thrown away in her dustbin which since then had been cleared. It looked as though these might be Vera Page's beret and her swimming certificates.

Investigation showed that there was also an unlocked and empty coal shed in the area. Was this the scene of the murder? Had the child's body lain in this unlocked shed for forty hours, and had chance again stepped in and prevented anyone from opening the door?

Many of the children in the district were wearing red berets at that time and there was nothing to prove that the one found belonged to Vera Page. The candle end had gone beyond recovery, so had the pieces of paper. The most thorough and minute examination of the coal shed revealed nothing to show that anyone had entered it, or that a body had been left there.

We had one other clue. In the crook of the child's arm when she was found there was a finger bandage composed of boric lint and a piece of bandage. Without any doubt the murderer had had this on one of his fingers when he put the body down in the garden. But the most careful scientific examination of both bandage and lint did not help us, for they were of an ordinary type that could be bought anywhere for a few pence.

So ended this tragic case. No more information that could assist us was forthcoming. We could get no answer to our questions, nor could we answer another: Where had the murderer himself been during those forty hours?

Possibly he had stayed with the dead child. It is, however, more than possible that somewhere the murderer of Vera Page goes about his day's work without any knowledge that he is a murderer.

George Cornish

AFTERWORD

Discussing the case in *Written in Blood* nearly sixty years after it happened, I was able to supply the facts that Cornish was unable to reveal.

On the morning of 15 December 1931, a milkman entering a garden in Addison Road, Holland Park, saw the body of a child lying on the lawn. She was identified as 10-year-old Vera Page, who had been missing from her home at 22 Blenheim Crescent, in the Notting Hill area of London, since the previous evening. She had been raped and then manually strangled. When the body was moved, a finger-stall fell out from the crook of the arm.

A number of clues enabled the police to reconstruct roughly what had happened. Vera Page had last been seen alive at a quarter to seven on the previous evening; she had been on her way back from the house of an aunt, and had been seen looking in the windows of shops decorated for Christmas. Spilsbury's examination indicated that she had been raped and strangled not long after she was last seen, close to her home. Since she was a shy child, it seemed clear that she had been murdered by someone she knew and trusted. This man had probably taken her to a warm room – decomposition had already set in – and raped and killed her there. Then he had hidden the body in a coal cellar – this was indicated by coal dust on her clothes. The cellar had no electric light; this was suggested by spots of candle grease on the child's clothes. Some time around dawn, the murderer had retrieved the body and taken it to the garden in Addison Road, probably using a barrow. It had rained for much of the night, but the child's clothes were dry. As he removed his hands from under her arms, the bandage had slipped off his finger.

The murder caused intense public indignation, and the police mounted an enormous operation to track down the killer. Door-to-door enquiries were made over the whole area, and they quickly located a suspect. He was a 41-year-old labourer named Percy Orlando Rush, and he lived in a flat in Talbot Road, close to Vera Page. Moreover, his parents lived in the same house as Vera Page, so he often saw her. On the evening of the murder, his wife had been visiting her mother, and had not arrived home until later. So Rush could have murdered Vera Page, then taken her down to the coal cellar in the basement before his wife arrived home. Moreover, Rush had a wound on his left little finger, and had been wearing a finger-stall until recently.

The finger-stall was examined by Dr. Roche Lynch, the Home Office analyst. He found that it had covered a suppurating wound, and that the bandage had been soaked in ammonia. Percy Orlando Rush worked in Whiteley's Laundry, near Earls Court, and his job involved placing his hands in ammonia.

There was another damning piece of evidence against Rush. At dawn on 15 December, a man of his description had been seen pushing a wheelbarrow covered with a red cloth near the garden where the body had been found. When the police searched Rush's home, they found a red table-cloth.

From the point of view of forensic science, the most interesting clue was provided by the candle grease. In the previous year, an Austrian engineer had invented a new method of testing candle wax. It was melted, with careful temperature control, on a microscope slide, and allowed to cool. Examined thtough a microscope under polarized light, the wax would reveal its "fingerprinting", a characteristic crystalline structure. The wax on Vera Page's clothing was examined in this way, and compared with candles in her own home. They proved to be quite different. But it was identical with the wax of a candle found in Rush's home. So were certain spots of candle grease on Rush's overcoat.

But the crucial piece of evidence was the bandage. And here Superintendent George Cornish recognized that he may have made a mistake. He had let his suspect know about the finger-stall. And when he asked Rush for samples of bandage from his own house, Rush had handed them over with a faint smile that Cornish found disturbing. In fact, Roche Lynch's microscopic examination of the bandage established that it was not the same as that of the finger-stall.

Cornish's men scoured every chemist's shop in west London to try to find if anyone could recall selling bandages to Rush or his wife. If he could establish that Rush had bought some other type of bandage, and it proved identical with the finger-stall, then his case was complete.

Unfortunately, this attempt was a failure. The circumstantial evidence against Rush was overwhelming. But unless the bandage could be traced to him, the case had a fatal flaw. This became clear at the coroner's inquest, conducted by Dr. Ingleby Oddie, on 10 February 1932. Rush proved to be a short, thick-set man who wore horn-rimmed glasses and a black moustache. His evidence was punctuated by angry cries of "Liar!" from the spectators. But Rush stuck to his story that he had ceased to wear his finger-stall some days before the disappearance of Vera Page; he explained that he wanted to "harden" the wound. All the coroner's questions – and those of jurymen – make it clear that they were convinced of Rush's guilt. But no one had actually seen Rush with Vera Page, and after only five minutes, the jury decided there was insufficient evidence to charge him with her murder.

C. W.

Winnie Ruth Judd

When I was driving across America in 1967 – from New York to Seattle – I called upon the poet and novelist August Derleth at his home near Sauk City, Wisconsin, and spent the day with him. I was fascinated to observe on his bookshelf a set of books about murders in famous American cities: *New York Murders*, *Chicago Murders*, *Denver Murders*, and so on. As a historian of crime, I looked at them with a certain predatory envy. There were nine volumes, all dating from immediately after the Second World War, and now obviously out of print. But in the course of my six-month stay in Seattle, I learned of a California bookseller who specialised in locating second-hand books, and in due course became possessor of the set. They contain some marvellous items, some by distinguished writers like Damon Runyon (on Ruth Snyder) and Erle Stanley Gardner (on the murder of William Desmond Taylor.)

The gruesomely fascinating case of Winnie Judd is little known outside America – one very good reason for including it here. Another is that this is a first-hand account by a reporter who worked on the case and who met the murderess. The decision to include it was taken after some hesitation, for it is, from the point of view of the present anthology, rather too long. But after reading it again, I decided that its air of immediacy is irresistible.

Incidentally, the reference to the use of rattle-snakes as a murder weapon refers to the case of Robert James, which will be found later in this book.

The chamber of commerce doesn't mention it. But there is something about Los Angeles that makes citizens knock each other off in curious and fascinating ways. They use ice picks, hammers, home-made bombs and rattlesnakes. They bury their victims in cisterns, chicken yards and basements. They even ship them about by rail. The most notorious exponent of the latter method was a copper-haired lady named Winnie Ruth Judd.

I have heard various explanations of this bloody phenomenon. One amateur criminologist blamed the weather, said it had something to do with the seasons, or lack of them. Another thought that the remarkable advertising campaigns of funeral parlors were at fault. He said that when people continually read billboards like "Bury Your Loved Ones in High Dry Ground," and "Whatever You Do in Times Like These Don't Ration Grief at the Grave," they begin to look on death as something to be welcomed. Still another felt that certain newspaper editors who tack fascinating labels on every murder, no matter how cheap or grisly, should be taken to task.

I am one who holds with this latter theory. In my time, at the insistence of managing editors, I have taken some run-of-the-mill killing worth no more than two paragraphs and whooped it up into three columns. There was a poor old witless janitor who could no longer stand his wife's tongue lashings, hit her with an axe and then stuffed her in a trunk in his garage. We made him an engineer. We made his wife beautiful. And we called it the "Thin Man" murder. He was thin. Then there was a Pasadena killing around the corner from the Shrine temple. In front of the temple were two stone sphinxes. It would have been necessary for the sphinxes to walk a block to witness the crime. But that didn't bother us. It became the Sphinx Murder. Only the

Sphinx, who saw this dark and gory crime, knew the secret of the riddle.

Such goings on in the press could arouse a competitive spirit in murderers, could set them to trying to outdo each other. Such a thought makes me uneasy, makes me thank God that I deserted a rewrite desk for one of my own – that I stopped writing about real killings and took up imaginary ones.

However, I was not the one who, back in 1931, called Winnie Ruth Judd the "Velvet Tigress" and the "Wolf Woman." Nor did Tom Treanor, who just missed capturing her single-handed; nor Lionel Moise, who took Tom's failure so much to heart.

Now, in 1947, Winnie Ruth is locked up in an asylum in Arizona. Moise is still making big reporters out of little ones in New York. And Tom Treanor sleeps in a French cemetery. When he was killed in 1944 during the invasion of France, no one mentioned his part in the Winnie Ruth Judd murder case. And no wonder, in the light of all the things he had done, all the great stories he had covered and written since he started as a cub on the old *Los Angeles Express*. I bring it up because it illustrates how wrong guys can be about other guys. In 1931 we thought Tom was in the wrong racket. We thought he should have taken his father's advice and gone into the cement business. Moise, city editor of that now forgotten paper, suggested it many, many times and in a loud voice.

Tom had just realized his ambition to become a reporter that day in '31 when the Winnie Ruth Judd case broke. He was a tall, merry, eager youth who resented the fact that he looked a lot like Charles Lindbergh. Tom had been writing a radio column for the paper when Moise became city editor. Hating radio, he turned his charm on Moise and that gentleman finally gave in and put him to covering Rotary luncheons and postoffice clerk's conventions at fifteen bucks a week.

We were in the middle of a fight with the police department

that bright October afternoon. Most of the staff was out digging up mean things to say about the cops. I was on rewrite putting the mean things together. Moise was on the desk making them even meaner. Tom was hanging around. The phone rang. Moise answered it, made a couple of notes and hung up. He beckoned to Tom.

"Go down to the SP station," he said. "Something is up. We do not know what because the coppers are not speaking to any gentlemen from the *Express.*"

Something certainly was up, we discovered when Tom called back. A baggageman named Andrew V. Anderson had become curious about a couple of trunks in the baggageroom. The trunks had arrived a while before on the Golden State Limited. They had been shipped from Phoenix, Arizona and it was evident from the aroma rising from them that all was not well inside.

Mr. Anderson wasn't looking for murder evidence. He was looking for illegal shipments of venison into the state.

Blood dripped from the big black trunk onto the station platform. Mr. Anderson looked. Mr. Anderson sniffed. Mr. Anderson stuck around and waited.

Around noon a copper-haired young woman and a red-haired young man in a collegiate sweater and corduroys walked into the baggage room. The young woman handed two baggage checks to the man at the window.

"I want my trunks," she said coolly.

The man glanced at the stubs, nodded and disappeared, to come back a moment later with Mr. Anderson.

"Sorry," said Anderson. "You'll have to open the trunks."

The young woman hesitated. She tried to look hurt. Then she sighed and said, "My husband has the keys. I'll have to call him."

"We'll be right back," said the red-haired youth. He took her arm and off they went. Being a suspicious man, Mr. Anderson followed, got· the license number of the roadster the red-haired youth was driving, then went back to wait. He waited three hours. More blood ran out of the big trunk. The noxious fumes thickened. He decided it was time to call the cops, which he did.

Detectives Paul Stevens and Frank Ryan answered the call. They looked at the big black trunk and the smaller steamer trunk. They hefted them.

"Deer meat all right," said Mr. Ryan. "Get me a crowbar."

Crowbar in hand, Ryan set to work on the larger trunk. He pried off the lock and lifted the lid.

Tom wasn't on hand when the trunk was opened so I'll have to quote from a newspaper account what happened then. According to the newspaper version, Mr. Ryan said in a hoarse whisper, "That's not venison. It's a human body." If my memory of Mr. Ryan's speech is at all accurate, he said something much more pungent.

But undoubtedly his whisper was hoarse. Wedged in a crouching position and wrapped in a sheet was the body of a woman – a brunette about thirty years old. She was wearing orange silk pajamas.

"Taken aback momentarily," the newspaper account continues, "the officers stared at the grisly find. Then they set to work on the steamer trunk. By this time a small crowd had gathered. The lock gave way and the lid was raised. A man in striped overalls fainted. From the trunk protruded a human foot. Ryan took hold of it. A leg appeared – a leg severed at the knee."

The story I have at hand doesn't say how Mr. Ryan felt about it. I imagine he was more than taken aback, standing there holding a leg in his fist. Apparently he didn't faint. Because when Tom reached the station and joined the little group, Mr. Ryan was still on his feet directing activities. He had found another leg and the upper torso of a woman with head and arms attached. A few parts of the body, to wit, the upper legs from the knees to the hips, and the lower torso, were missing. He had also found evidence that the bodies were those of Agnes Ann LeRoi, thirty, twice-divorced nurse, and Hedvig Samuelson, twenty-three, a tubercular school teacher, both of 2929 North Second Street, Phoenix. The trunks were full of letters addressed to the dead women and snapshots of the pair.

Had Mrs. Judd disposed of the trunks, she might have got away with the murders. There was nothing in her history to indicate that she would start knocking off her friends. An ex-nurse, recovering from tuberculosis, she had lived a quiet life of respectability. Her husband was a Los Angeles physician. She had been a good wife, a model wife, and was only separated from him by her illness.

Into those trunks she had packed not only the bodies but letters revealing her close friendship with the dead women.

Police read the letters, looked at the photographs and the records revealing that Mrs. Judd had shipped the trunks to herself in Los Angeles. They were certain who the murderer was.

But there were mysterious aspects to the case.

Where was the rest of Miss Samuelson's body? (She occupied the steamer trunk.)

How could a woman as small and slight as Mrs. Judd was, have butchered that one body so neatly?

Did she have help?

Where in hell was she?

The first question was answered within a few hours. The woman who took care of the station restroom appeared carrying a suitcase. In it were the missing pieces of Miss Samuelson's body.

Whether Mrs. Judd had help or not is still a moot question. At first she said she didn't. Later on, at her sanity trial, she intimated she did. But she wasn't specific.

It wasn't long before the police were on Winnie Ruth's trail. Armed with a license number, they traced the roadster to one Burton J. McKinnell, twenty-six-year-old University of Southern California law student. Mr. McKinnell was Mrs. Judd's brother. He had an apartment in Beverly Glen, a very pleasant canyon north of Beverly Hills which was the scene, many years back, of two fine murders. When I was a novice reporter I accompanied an *Examiner* man named George Van Sands up the canyon on a hunt for a woman's body. Mr. Van Sands found her accidentally. It was a hot day and he bent down over a water tap and turned it on. He seldom touched water after that experience, for the woman, a Mrs. Young, was in the cistern. But that is another story.

Burton was not at home. The police searched the place, came up with the name and address of one Dr. William C. Judd, of 823 Seventeenth Street, Santa Monica. They hot-footed it to that address. At the curb stood Mr. McKinnell's roadster. Mr. McKinnell and Dr. Judd were waiting upstairs.

Both men, according to newspaper accounts, were quite calm. Dr. Judd admitted that Winnie Ruth was his wife, that the last time he saw her was in Phoenix, where she lived for her health.

Burton said she was his sister. "This morning," he continued, "as I left my classes at U.S.C., I found my sister waiting for me in front of the political science building.

"She had just arrived from Phoenix. We had not expected her. She was nervous and wrought up. About her left hand she wore a heavy bandage. When I inquired about it, reluctantly she told me she had been shot. Then she grabbed my shoulder and said, 'Burton, there are two trunks at the station. You must help me get them. We must take them to the beach and throw them in the ocean.'"

Mr. McKinnell admitted he was puzzled by his sister's behavior. His story continues:

"I was puzzled by the request and by the wound in my sister's hand but I accompanied her to the railroad station. When the baggageman refused to turn over the trunks without an inspection, I knew something was wrong.

"I asked Sis what it was she had in the trunks. She finally admitted there were bodies in them. I asked if they were men and women. She replied that the less I knew about it, the better. I drove her to Sixth and Broadway, gave her five dollars and that's the last I saw of her."

At the time there were men who felt that Burton McKinnell's attitude and actions were peculiar. They weren't, really. He was young and he was fond of his sister who was in a hell of a jam. What would you do if your sister asked you to help her get rid of a couple of bodies?

Dr. Judd was also a bewildered man. He hadn't heard from his wife. He hadn't the slightest notion why she was knocking off her friends and shipping their bodies around in trunks. To the day of his death, two years ago, I think he was still bewildered by it all.

There wasn't much the police could do about it but haul the two gentlemen in for further questioning and start looking for Winnie Ruth. They didn't find her for a while.

However, they did find another clue linking her to the murders. One of the toilets in the restroom of a department store wouldn't work. A plumber investigated. He found what was left of a long letter written by Mrs. Judd. I forget whom she wrote it to. And the boys in the newspaper morgues whose business it is to clip the papers seem to have mislaid all the stories pertaining to the letter. I remember it as a rambling, peculiar missive in which she admitted killing her friends during a quarrel. It isn't important because she showed up after a time to tell the story in her own inimitable way. I mention it only to show how inexperienced she was in the art of murder. You don't do things like that if you want to stay out of jail. You make it as tough for the masterminds as possible. Until she took it on the lam, Mrs. Judd left a trail my cocker spaniel, who has no sense of smell, could follow. Only when she started running did she use her wits. She might still be running if the bullet wound in her hand hadn't got infected.

According to the clippings I have at hand, the search for Winnie Ruth was the greatest, most exciting and most intense since the manhunt for William Edward Hickman a few years before. That is an exaggeration. There has never been anything like that hunt for Hickman – not in Los Angeles anyway. I remember a city in the grip of terror when Hickman was on the prowl – a city where it wasn't safe to venture forth at night because it was full of guys with guns who were ready to shoot on sight any young man with curly black hair.

It wasn't like that when they were looking for Winnie Ruth. The cops were excited, with the angry excitement of frustrated men, but the citizens bore up well. People phoned in now and then to say they had seen her in Mexico, or San Francisco, or Santa Barbara or at the corner of Hollywood and Vine, but people always do that. It makes them feel useful.

By the time the manhunt was well under way, we had the background of the crime from the boys in Phoenix. Mrs. Judd, it appeared, had been employed for a time in the same clinic where Mrs. LeRoi was a nurse. Off-duty, Mrs. LeRoi took care of Miss Samuelson, a former Alaskan school teacher who had come to Phoenix suffering from tuberculosis. For months the three women lived together in a bungalow on North Second Street. A few months before the murder, Mrs. Judd had moved to an apartment of her own at 1130 East Brill Street on the other side of town.

Even after Mrs. Judd moved, the three women were friendly. Every now and then they got together for a party. They had got together the night of October 16th, a Friday, at the Samuelson-LeRoi bungalow.

On Saturday, H. N. Grimm, a baggage-transfer man, was summoned to the North Second Street address. Mrs. Judd was there, apparently alone. She showed him a big trunk and said she wanted it taken to the station. Mr. Grimm hefted it. Too heavy, he said. Much too heavy to check on a ticket.

"What's in it?" he wanted to know.

"Books," said Mrs. Judd. "My husband's medical library."

Then she told him to take it to her Brill Street address. She said she'd put some of the books in another trunk. Mr. Grimm did what he was told.

Next day, Mr. Grimm got another call from Mrs. Judd. This time she had three pieces of luggage – the big trunk, a steamer trunk and a suitcase. He was not a curious man. To him baggage was baggage. It was his racket to move trunks. So he took them to the station, figuring that would be the end of it. Little did he wot what he was toting around. When he found out, he gulped and turned pale. You could have knocked him down with a feather, he admitted.

Mrs. Judd followed the trunks to the station. She bought a one-way ticket to Los Angeles. Fittingly, she rode in the first Pullman behind the baggage car in which were the trunks and their human cargo. When Tom Treanor learned about this he wanted to write a piece in rhyme. He pointed out that the song "The Baggage Car Ahead" was very well known and that if he didn't make use of it, someone else would. Moise was almost shocked into silence.

"Tommy," he said, "if you want to do something useful, go out and find Mrs. Judd."

Tom admitted that the idea appealed to him. But he pointed out that everybody and his brother was looking for her. Where should he look?

Moise checked the list of places where she might be. Before she went to Phoenix she had been a patient at La Vina Sanitarium in the hills back of Altadena. "Run out there and look around," suggested Moise.

I thought the idea was silly. I said the cops would have cased the joint by this time. Tom agreed with me. But Moise was insistent, so Tommy went.

Tom found the sanitarium easily enough. He drove in the gate and went straight to the superintendent's office.

"I asked if Mrs. Judd was hiding anywhere around the place," Tom told us when he returned. "He was very annoyed. I don't blame him, really."

"Did you look around?" Moise wanted to know.

"Of course not," said Tom. "The superintendent said she wasn't there. That's good enough for me."

It turned out that the superintendent had reason to be annoyed. The cops had asked him the same question several times. So had a couple of other newspapermen. He was a busy man with a hospital to run and he hadn't seen Mrs. Judd for a long time. How was he or anyone else to know she was hiding in an unused building up the hill back of the administration office?

You couldn't blame Tom for not finding Mrs. Judd. The police couldn't find her either. By Wednesday night they were convinced she had committed suicide and so stated publicly. As one police authority put it, "Undoubtedly she has thrown herself in the ocean where she intended to throw her victims. We will find her body on the beach in due time."

Dr. Judd disagreed. He was convinced his wife was alive, so he appealed through newspaper advertisements for Winnie Ruth to give herself up. He had employed two attorneys for her – Richard Cantillon and Louis P. Russill. He urged her to get in touch with them. He said every effort would be made to keep her off the Arizona gallows.

The following afternoon, while the coroner was conducting an inquest and a jury was blaming Mrs. Judd for the two murders, she called Mr. Cantillon.

"This is Mrs. Judd," she said. "Can you please put me in touch with my husband?"

Mr. Cantillon gave her the telephone number of Attorney Patrick Cooney. He said he and the doctor would wait in Cooney's office for another call. That was because Mr. Cantillon was very popular with the press and a number of reporters were in the outer office drinking his gin. I was one of them. Tom was another.

We tried to tail Mr. Cantillon but he gave us the slip. He and the doctor waited an hour. Then Mrs. Judd called again. For fifteen minutes the doctor argued with her and finally she said all right, she was fed up with hiding out and would meet him in the lobby of the Biltmore Theatre. That's where Judd met her. That wasn't where the cops and the reporters met her. Two hours later Mr. Cantillon, looking very smug, led us to the undertaking establishment of Alvarez and Moore at Court and Olive streets. We found Winnie Ruth lying in

74

bed in an upstairs room looking pretty sick and bedraggled. Her wounded hand was infected and the wound had been freshly dressed. But she was quite calm.

Downstairs there were several bodies waiting for burial but that didn't worry her. It didn't worry us either. It gave us the opportunity for considerable fancy writing – such a fitting setting – such an eerie setting – candles and faded flowers and coffins and corpses – and upstairs a dame talking her head off to the cops. I give you her story in her own words:

"I met Mrs. LeRoi shortly after I arrived in Phoenix. We soon became fast friends. She told me about herself and I told her about my life.

"Anne invited me to her home. There I met her pal, Hedwig Samuelson, whom we all called Sammy.

"Sammy was ill. Anne took care of her. In return, Sammy helped Anne financially.

"Anne was a stunningly beautiful girl and loved all men. Not in an immoral way but as friends and companions. She loved a good time. Sammy, on the other hand, cared for no man. She was consumed by a very unusual love for Anne.

"I got to know both of the girls very well. Finally when Dr. Judd left Phoenix to come to Los Angeles I moved in with Anne and Sammy. We were very happy together.

"During my early months in Phoenix I had made the friendship of a millionaire lumberman. Jack was a splendid fellow, a good scout and a true friend to me.

"I introduced Jack to Anne. He seemed to like her. After I moved over with Anne and Sammy, Jack often came to the house in the evenings. We would have parties. He would bring his men friends.

"Jack, although he seemed to like Anne, was also kind to me. At first this was all right. Then Anne began to resent it. Finally I moved to my own apartment. Anne became very cool to me.

"There was another little nurse at the clinic and she was very cute. Her name was Lucille. Jack found out that Lucille was going on a hunting trip to the White Mountains. Jack planned a similar trip. He asked to meet Lucille, said they might make it a party. On Thursday evening, October 15th, I invited Lucille to my apartment for dinner. Then I asked Jack to come up. He brought two men friends. We had a happy evening. Anne learned about the party, for Jack had stopped by to see her on the way to my house. He had taken Anne and Sammy a radio.

"The next day, Friday, Anne went to lunch with me. She insisted that I come over to see her and Sammy that evening. I tried to renege but she insisted. I had special work to do at the clinic. I didn't get to the Second Street bungalow until after nine o'clock.

"Anne and Sammy were tired. They insisted I stay all night. I slept on the davenport. In the morning, Saturday morning, we were all three in the kitchen in our pajamas getting breakfast. Anne started to upbraid me for introducing other girls to Jack. She was angry because I had introduced him to Lucille. Sammy was furious because my action brought sorrow to her beloved Anne.

"Our words became heated. We were shouting at each other. Finally Anne screamed, 'Ruth, if that Lucille goes hunting with Jack I'll tell him things about other girls you have introduced him to.'

"The threat infuriated me. 'Anne,' I said, 'if you do a thing like that I will tell Jack about you.' At these words Sammy sprang to her feet, ran into the bedroom and came out with a little black-handled gun I had left behind with some other things when I moved to my own apartment.

"Sammy's face was drained of blood. Her eyes pierced me through. She pulled the trigger of the little gun. I threw up my arms. The bullet struck me in the hand. I threw my whole weight against Sammy and grabbed the gun. She fell behind the breakfast-nook table. I was over her. I shot twice.

"Anne screamed and ran at me with the ironing board. I pointed the gun at her and fired one shot."

That, according to Winnie Ruth, was it.

She had two bodies on her hands and she didn't quite

know what to do with them. While thinking it over, she went to work.

"I told the people at the clinic I was sick," she said. "I also told them Anne was sick. Then I went back to Anne's house."

Winnie Ruth was a busy girl that day. She packed both bodies in the one big trunk and had Mr. Grimm take them to her apartment. Then she cut Sammy up with a meat saw and a butcher knife and put most of her in the steamer trunk and the rest in the suitcase. Anne stayed in the big trunk.

After she left her brother in Los Angeles, Winnie Ruth started walking. She walked twenty miles to La Vina Sanitarium and hid in a vacant cottage. At night she crept to the kitchen to swipe food. Her hand began hurting, so she lit out, intending to give herself up, she said. En route she got hold of a newspaper, saw her husband's advertised appeal and called Mr. Cantillon.

Mrs. Judd stuck to that story all the time she stayed in the Los Angeles county jail. We liked it enough to try to buy an elaborated version of it. But the *Express* wasn't doing too well and another paper outbid us. However, the dickering gave me the chance to see a good deal of Winnie Ruth. I got the impression that she was a pretty cold-blooded article and so did the other guys who talked to her. We all figured she wasn't too sane, which, it turned out, she wasn't.

How true her story was, I can't say. Later on, at her trial, the Arizona authorities called her a liar. They said it wasn't self-defense but premeditated murder. They proved to the satisfaction of the jury that she went to see Anne and Sammy with a gun in her pocket on the night of October 16th, that she shot both women and then shot herself in the hand. Motive? Jealousy over the close friendship of her two victims, and jealousy over the attentions paid to them by some of Mrs. Judd's gentlemen friends.

The jury decided she should hang. She was in the death house waiting for the noose when the psychiatrists came to her rescue and called her insane.

Undoubtedly, the psychiatrists were right. All the evidence presented by the state pointed toward insanity. Premeditated or not, the murders were not committed by a normal woman, but by an insanely jealous one.

All of us who worked on the case wanted to keep Mrs. Judd in Los Angeles for trial. Things were dull around the courts at the time. But the boys in Arizona claimed priority and won.

It was Moise's idea that I join the caravan of officers and reporters on that trek to Phoenix. It was Tom Treanor's idea that he go along. He had a good car. I didn't. Moise gave in. Moise said maybe it would be good experience for Tommy. If Tom had stayed home you wouldn't find this squib in the files of one of the newspapers: "That night, in a surprise move, Sheriff McFadden started to Phoenix with her by motor. It was one of the most amazing treks in the annals of the west. Trailed by cars bearing newspapermen, the sheriff's automobile wended its way along shadowy, little-used roads throughout the night –" Why? Here's why.

Amazing is a mild word for that trip. There we were trailing the sheriff's car through the night when we found ourselves at Lake Elsinore.

If you ask any native how to get from Los Angeles to Phoenix he will certainly not mention Lake Elsinore. You just don't go that way. Yet here we were at Lake Elsinore. Someone had blundered.

"Now what do we do?" one of Mrs. Judd's escorts asked.

Mrs. Judd sat back calm and uninterested.

"We keep on this road to San Diego," a reporter suggested.

Tom stepped forward. "No, we don't. We take a short cut. I know a way that will save us hours of driving."

It was late and it was dark and everyone was cold and hungry and Tom sounded like a man who knew the country. They told Tom to lead on. He led.

The road got worse and worse. I was growing dubious. Tom assured me that all short cuts had shortcomings. Around two in the morning a settlement hove in sight. The sheriff honked at us and we stopped. The sheriff, too, was getting dubious. So was everyone else.

"Don't you worry," said Tom. "I know this country like a book. By the way, would you all like something to eat?"

Mrs. Judd said she could use some coffee. Tom disappeared behind one of the darkened buildings. Then things began to happen. Lights went on. Men came running. Stoves were lit. Food was produced. We were, it seemed, at Warner Hot Springs, and the management was more than glad to see us. I thought it odd but I said nothing. Tom kept out of my way.

The sheriff must have thought it odd too because I heard him asking the man who ran the place if we were on the right short cut. The man looked over at Tom and said yes, he guessed we were. If we kept going we'd hit the road to El Centro after a while.

"Isn't there a better way?" asked an officer.

"Not from here, there isn't," said the man.

"Maybe we should have gone to San Diego?"

"You're here," said the man. "So there's no use worrying."

When we got moving again I had it out with Tom. He confessed. This was a short cut of a sort, he said. It took a little longer in time, was all. "Anyway," he said brightly, "my father owns Warner Hot Springs. Think of the publicity we can give the resort in the *Express*."

We lost the caravan at dawn and we never caught up with it. We missed the triumphal return of Winnie Ruth Judd to the scene of the crime.

Just before we hit the El Centro road, a tire went flat. Les Wagner, of the United Press, paused to ask if we needed help. Tom waved him on. The other cars flashed by. Tom got out and opened the turtle back to get his tools. "How do you like that?" he said. "I haven't any jack."

79

That didn't daunt him. He was an inventive fellow and in two hours he rigged up a workable jack out of some rocks and a log and we got the tire changed. We stopped at the first gas station to phone the office. Tom stood at my elbow while I put the call in.

"Remember to mention Warner Hot Springs," he urged. "Tell Moise we went that way to escape the lynch mobs on the main highway."

What else could I do? And that's how the story came out, with a Warner Hot Springs dateline. Whether it brought the resort any extra business or not, I never found out.

Moise was satisfied. He liked the idea of the mobs waiting in the dark. He told us to hurry after Winnie Ruth to be on hand if any stray lynchers got her and we started hurrying. Out of El Centro we ran out of gas and had to push the car two miles. That was because Tom assured me his gas gauge didn't register accurately when it showed empty.

I didn't speak to him from El Centro to Phoenix. When we got there the tumult and the shouting had died. Tom wasn't at all upset. He said I had a good imagination. He said I could probably write a better piece than if I had been on hand. "You have all the expense money," he pointed out. "Let us take a few dollars and get a little whisky. There must be a bootlegger in town."

I refused. I said that any guy who forgot his jack and who let his gas tank run dry didn't deserve a drink. I said I was going to call Moise and suggest that Mr. Treanor be sent back to sacking cement. I called. I didn't get a chance to complain about Tom.

"By the way," said Moise. "Whose idea was that lynchmob story? We had it exclusive. It was a honey."

"Treanor's," I said. "And it was his idea to go around by Warner Hot Springs."

"I knew he'd come through," said Moise. "That boy has the makings of a great reporter. I need you here on rewrite. Give him the expense money and hop a train. He can handle the story from now on."

*   *   *

In due time, Winnie Ruth was tried, found guilty, then saved by the psychiatrists. They locked her up in the Arizona state hospital and that should have been the end of it. The tumult and the shouting died. Mrs. Judd was forgotten.

Apparently the peace and quiet of the hospital palled on Mrs. Judd. In October of 1939, she turned up missing. Six days later she was found hiding in an orange grove near Tempe.

In December of the same year, Mrs. Judd escaped again. For two weeks police in three states sought her. On the fifteenth of the month, a slim, bedraggled woman, shoeless and unkempt, walked into a drugstore in Yuma and asked for food. The drug clerk recognized her and called the cops and the saga of Mrs. Judd was ended.

"The door was open and I walked out," Mrs. Judd told police. "I kept on walking until I reached Yuma. Here I am."

That was Mrs. Judd's last escape. Since then she's been a model patient, quiet, tractable and good-natured. She seems perfectly satisfied to spend the rest of her life behind the hospital walls. Which is just as well – there's nothing else she can do.

Geoffrey Homes

How We Trapped Al Capone

Where law enforcement is concerned, the imprisonment of Al Capone on tax evasion charges was one of the most important events of the early 1930s. Capone, born in Brooklyn in 1899, had been summoned to Chicago by his boyhood hero Johnny Torrio, who was the chief lieutenant of mobster Big Jim Colosimo. In January 1920, America was turned into a gangsters' paradise by the passing of the Volstead Act, better known as Prohibition. Colosimo lost no time in extending his activities to bootlegging. But in May 1922, Colosimo was shot through the head by an unknown assailant – almost certainly hired by Torrio. It was widely believed that the killer was Al Capone. In November 1924, Torrio arranged the assassination of Irish mobster Dion O'Banion. O'Banion's remaining lieutenants swore vengeance, and in January 1925, Torrio narrowly survived an assassination attempt by Bugs Moran, and decided to return to Italy, leaving Capone in charge of his crime-empire. Capone's men succeeded in killing O'Banion's chief lieutenant, Hymie Weiss, in October 1926. And on February 13, 1929 – St. Valentine's Day – five Capone gangsters, two of them dressed as policemen, marched into Moran's garage and lined up seven men (including an innocent bystander) against the wall, then shot them down. Moran was not among them, but decided to retire. Which left Capone as the most powerful gangster in Chicago, with so many corrupt policemen in his pay that he was apparently above the law.

Now read on . . .

W hen my wife and I left Baltimore for Chicago in 1928, all I said was, "Judith, I'm after a fellow named Curly Brown." If I'd told her that Curly Brown was an alias of Scarface Al Capone, she'd have turned the car around then and there and made me take up some respectable trade like piano tuning. My assignment was to find clear proof of income-tax evasion by Capone. In previous years he had filed no tax return or had reported insignificant income.

Art Madden, our Chicago agent-in-charge, told me that hanging an income-tax rap on Alphonse Capone would be as easy as hanging a foreclosure sign on the moon. The Grand Panjandrum of the checkered suits and diamond belts had Cook County in the palm of his hand. He did all his business anonymously, through front men. To discourage meddlers, his production department was turning out fifty corpses a year.

For a base of operations the government gave me and my three assistants an overgrown closet in the old Post Office Building, with a cracked glass at the door, no windows, a double flat-topped desk and peeling walls. I spent months in fruitless investigation through banks, credit agencies and newspaper files.

I prowled the crummy streets of Cicero but could get no clue to show that a dollar from the big gambling places, the horse parlors, the brothels or the bootleg joints ever reached Scarface Al Capone. Jake Lingle, a Chicago *Tribune* reporter, had been seen with Capone in Chicago and Miami and, from the tips I got, he wasn't just writing interviews. So I saw the *Tribune* boss, Robert R. McCormick, and told him Jake Lingle's help would be appreciated by the United States government. "I'll get word to Lingle to go all the way with you," said the colonel. Lingle was assassinated next day in a subway, right in the busiest part of the city.

I was stuck, bogged down. Sixteen frustrating months dragged by. Capone was all over the front pages every day. It was common talk that he got a cut on every case of whiskey brought into Cook County; that he ran a thousand speakeasies, a thousand bookie joints, fifteen gambling houses, a string of brothels; that he controlled half a dozen breweries. He had bought a Florida palace on Palm Island and was spending $1000 a week on banquets. He tore around in sixteen-cylinder limousines, slept in fifty-dollar pajamas and ordered fifteen suits at a time at $135 each. His personal armed forces numbered seven hundred, equipped with automatic weapons and armored automobiles. But evidence of lavish living wasn't enough. The courts had to see *income*.

One night, in a desperate mood, I decided to check over all the data which my three assistants and I had piled up. By one o'clock in the morning I was bleary-eyed, and while gathering up my papers I accidentally bumped into our filing cabinet. It clicked shut. I couldn't find the key anywhere. "Now, where'll I put this stuff?" I wondered. Just outside, in a neighboring storeroom, I found an old filing cabinet full of dusty envelopes. "I can lay this old junk on the table," I thought to myself. "I'll put my own stuff in overnight."

In the back of the cabinet was a heavy package tied in brown paper. Just out of curiosity I snipped the string and found three ledgers, one a "special column cashbook." My eye leaped over the column headings: "Bird cage," "21," "Craps," "Faro," "Roulette," "Horse bets." Here was the diary of a large operation, with a take of from $20,000 to $30,000 a day. Net profits for only eighteen months (the books were dated 1925–26) were over half a million dollars.

"Who could have run a mill that size?" I asked myself. The answer hit me like a baseball bat: only three people – Frankie Lake, Terry Druggan or Al Capone! But I had already cleaned up the Druggan-Lake case. Two from three leaves one.

The ledgers had been picked up in a raid after the murder of Assistant State's Attorney William McSwiggin in 1926. They came from one of the biggest gambling palaces in Cicero, The Ship, where diamond-studded crowds from Chicago laid down $30,000 a year in wagers. Here was a record of *income*. If I could hang it around the neck of Al Capone, we'd have a case at last.

Scarface must have found out that we were closing in. On the inside of the gang I had planted one of the best undercover men I have ever known, Eddie O'Hare. One afternoon word reached me that Eddie wanted to see me at once. When we met, he was red-faced and excited. "You've got to move out of your hotel, Frank. The big fellow has brought in four killers from New York to get you. They know where you keep your automobile and what time you come in and go out. You've got to get out this afternoon!"

"Thanks for tipping me off, Eddie," I replied. So I phoned Judith I had a surprise for her – we were moving to the Palmer House, where she had once said she'd like to live. I left word at my hotel we were going to Kansas and drove to the Union Station – but right on through and around to the Palmer. Judith was completely confused and I hoped Al's torpedoes were, too.

Later Eddie met me with another report: "The big fellow's offering $25,000 reward to anybody who bumps you off!" When the story broke in the papers that Capone had put a price on my head, Judith took it with amazing calm. She simply said, "We're going straight home to Baltimore!" I finally won her over by promising she could be with me as much as possible. Women always think they're bulletproof.

Meanwhile I was working on the handwriting in the ledgers of The Ship. I think we must have collected handwriting samples of every hoodlum in Chicago – from voting registers, savings accounts, police courts. The painful process of elimination finally left me with a character named Lou Shumway, whose writing on a bank deposit slip was a dead twin to that in the ledgers. I heard from a tipster that Shumway was in

Miami, probably working at Hialeah or the dog tracks. All I had to go on was a description: "Shumway is a perfect little gentleman, refined, slight, harmless – not a racetrack sport at all."

In February 1931, I stood by the rail at Hialeah looking at the man I had been stalking for nearly three years. Scarface Al Capone sat in a box with a jeweled moll on either side of him, smoking a long cigar, greeting a parade of fawning sycophants who came to shake his hand. I looked upon his pudgy olive face, his thick pursed lips, the rolls of fat descending from his chin – and the scar, like a heavy pencil line across his cheek. When a country constable wants a man, I thought, he just walks up and says, "You're pinched." Here I was, with the whole U.S. government behind me, as powerless as a canary.

Two nights later, I spotted the "perfect little gentleman" my tipster had described, working at a dog track. I tailed him home, and picked him up next morning as he was having breakfast with his wife. He turned pale green. When I got him to the Federal Building, I said cold-turkey: "I am investigating the income-tax liability of one Alphonse Capone."

Gentleman Lou turned greener yet, but he pulled himself together and said, "Oh, you're mistaken. I don't know Al Capone."

I put my hand on his shoulder. "Lou," I said, "you have only two choices: If you refuse to play ball with me, I will send a deputy marshal to look for you at the track, ask for you by name and serve a summons on you. You get the point, Lou. As soon as the gang knows the government has located you, they will probably decide to bump you off so you can't testify.

"If you don't like that idea, Lou, come clean. Tell the truth about these ledgers. You were bookkeeper at The Ship. You can identify every entry in these books – and you can tell who your boss was. I'll guarantee to keep it secret until the day of the trial that you are playing ball with me.

You will be guarded day and night, and I'll guarantee that Mrs. Shumway will not become a widow." Lou quivered like a harp string but finally gave in. I spirited him out of Miami and hid him in California.

But we still had to show that *income* actually reached the pockets of Al Capone. A painstaking checkup on all the recorded money transactions in Cicero finally showed that one "J. C. Dunbar" had brought gunnysacks full of cash to the Pinkert State Bank and bought $300,000 in cashier's checks.

Agent Nels Tessem and I caught up with "Dunbar," whose real name was Fred Ries, in St. Louis. We tailed a messenger boy with a special-delivery letter and slapped a subpoena in Ries's palm. He was annoyed, especially since the letter was from Capone's headquarters telling him to flee to Mexico. He wouldn't talk at first. But after a week in a special vermin-ridden cell in a jail we picked out for him – we knew he had a pathological fear of bugs – Ries cried uncle. We sneaked him before a Chicago grand jury in the middle of the night. His testimony put the profits of The Ship squarely in the pockets of Scarface Al! I packed my scowling little treasure off to South America with government agents to guard him until we should need him in court.

In the autumn of 1931, two weeks before the Capone trial, Eddie O'Hare reported to me: "Capone's boys have a complete list of the prospective jurors. They're fixing them one by one – passing out thousand-dollar bills, promising political jobs, giving donations to churches. They're using muscle, too, Frank." Eddie handed me a list of ten names and addresses. "They're right off the jury list – names 30 to 39!"

Next morning I went with U.S. Attorney George E. Q. Johnson to the chambers of Federal Judge James H. Wilkerson, who was to sit in the Capone trial. The judge was reassuring – somehow he seemed like a match for Scarface Al. Sure enough, the ten names Eddie had given me tallied with the judge's list. But the judge didn't seem ruffled. He said calmly, "Bring your case into court as planned, gentlemen. Leave the rest to me."

The day the trial started, I fought my way through reporters, photographers and sob sisters. Al Capone came into the courtroom in a mustard-colored suit and sat down at the counsel table just a few feet from me. Phil D'Andrea, Al's favorite bodyguard, sat beside him, sneering at the crowd. As Judge Wilkerson entered in his black robe, Capone, behind the mask of his moonface, seemed to be snickering over the jury of new-found friends and intimidees who would soon send him back to the overlordship of Chicago.

Judge Wilkerson called his bailiff to the bench. He said in crisp, low tones, "Judge Edwards has another trial commencing today. Go to his courtroom and bring me his entire panel of jurors. Take my entire panel to Judge Edwards." The switch was so smooth, so simple. Capone's face clouded with the black despair of a gambler who had made his final raise – and lost.

The trial marched on. My gems, Gentleman Lou Shumway and the bug-bedeviled Ries, stood their ground on the witness stand, though Capone and Phil D'Andrea were staring holes through them the entire time. I kept my eyes on D'Andrea. When he got up to stretch during a recess I could have sworn I saw a bulge in his right hip pocket. But no, I thought, there wasn't a crumb in the world who would dare to bring a gun into federal court. I saw him stretch again. I had the boys send in word that a reporter wanted to see him. I followed him out of the courtroom. Nels Tessem and Jay Sullivan, my colleagues, led him down the corridor. As we passed Judge Wilkerson's chambers I shoved him inside. "Give me that gun!" I snapped. D'Andrea handed it over. "Give me those bullets!" He ladled out a handful of ammunition.

Judge Wilkerson interrupted the trial to cite D'Andrea for contempt and send him away for six months. Capone growled, "I don't care what happens to D'Andrea. He's a damn fool. I don't care if he gets ten years." Al was cracking.

The trial wound up in mid-October. As the jury returned I felt sure we had won. "Gentlemen," intoned Judge Wilkerson, "what is your verdict?"

"Guilty!" The courtroom broke up like a circus after the last performance. Reporters ran out of court. Lawyers ran. Mobsters ran. Everybody seemed to be running but Scarface Al Capone. He slumped forward as if a blackjack had hit him.

When I got home, Judith cried, "You did it! I knew you were going to do it all the time!" Then she sighed. "Now can we go back to Baltimore?"

Frank J. Wilson

The Ma Barker Gang

In the mid-1950s, Kurt Singer, a distinguished biographer of, among others, Goering and Hemingway, had the excellent idea of persuading leading policemen from all countries to write about "my greatest crime story". The volume of that title was so successful that he went on to compile a second volume, *My Strangest Case*. This contains some classic first-hand accounts of crimes, including the following chapter on the Ma Barker gang written by J. Edgar Hoover. During the 1930s and 40s, Hoover was probably the most famous policeman in the world. Born in 1895, John Edgar Hoover became a clerk in the Department of Justice, and was appointed head of the Enemy Aliens Registration Department during World War One. After the war, his job was "Red hunting" – for the 1917 revolution in Russia had set off one of America's periodic outbursts of violent anti-communism. His success in arresting and deporting communists and anarchists led to his appointment, in August 1921, to the newly-formed Federal Bureau of Investigation. Hoover became head of the Bureau in 1924, at the age of 29. He soon organised the FBI into a formidable unit, and in the 1930s, used it with deadly effect against the new breed of bank robbers and gangsters – Ma Barker, Machine Gun Kelly, Pretty Boy Floyd, Baby Face Nelson, John Dillinger – who were spawned by the Great Depression that followed the Stock Market Crash of 1929. Hoover died in 1972.

This account of the end of the Barker gang forms

an interesting companion-piece to Frank Wilson's account of the downfall of Al Capone.

They never came any tougher than "Ma" Barker and her brood, and that goes, too, for the other half of the gang – the hoods led by Alvin Karpis. I should know, for I helped to hunt them and, finally, to eliminate them. Of all public enemies they were unquestionably the vilest – a throng of wanton killers, vicious, depraved and incredibly ruthless.

We know all about murder and its motives at the Federal Bureau of Investigation, and possess the records of many men and women who have killed often and inhumanly but yet had a side to their nature that was not wholly despicable.

It is something that cannot be said of "Ma" Barker, her four sons and Karpis, and the mobsters they commanded. Without a single exception they were monsters, and pity was a word of which they had never heard. They moved in a welter of blood; mail robberies, bank hold-ups, kidnapping and pitched machinegun battles; they loved nothing better than to kill a police officer, and if some innocent bystander fell to the same hail of bullets that did not matter either. They executed their own traitors, bought over unfaithful police officials, "fixed" paroles and prison breaks. Their anarchy fouled the very roots of law and order.

I remember their heyday and the various impressions I received from the tortuous investigation, the interrogation of witnesses, and the study of reports which came in from special agents all over the country. "Ma" Barker, for instance, renting an apartment from an unsuspecting landlord, knowing that if he looked into her hard eyes he would guess the truth; a drunken doctor shaving the fingertips of a crazed hoodlum no longer under an anaesthetic; Karpis, the slit-eyed killer, explaining how he was going to wipe out top F.B.I. agents in Los Angeles, Chicago, New York and myself in Washington by using automobiles and planes, and hating it like hell because somebody had called him a rat;

an afternoon search in St Paul when we were sure we had the gang dead to rights and a flood of sound unexpectedly broke out – church bells, kids yelling and a dog howling.

Yes, Alvin Karpis, otherwise Francis Albin Karpavicz, had dreams of gunning the F.B.I., and never more vivid than at the moment we grabbed him.

So intensely did the Barker-Karpis alliance live by the gun that it is impossible to give an orderly picture of their stained history. They intertwined murder with corruption, but it is probably right to ascribe to "Ma" Barker the gang's inspiration for organised crime. She was born Arizona Donnie Clark of very mixed blood – Scots, Irish and Indian. She grew up in the Ozarks, the wild, mountainous region of Missouri and among people who were as stark as the scenery. She is supposed to have coached her four sons, Herman, Lloyd, Fred and Arthur, on the principle of how to do business with bankers – with a tommy-gun. But in the beginning she herself had no criminal experience on which to draw. She indulged them, though, wilfully and wickedly, and it is beyond dispute that the four Barker boys owed their criminal careers to their mother. She was both resourceful and ruthless and they looked to her for inspiration and guidance, if those are terms which can be used in respect to a she-wolf and her vicious whelps.

A theme that repeats itself with great frequency in the Barker-Karpis combination is the strength it derived from friendships that took root in various penitentiaries and Federal prisons. For example, Fred Barker and Karpis learned to understand and admire each other while both were imprisoned in the Kansas State Penitentiary. Karpis, allegedly dubbed "Old Creepy" because of the feeling he inspired in other mobsters with his cold, fishy stare, was smart enough to take advantage of conditions in Kansas. Convicts assigned to the coal-mines there were rewarded for extra production by having days lopped off their time, but Karpis found that working alongside him were a number of lifers.

It did not take him long to figure that for these men there was no incentive. They could, however, be stimulated into more active mining with money and such small services as he was able to render, and soon Karpis was buying the extra coal output of a half-dozen lifers and thus appreciably shortening his own sentence.

It was the kind of trick that appealed to Fred Barker, and their jail friendship was translated into a partnership on their liberation, and they committed their first murder together. It was a cowardly affair. Two days before, they had used a De Soto to pull off a robbery, and when Sheriff C. R. Kelly, of West Plains, Missouri, saw the car in a garage he recognised it as suspect. He walked over to question the occupants and was cut down by a blast of gunfire before he could draw his own weapon.

Fred Barker, Karpis, "Ma" Barker and her paramour, Arthur V. Dunlop (alias George Anderson), occupied a cottage in Thayer, Missouri, but with the murder of the sheriff they fled to St Paul, leaving behind their latest haul. They took over a furnished house, and had not long settled in when they were joined by William Weaver, known variously as "Phoenix Donald" and "Lapland Willie." Weaver had been paroled from Oklahoma State Penitentiary, where he had been serving a life sentence for murder during a bank robbery, and where he had met "Doc" Barker and Volney Davis, jointly convicted for the slaying of a night watchman.

"Ma" Barker and Karpis were satisfied with Weaver's credentials, but although the gang lived quietly, and as inconspicuously as possible, it was noticed that whenever they left the house together one of them carried a violin case. All five knew how to play the instrument inside, but it didn't make them musicians!

It was uncanny the way the Barker-Karpis gang throughout its lifetime was able to smell danger before it was too late. When the St Paul police raided their hide-out early one morning it was to find an empty house. It had been a hasty departure, and for some reason we were never able to discover they decided that Arthur Dunlop was a squealer. The day after the gang left St Paul Dunlop's nude, bullet-riddled body was found on the shores of a lake near Webster, Wisconsin. Close by was a woman's blood-stained glove.

Kansas City was the next stop, and here the gang was reinforced by the addition of Thomas Holden and a fellow mobster, both of whom had escaped from Leavenworth; Harvey Bailey, a notorious bank robber; Larry DeVol and Bernard Phillips, a renegade policeman turned bank bandit. In June a bank at Fort Scott fell to the gang and some of the loot was used to stage an elaborate "Welcome Home" party for a classmate of Fred Barker at Kansas State Penitentiary.

The celebrations had not long been over when late in the afternoon of July 7th, 1932, F.B.I. special agents stepped out from some bushes surrounding the Old Mission Golf Course and put the bracelets on Holden, Bailey and another gangster. The other member of the foursome, Bernard Phillips, happened to be absent when these arrests took place and went streaking with the news to "Ma" Barker. The gang took off in such haste for St Paul that a raiding party found they had left their quarters just as dinner was about to be served!

St Paul once more – and another murder! It stemmed from the arrest of Harvey Bailey, who was tried for participation in the Fort Scott bank robbery. He was defended by J. Earl Smith, a criminal attorney of Tulsa, Oklahoma, but the evidence against him was too strong and he was convicted. Shortly afterwards a mysterious telephone call lured Attorney Smith to the vicinity of the lonely Indian Hills Country Club, fourteen miles north of Tulsa. The following morning Smith's body was found, full of bullet holes.

To offset casualties that occurred for one reason or another the gang was ever on the look-out for new recruits, but they had to measure up to tough requirements. During the next few weeks two newcomers were roped in, Earl Christman, confidence man wanted in several states, and Frank Nash, who had slipped out of Leavenworth. Christman brought his moll with him. They took part in an audacious daylight raid on the Cloud County Bank at Concordia, Kansas, that yielded over 240,000 dollars.

With all this coin to play with the Barker-Karpis organisation turned to the task of springing some of its old hands now tucked away. It was successful in getting "Doc" Barker paroled from the Oklahoma State Penitentiary and in securing from the same institution an incomprehensible "two years leave of absence" for Volney Davis. An attempt to secure the release of Lloyd Barker, another brother, doing twenty-five years in Leavenworth for mail robbery, failed.

Looking for Christmas money the gang descended on Minneapolis and murdered three in taking the Third North-Western Bank for a heavy score. Two policemen who got in their way were chopped down by machine-gun fire, and, as they were about to leave, one of the Barker-Karpis mob thought a civilian was trying to memorise the licence number of their automobile. He too died from a stream of hot lead.

It was in Reno, Nevada, that the gang holed up to enjoy the stolen money, and while there Volney Davis made a trip to Missouri to pick up his favourite moll, who had escaped from a Mid-Western penitentiary. She stayed with Davis when the mob shifted its headquarters first to St Paul and in April of the following year to Chicago, from which city they struck successfully at the Fairbury National Bank, Fairbury, Nebraska.

In this raid, however, Earl Christman was so badly wounded that he was rushed to the home of Verne Miller. He died despite medical care and one night was secretly buried. Christman's mother wanted to know where her son's body rested, but nobody would tell her.

It was about this time that Fred Barker began to yearn for a mate, and found one in the widow of a well-known bank robber killed while following his "profession." She had a history that satisfied even "Ma" Barker.

Either Christman's death or a belief that it had got into a rut persuaded the gang that new ideas were needed, and a fling was taken at kidnapping. The first victim was William A. Hamm, junior, of the Hamm Brewing Company, St Paul. The ransom collected was 100,000 dollars, and those who played the principal parts in the snatch were Fred and "Doc" Barker, Karpis, Charles J. Fitzgerald and a widely known underworld character – Fred Goetz, alias "Shotgun Zeigler," purportedly a former engineering student and football star at a Mid-Western university.

Wherever the gang moved it cast a shadow of murder, and two further slayings were added in quick succession to the lengthening list. In a stick-up of the Stockyards National Bank, South St Paul, a police officer was killed outright and another crippled for life; the loot was 30,000 dollars. In Chicago the mob pounced on two bank messengers, but again they got very little, and in fleeing became involved in a minor mishap with their car. Unaware of the robbery which had taken place only a few minutes earlier, Patrolman Miles A. Cunningham approached the bandit car at an intersection on Jackson Boulevard to inquire into the accident. Without warning he was blasted to death with a machine-gun.

By the end of the year the mob, now idling in Reno again, was more motley than ever. "Ma" Barker was there and so, too, was Fred, with the widow of the bank robber, who still stuck to him. A seasoned shoplifter had teamed up with William Weaver and Karpis, Volney Davis and Fred Goetz had their molls with them. Towards the end of the year all of them set out for St Paul. They had planned to rob the Commercial State Bank, but on the way they got another idea. Instead of a hold-up – the danger was great and the reward uncertain – why not snatch the bank president, Edward George Brenner? The task would be much easier and it would open the bank vaults for whatever sum they demanded.

On the night of January 13th the gang gathered at the apartment of William Weaver and his paramour for a final check-up. Everything had been worked out, and those who were to do the job were soon able to leave. But as they drew away from the kerb another car, containing several men, one of them in uniform, fell in behind them. One of the bandits yelled "It's the cops" and instantly guns began to blaze. The bandit car sped away at last, leaving behind two badly wounded employees of Northwest Airways – the "cops" the gang thought they had spotted.

This fiasco did not upset the original plan, it only delayed it, and four days later five members of the Barker-Karpis outfit "took" Brenner as he halted his car at a street signal after dropping his nine-year-old daughter at a private school. There followed almost a month of complicated negotiations, with the F.B.I. keeping close watch but deferring to the family wish to effect the bank president's release before taking action. The gang collected 200,000 dollars in five- and ten-dollar bills. Brenner was then released in the vicinity of Rochester, Minnesota.

It was at this juncture that things began to get complicated for the gang. Fred Goetz offended some of his gangland pals and was executed by two blasts from a shotgun which blew off his face. There is no evidence to show if it was the vengeance of the Barker-Karpis mob, but it was certainly effective! Soon the strain of associating with the mob – their unbridled violence and the frenzy of escaping from one hide-out to another to avoid the special agents they knew were hunting them – proved too much for Goetz's moll. She became deranged and was placed in an asylum.

Converting the hot Hamm and Brenner snatch money to clean bills was a problem far from easy to solve, and the tortuous negotiations and fixing that were required almost transcend belief.

First to offer assistance was a suspect Chicago politician and ward heeler known as "Boss" McLaughlin. He was not too bright, though, and our special agents picked him up in quick time. His wife telegraphed both the President of the United States and the Attorney-General protesting against his arrest. Nevertheless, McLaughlin stayed in jail.

Next to be recruited to handle the hot money was a certain Dr Joseph P. Moran, who had once served time for abortion and of late had looked after any hood who needed his services. In turn Dr Moran got his nephew to help him, and apparently the arrangement was that Dr Moran would get hold of enough of the ransom funds to put his nephew through medical school!

Yet a third character emerged in the negotiations. He was a fifty-year-old Chicago gambler with connections reaching all the way to Havana. He managed to exchange nearly 100,000 dollars of the tainted money for Cuban gold, which a well-known bank then converted into one-thousand-dollar American bills at a discount of a quarter of one per cent!

During this time Dr Moran (he was to disappear later, and according to reliable underworld reports his weighted body was dumped by his "pals" into Lake Erie) operated on Fred Barker and Alvin Karpis in an attempt to obliterate their fingerprints and change their looks. Both realised time was running out, but what they suffered on the operating table did no good. They could not hide their identity as public enemies; they nor other members of the gang for whom there was no escape from justice.

Volney Davis, "Doc" Barker and Harry Campbell also underwent the agonisingly painful Moran "refresher" treatment to no avail. The gang did not stay in one place long. They doubled back on their tracks, dodged to this city and that county, but they could not throw off the pursuit of F.B.I. agents and decided to split up into small units. They then scattered to locations as widely separated as Glasgow (Montana), Allandale (Florida), Las Vegas, Miami, Cleveland and Havana. It was the beginning of the end.

On the night of January 8th, 1935, special agents arrested "Doc" Barker in Chicago. He was traced through a woman with whom he had become infatuated. When the apartment of the couple was searched a sub-machine-gun was found which had been stolen from a guard at the time of the St Paul payroll robbery.

The same night special agents surrounded the apartment occupied by Russell Gibson and another mobster and their girl friends. Ordered to surrender, all but Gibson complied. Armed with a Browning and a Colt automatic he tried to get out through a rear door, but it was being watched. Gibson fired and missed, and that was the end of him. As his body was carted to the morgue the F.B.I. were collecting a small arsenal inside the apartment.

Oddly enough, it was an alligator which put the finger on "Ma" and Fred Barker! In "Doc" Barker's apartment agents found a map of Florida and a circle round Ocala and Lake Weir. Earlier they had been tipped off that mother and son were hiding out in some southern area that sheltered an ancient alligator known to the natives as "Old Joe." Now they knew for certain, and at five-thirty on a crisp January morning, with the mists hanging over Lake Weir, a picked group of special agents surrounded a cottage on the shore in which "Ma" Barker and her son were holed up.

"We are special agents of the Federal Bureau of Investigation," called out the leader. "I'm talking to you, Kate Barker, and you, Fred Barker. Come out one at a time and with your hands up!"

Further commands were issued, but in the cottage all was silent. The minutes ticked by, and once again the Barkers were ordered to come out singly, unless they wanted to be driven out by tear gas and any other means deemed necessary.

After fifteen minutes "Ma" Barker shouted: "All right, go ahead!" For a moment it looked as if mother and son had decided to throw in their hands, but then a machine-gun began to speak from the house and it swept the surrounding trees and tore into the undergrowth. It sparked off a battle that went on for hours. Tear-gas bombs were tossed into the cottage and a deadly fire from automatics was concentrated on the firing points within. It was a fight to a deadly finish, and when the F.B.I. were at last able to enter the cottage they found "Ma" Barker dead, still grasping a machine-gun in her left hand. Fred was doubled over in death, a .45 Colt automatic beside his stiffening body.

There was enough ironware in the cottage to keep a regiment at bay; two Thompson sub-machine-guns, Browning .12 gauge shotgun, Remington shotgun, two .45 automatics, two Winchester rifles and a .38 Colt automatic, along with machine-gun drums, automatic-pistol clips and ammunition for every weapon.

There was a letter, too, from "Doc" Barker, in which he wrote: "I took care of that business for you boys. It was done just as good as if you had did it yourself. I am just like Standard Oil – always at your service. Ha, ha!"

"That business" referred to by "Doc" was, as to be expected, a slight case of murder! The victim, if such a term can be used, was William J. Harrison, who had moved within the orbit of the Capone syndicate before he joined the Barker-Karpis mob. Later his reliability became suspect, and from his Florida hole Fred Barker had ordered Harrison's execution. "Doc" Barker had seen to it. They took Harrison to an abandoned barn near Ontarioville in Illinois on a wild, dark night and shot him. The body, and the barn itself, was then saturated with paraffin and a match was tossed in.

As the F.B.I. ring narrowed Alvin Karpis and Harry Campbell, with their women, scuttled from Miami to Atlantic City. There a gun battle with the police took place and Karpis and his crony came temporarily to rest in Toledo, Ohio. Meanwhile, Volney Davis was picked up by special agents in St Louis. He was found to be carrying a counterfeit hundred-dollar bill, and was quick to explain that he "wasn't shoving the queer." He carried the bill with him, he said, to offer as a bribe should he be arrested by law-enforcement officers!

One of the gang surrendered in Kansas after a gun fight,

and then William Weaver and his moll were cornered and captured in a house in Allandale, Florida. Although the Barker-Karpis organisation had not merely been split open but virtually destroyed, Karpis and Campbell still had some fight left in them, as can be seen from what followed. It was so fantastic that it is hardly believable.

Karpis picked up a few hoods, among them several ex-convicts, and a gambler who must have believed in his luck. On April 24th, 1935, three heavily armed raiders pounced on a mail truck at Warren, Ohio, and got away with 70,000 dollars and then pulled off a robbery worth 30,000 dollars against the Erie train – Detroit to Pittsburgh. Introduced was a new tactic in robbery – the thieves escaped by aeroplane.

These exploits were followed by an alliance that only a script writer could dream up. Karpis and his crony fled to Hot Springs, Arkansas, where they were afforded protection by the chief of police and the chief of detectives. While an F.B.I. "wanted" poster for leaders of the mob aged and yellowed in the very centre of the jail door at Hot Springs, Karpis and his pals roamed at will through the streets of the spa. Nor was that all, for Karpis bedded up with an adroit woman who not only kept him happy, but also one of the law-enforcement officers as well. She divided her time between the two and owed her vast experience to the fact that she had begun operating brothels at the age of seventeen.

Eventually Hot Springs became a little too warm for Karpis. He was well aware he was being hunted, and in the early part of 1936 he again got on the move. With him was a crony who brought his girl along – a twenty-one-year-old prostitute. This time Karpis's destination was New Orleans, and although he may have thought he had again slipped the net it was in that city he had a rendezvous with justice!

Evil and merciless, Karpis had dealt out so much death that he had every reason to declare, as he had often done, that he would never be taken alive. We knew he was a problem, and planned the raid carefully. It was approximately five-fifteen in the afternoon of May 1st, 1936. Four assistants and myself were to enter by the front door. Other squads were deployed at each side of the building and at the rear. We were about to move in when a man on a horse moved into the lane beside the through traffic.

We waited, anxious to avoid attention, until the horseman had passed down the street. Now was the time for action, but then two men stepped from the doorway and walked briskly down the steps. We recognised Alvin Karpis and his crony. As they made their way towards their car, a little boy on a bicycle scooted between the pair and our vantage-point. We did not want the child hurt, as he might be if shooting started at that moment, so we moved out and hurried forward, calling for the surrender of the fugitives as they were getting into the car.

Perhaps Karpis had come to believe in his own indestructibility. I am sure he had never expected to meet the top G-man and a squad of what he had been pleased to call "sissy" agents. His expression was divided between amazement and fright and his colour was ashen. Neither he nor his shaking companion raised as much as a finger. There was no gunplay, not the remotest chance of any. Like all their breed they derived their courage from getting the drop on their victims. When they were on the wrong end of a gun the fight went out of them – as it does with every hoodlum, who is a coward at heart. Karpis told me that he thought he would never be taken alive – but then Karpis did not know Karpis.

Six days after his arrest we picked up the rest of the gang in Toledo. It was the end of an era of violence.

J. Edgar Hoover

Crime of the African Crater

It would be a pity to confine a book of this kind to famous crimes of Europe and America, as though other parts of the world did not exist. Benjamin Bennett's *Famous South African Murders* appeared in 1938, and contains some fascinating cases, including that of Detective Coetzee, who turned murderer when a girl with whom he had become involved tried to convince him that he was the father of her unborn child, and the account of the serial "killer of the White Mountain." Most of the cases in the book are too long to include here, but the rather odd "crime of the African crater" – presumably a sex crime – is an interesting example.

Nakuru, a little town in Kenya, hard by the shores of a lake, surrounded by mountains, sloping pastures and extinct volcanoes, awoke on the morning of Saturday, October 8, 1932, with misgiving.

For thirty-six hours three of its young people had been missing. Unaccountably. They left Nakuru by car on Thursday evening, October 6, presumably to visit a cinema, and were seen driving along the Eldama Ravine Road.

Then they had vanished as though into thin air. When they failed to return the first night, it was believed they were staying with friends. But this was soon disproved. They were not in Nakuru.

The blue Chevrolet in which they set out had not been seen

on any of the roads in the neighbourhood, or even farther afield. The possibility of their organizing an impromptu hunting-trip to popular Lake Baringo was considered – and ruled out.

Driving the car was Charles William Ross, nineteen-year-old son of the late Major Ross, soldier and noted big-game hunter of British East Africa. Educated in his early years at a school in England, he had gone to live in Kenya in 1927, and was employed by the Kenya Farmers' Association, whose headquarters were at Nakuru.

Ross's companions were two young women, Margaret Keppie and Winifred Stevenson. Miss Keppie, a qualified chemist and druggist and member of the Pharmaceutical Society, had arrived in Kenya four months previously from Leeds, England, where she lived with her parents. She first joined the Nairobi firm of Messrs. Howse & McGeorge and was transferred to the Nakuru branch. A week before, her engagement to a fellow employee was announced.

"Winnie" Stevenson, twenty years of age, was the daughter of Mr Harry Stevenson, known in Nairobi, capital of Kenya, as Harry Venson, entertainer. A bright, vivacious girl and accomplished linguist, speaking the native languages of Swahili and Kikuyu fluently, she was generally understood to be Ross's sweetheart. He was known to be devoted to her.

Anxious consultations were held among the parents and friends of the missing trio as Friday passed without word or trace of them. Anxiety gave way to alarm when the strange tales of Ross's eccentricities and unusual behaviour were revived. Though mostly shy and reserved in the company of women, he was said to have exhibited vicious sexual tendencies which, apparently, were satisfied only by sadistic frenzies or indulgence in orgies of bloodshed.

A story was told of his stabbing of animals after he had shot them and then smearing himself with the blood.

He was accustomed, as well, to wander off by himself and mingle with the natives of the Colony, converse with them in their own dialects and participate in their quaint customs. The men of one tribe called him their young "White Chief".

The police were called in and interviewed Ross's step-father, Major Matthew W. Whitridge, at his home, Maji Mazuri, some miles from Nakuru. He was unable to enlighten them. But he instructed Gordon, Charles Ross's twenty-one-year-old brother, to drive along the Eldama Ravine Road on his motor-cycle and keep a look-out for the blue Chevrolet.

About seven miles from Maji Mazuri he found his brother. Dressed in a navy blue suit and light blue shirt, he was grimy and dishevelled as though he had spent several days in the open. Ross did not seem at all surprised when his brother rode up and alighted.

He pointed to the car. It was ditched. "Can't get the bus out," he remarked casually, "and I have been pottering around here."

Not a word did he volunteer about his two companions. Together the brothers attempted to reverse the car out of the ditch on to the road. The engine roared and strained, but the wheels would not grip. They waited in vain for a passing motorist to come to their assistance. In desperation, Gordon Ross suggested that he ride into Nakuru and arrange for a car to haul the Chevrolet on to the road.

His brother point-blank refused. "What's the use of going down there?" he asked evasively. "Let's potter around here a bit longer."

He seemed strangely preoccupied and disinclined to leave the neighbourhood. Finally, however, he consented and agreed to be driven home on the motor-cycle. On the journey, Gordon Ross told his brother that Assistant Police Inspector May was making inquiries about the disappearance of Miss Keppie and Miss Stevenson. The news did not appear to disturb or interest him unduly.

"I didn't go out with them," he rejoined, "and I know

nothing about their disappearance. I was just coming back home from Nakuru."

The motor-cycle trip continued to within three miles of Maji Mazuri. The road was rough and both driver and passenger were severely jolted. Charles Ross asked to be allowed to walk the remainder of the distance. His brother pulled up for him to dismount, then pressed on alone to report to Major Whitridge. He returned to escort Ross home.

About half an hour later Major Whitridge, keeping observation on the road, saw the two approaching. He stood behind the door and waited. As Charles Ross entered he gripped his arm and demanded to know whether he was armed. For a moment the youth hesitated, then, shrugging his shoulders, replied, "Yes, I am."

"Disarm him, Gordon," said Major Whitridge, holding Charles Ross so that he was powerless to draw his revolver. Gordon ran his hands through his brother's pockets and found a revolver with six .32 cartridges in the chambers. Major Whitridge pocketed it.

"Now," he demanded, "what did you do with the two girls you took out on Thursday night?" The family had by then gathered in the dining-room. Mrs Whitridge, too, begged her son to tell where he had left the companions of his Thursday night drive.

He had not the remotest idea where they were, he replied, and had gone out shooting "for a party". "If Winnie Stevenson was with me she could have driven the car home herself," he added impatiently.

"You are responsible for the girls you took in the car," Major Whitridge rejoined, "and the police have been here making inquiries and looking for you. You will accompany me at once to Inspector May."

"But I tell you I can't remember taking the girls out at all," young Ross persisted. "And I'm not going to Inspector May either. If he wants to see me, he can come here."

After further argument and persuasion, Ross agreed to

accompany his stepfather and brother to the police camp at Eldama Ravine, near Nakuru. They reached the camp at 3.15 on the Saturday afternoon. Ross was handed over to Assistant Inspector A. Poskitt and detained.

News of young Ross's reappearance was communicated to the Nakuru police. A search-party scouring the country-side hastened to the spot where the Chevrolet was found ditched.

Among the searchers was Mr M. Ritchie, the Nakuru manager of Messrs. Howse & McGeorge. Working his way carefully to the bottom of a ravine below a forty-foot cliff, he came across the body of his employee, Margaret Keppie. She was shot through the head and had evidently been dead some time.

The body was removed to Nakuru. Fears for Winnie Stevenson grew apace. Every inch of ground at the foot of the cliff and in the vicinity of the ravine was combed. Yet not the slightest trace was found of the second girl when darkness fell on Saturday and ended the day's painstaking search.

On the Sunday nearly every man in Nakuru and many of the women and children banded themselves into search-parties. The authorities instructed members of the Nakuru section of the Kenya Defence Force to assist, and requested the trackers of a native tribe, who knew the countryside well, to organize a separate party.

The murder of Miss Keppie and the futile efforts to trace Miss Stevenson roused the whole of Kenya. An aeroplane left Nairobi to survey the Nakuru area from the air.

One of the search-parties in the bush stumbled across a camping-place that seemed to have a sinister link with the tragedy. There were the remains of a fire, a quantity of fresh provisions, a number of shawls, articles of women's clothing and toilet requisites. All appeared to be brand new and recently deposited. A revolver and two empty cartridge cases lay on the ground. From a nearby tree dangled a piece of rope.

Had Ross camped there? If so, at whom was the second shot fired? Could Winnie Stevenson have suffered the fate of her companion? The search went on, grimly, tirelessly.

Back at Nakuru on the Sunday afternoon the body of Margaret Keppie was borne to a little chapel covered with Golden Shower under the lea of the great hill where her life was taken. Rain fell as the coffin was lowered in a shower of beautiful flowers.

Darkness came on once more. Monday dawned. Nakuru was deserted. European business men, Indian bazaar merchants, clerks and official left shops, offices and desks to continue the search. Women carried on what work and business there was to be done.

Ross was charged before the Nakuru Resident Magistrate with the murder of Miss Keppie and kept under strict guard in goal. He refused to reveal where Miss Stevenson was, maintaining stubbornly and impatiently that he knew nothing of her movements.

The police, in a despairing effort to ascertain the prisoner's movements on the Thursday night, issued a notice:

> "Will any person who saw an aluminium box body Chevrolet motor-car with a blue bonnet, number B 8633, between 8.45 p.m. on Thursday, October 6, and 11 a.m. on Saturday, October 8, communicate at once with the police at Nakuru or Nairobi.
>
> "The car may have travelled on any road within a radius of 150 miles from Nakuru. It probably contained three passengers.
>
> "Information is still urgently sought by the police as to the whereabouts of Miss Winnie Stevenson, missing from her home at Nakuru since the evening of Thursday, October 6."

As the days passed without the efforts of the searchers meeting the slightest success, the people of the town became incensed against the youth who maintained an obstinate silence and an air of unconcern when, it seemed certain, he alone could clear up the mystery and spare the parents of Miss Stevenson untold agony.

The rumblings of anger swelled. There was talk of "rushing" the gaol and of submitting Ross to a public third-degree grilling. To avoid the possibility of the townsfolk taking the law into their own hands, the police decided to remove their prisoner to Nairobi.

Before he left Nakuru, however, the authorities allowed Winnie Stevenson's mother to see Ross in his cell and plead with him to tell her the fate of her daughter. Her entreaties had no effect. He simply did not know, he declared, and that was the end of it.

After she had been led away, sobbing, Ross ate a hearty meal and that night slept peacefully as an innocent child, not like one loaded down with a ghastly secret he feared the world to know.

When the search-parties and pilots began to despair of ever solving the riddle of Miss Stevenson's disappearance, hopes were suddenly revived. A woman of the Kikuyu tribe, named Mukenye, who was credited with much success in her practice of witchcraft and divination, proclaimed that she had a clue for the white people. Two European women from Nakuru and then a reporter visited her to hear her claims.

Crooning weirdly, she poured oil and water into the palm of her hand. Thus aiding her divinations, she croaked out her discovery. Margaret Keppie, she said, had been shot on the Saturday morning, but her companion lay in the Menengai crater. She was alive – but completely hidden.

"None can save her," said Mukenye oracularly, "except one man."

The Menengai crater, close to Lake Nakuru, home of many flamingos, is almost nine miles in diameter, and commands from its rim a view of Rift Valley. The saucer-like walls contain great crevices, and thick jungle growth makes progress difficult. Though many scoffed at the native woman's psychic claims and directions, over a thousand people from Nakuru scoured the Menengai crater on Thursday, October 13, from dawn to dusk.

The great body of searchers split up into two sections one working round the crater lip to the south, and the other to the north. Not a thought was given to personal inconvenience and the peril from deadly snakes infesting the crater.

But reluctantly even the warmest supporters of Mukenye were forced to admit that she had put them on a false trail.

Eventually Ross, yielding to persuasion, and tired of putting off his questioners, agreed to show where his sweetheart was. Late on Friday night, October 14, he was taken from the Nairobi prison, handcuffed and, under armed guard, escorted back to Nakuru.

The following morning he directed Mr Neil Stewart, Superintendent of the C.I.D., and Mr S. L. Vincent, Assistant Superintendent of Police, Nakuru, to a secluded spot off the main road, just outside the Menengai crater. Beneath a coating of leaves and grass lay the decomposed body of Winnie Stevenson.

She had been shot to death within a mile of her home. Her family and friends passed near the spot daily.

Ross then asked to be allowed to dictate a statement. On the return of the party to Nakuru he appeared before the District Commissioner and admitted his crimes in these words:

"I promised to show the police where the body of the girl was on condition that I was shot immediately afterwards. I admit killing both Miss Keppie and Miss Stevenson for *nothing*.

"It happened at 9.30 on Thursday night. I shot Miss Keppie near the camp. She was sitting next to me at the time and grabbed at my revolver which I kept in my left-hand pocket.

"I ordered her out of the car and took her about thirty yards from the camp. She was a yard from me when I shot her. I threw her down a sort of square pit nearby.

"After that I returned for Winnie. She was sitting in the car. When I took Miss Keppie away, I had ordered her to get into the car. She had not moved when I got back. She was terrified. She wanted to go home. I told her I would lead the way and she could follow.

"When we were near her home she said she could not go any farther. She lay on the grass under a tree. She did not know what was going to happen to her. I shot her in the side of the head.

"I had no reason for shooting her either. I covered her up and returned to the car, where I remained until the Saturday morning. I ate some oranges and drank lemonade. Then I threw everything out of the car and made up my mind to go home.

"I reached the ditch and stuck. I reversed the car and backed out. Next, I rushed the ditch but the clutch burnt out and something broke . . ."

That was all. Not a twinge of pity did he show for what he had done, as he said, *"for nothing"*. Obviously he did not tell all he knew in his confession and some of his statements did not ring true.

Was it likely, for example, that Miss Stevenson would have sat paralysed with fear in the car – under instructions to wait – while Ross took Miss Keppie into the bush and shot her? Would she not have heard the shot and attempted to drive the car away? Or would she not have escaped into the night?

Then again, what was the truth behind the unworn women's apparel at the camp? Ross was believed to have been escorting the girls to a cinema, not to a camp to live in the open for several days. Could the strange collection of clothing have had some bearing on the youth's sexual peculiarities?

We can only guess at what occurred before the dastardly murder of the unfortunate girls. Perhaps it is better that the truth shall never be known . . .

On October 18, Ross, manacled to a warder, was charged

with a second murder. On November 4 he was committed for trial.

Ross stood his trial at Nairobi on November 28, 1932, before the then Chief Justice of Kenya, Sir Jacob Barth, and a jury. He was pale and haggard. His composure and self-assurance had gone.

The Attorney-General, Mr A. D. A. Macgregor, K. C., led Mr R. F. Branigan for the Crown. Ross's counsel were Mr Humphrey Slade and Mr M. J. Hogan.

The trial aroused great interest far beyond the borders of Kenya. A battle royal was waged between the law and science over the responsibility of the drawn youth in the dock, for his terrible deed. Both in England and South Africa the newspapers gave great prominence to the proceedings.

The task of the Attorney-General was not to pin the crime to the prisoner, but to destroy the only possible defence – that he was not in his sane senses when he committed the murders.

It was a painful story the witnesses for the defence told; as horrible, too, as anything Edgar Allan Poe imagined. They described Ross's desire to butcher animals for the mere sake and delight of killing.

At times he was stated to have slaughtered a number of animals and to have left the carcasses untouched. Again, he had been known to rush wildly up to the dead beasts, stab and slash at them in a frenzy – and then cover himself with the blood.

Other testimony concerned the behaviour of Ross's father, a psychopathic case from the description of those who knew him in his lifetime. Two men who served under him in the Boer War recalled his savagery and ungovernable temper.

He shot prisoners without mercy. Once when a native dared insist on payment for eggs supplied, Major Ross had drawn his revolver and emptied it into the man's head. So brutal was he to all who crossed his path and so ruthless with his men, that they were goaded to revolt.

Only then did they see something human in the pitiless soldier. He went to his tent and sobbed.

No woman could have faced a greater ordeal than Ross's mother when she entered the witness-box to reveal the intimacies and tortures of her life with her former husband, and to convince the jury that the son of such a father could not be normal.

Her life had been one of unending horror. Her husband thrashed her unmercifully. Frequently he threatened to shoot her. Once, in a towering rage, he seized her baby and attempted to put it on the fire. A moment later he dropped on his knees and begged forgiveness.

Her son, Charles Ross, was sensitive and during recent weeks a change had come over him. He was rude to her and his stepfather. He lost his good manners and charm.

"I have lost my boy in the last six months in every way," sobbed the grief-stricken mother.

The evidence of Mr E. R. Pratt, head master of the Nakuru school Ross attended after his arrival in the Colony from England, was that the lad was untruthful, often guilty of petty misdemeanours, and had a misdirected sense of adventure. This, of course, did not indicate abnormality; neither did the testimony that he was found with the servants in the kitchen of a man with whom he stayed for several months.

Other witnesses, however, described incidents suggesting that Ross had committed acts which were certainly not those of a normal person. He had been seen to kick a cat to death. When out fishing, he would squeeze his first catch and mumble senselessly to himself. One rainy night he went to the Menengai crater and killed a hyena. His hands and clothes were covered with blood and slush.

It was also proved that he suffered from a venereal disease in 1930 and again when he was taken into custody. The clothing he wore on the fatal car journey on the night of October 6 was examined at the Government laboratories and traces of semen were noticed on the waistcoat and trousers.

Dr R. F. G. Dickson, Medical Officer of Health to the Nairobi District Council, Doctor to H. M. Prisons and in charge of the Infectious Diseases Hospital, was prepared to state, from his observations of Ross, that he showed indications of insanity, and possibly did not know the difference between right and wrong when he committed his crimes.

"On what facts in the evidence," the Attorney-General questioned Dr Dickson, "do you base your theory of the prisoner's insanity?"

"I base it," replied Dr Dickson, "on his alternating moroseness and excitement; his solitariness and shyness; that he sat by himself for hours on a rock meditating; that he went hunting by himself; did not like the society of girls and left them. In addition to all that, there were his emotional outbursts and his quite unnecessary attacks with knives on dead animals."

The Attorney-General was not satisfied. "We have heard about the prisoner's moroseness," he said, "and of his slow, smouldering temper and sulking. But are those conditions symptomatic of insanity?"

"They may not be symptomatic of legal insanity," the doctor retorted, "but they are of insanity as I know it."

An X-ray photograph of Ross's head was used by Dr H. L. Gordon, mental specialist and leading witness for the defence, to illustrate the youth's abnormality. The smallness of one section of the brain, he pointed out to the Court, was associated with certain forms of mental deficiency. The pituitary gland, that part of the brain containing the essential to life, had reached its limit of growth.

Besides, there was a depression in the skull which somewhat cut the brain. The curious mottled appearance at the back of the skull, clearly shown in the X-ray photograph, Dr Gordon had not seen before, although it was not unknown in the skulls of South African natives.

Dr Gordon deduced, from the evidence of Major Ross's conduct, that he conformed to the type suffering from a constitutional psychopathic inferiority or pronounced mental instability. Had he attempted to put one of his children on a fire and his wife, then about to give birth to her son, Charles, had witnessed it, there was a scientific possibility that the child might be affected in later life.

From his examination and tests of Ross, Dr Gordon found his brain capacity equal to that of a lad of fourteen or fifteen years, and his intelligence quotient 65.7. A quotient below eighty was abnormal. He was, thus, midway between the feeble-minded and the moral-deficient.

"Do you think," Mr Humphrey Slade asked, "that mere overwork could have caused a temporary upset in a case such as the present?"

"Yes," Dr Gordon agreed, "but one has to qualify what one means by overwork. I think it would contribute. A strong sexual impulse might have that effect as well, particularly in the class of mental defectives to which I consider Ross belongs."

Mr Slade: Have you formed an opinion as to whether he has a strong or weak sex urge?

Dr Gordon: I have had evidence that he has a very strong sex urge. As a rule such an urge lasts until it is gratified. It might be momentary, or last a week or ten days.

"If," Mr Humphrey Slade suggested, "at some time between October 6 and October 8, he killed these two girls without apparent motive; and if, before or after the killing he underwent some sexual excitement, is there a possibility that, at the time of the murders, he was without the power of passing rational judgment on his action?"

"Provided he was suffering from what I have definite evidence he has got," replied Dr Gordon, "and that he had a strong sexual urge – of which he had no more understanding than he would have, say, of Relativity, he would be without control of his actions."

There was a sparkling duel between the mental specialist and the Attorney-General in cross-examination. The Attorney-General kept to the letter of the law; the legal interpretation of insanity, or uncontrollable impulse. The doctor answered pungently, with the conviction that the law had not kept pace with the advance of medical science and was still hedged about by the opinions and definitions of a half-century ago.

"I put it to you," the Attorney-General said, opening his cross-examination, "that there has been a good deal of hypothesis and speculation in your statement?"

"You disappoint me, Sir," Dr Gordon rejoined. "I thought the advantage I was placing before the Court was that I was facing it with concrete evidence as to mental deficiency."

"Quite, mental deficiency," commented the Attorney-General. "But as to legal insanity, hypothesis! There was the exception in the matter of the prisoner's very strong sex urge. On that you are emphatic?"

Dr Gordon: I am.

The Attorney-General: Assuming the continuousness of that urge at the time of this tragedy, are you equally emphatic that it deprived the prisoner temporarily of his control?

Dr Gordon: I am.

The Attorney-General: Your theory is that the murders were committed by him under an impulse caused by a sex urge he was unable to resist. I presume, Dr Gordon, you have studied the legal side of this problem, as well as the medical?

"I have tried to, Sir," Dr Gordon declared, "but it is very difficult to study the legal side."

"Are you aware," the Attorney-General went on, "of the attitude the courts have taken up towards the inability to control action? That the courts of justice of our country do not regard it as legal insanity?"

"That is not so," Dr Gordon contended. "The reverse is the case."

"You surprise me," was the Attorney-General's observation to this. But he was not to have the last say. Another question gave the doctor an opening to retaliate.

"What mental state was the prisoner in at the moment he killed Miss Keppie?" he asked.

"Oh, Sir!" Dr Gordon reproached. "How *can* I answer that? My opinion, from all the evidence before me, however, is that he was temporarily insane."

The Attorney-General impressed on the jury that Ross had not been proved *legally* irresponsible for his crimes in spite of the defence evidence adduced to portray his and his father's abnormalities.

The Crown was entitled to the verdict. Justice must be done, notwithstanding the contentions of medical science.

Mr Humphrey Slade argued that the crime was not a deliberate and calculated planned deed by Ross, but due to heredity and environment.

"You have been awkwardly placed in Court, gentlemen of the jury," he said. "You have not been able to see the prisoner well. I ask you to look at him now. You see a child, gentlemen, a child."

On December 1, 1932, the jury listened to the summing-up and exposition of the law concerning a defence of insanity, by the Chief Justice. For fifty-five minutes they were closeted, then returned with a verdict of "*Guilty*".

The announcement of the foreman in a hushed Court left Ross unmoved. He declined to add anything to counsel's plea for his life.

Sir Jacob Barth expressed agreement with the verdict and passed sentence of death.

For over a month Ross remained in the Nairobi prison calmly awaiting his end. He did not fear death. Most of his time was spent reading and marking passages in a prayer-book.

The date fixed for the execution was withheld from the public, and it was not until January 7, 1933, that the death warrant was signed.

At five o'clock on the morning of January 11, the gloomy condemned cell was converted into an impromptu chapel.

An altar was erected. Candles were lit. The Dean of Nairobi conducted Holy Communion.

Ross prayed fervently during the service. At its close he asked that the prayer-book, in which he found solace during his last days, be buried with him.

Ross met his end bravely and without complaint. He was laid to rest in a tiny cemetery just outside the prison walls, the victim of an abnormality whom Society could not allow to live.

Benjamin Bennett

Samuel Furnace: History's Greatest Manhunt

Like Rouse, Samuel Furnace decided that fire would provide a convenient means of escaping his debts – although these seem to have been relatively small. The crime was clumsy, and Furnace's own death far more unpleasant than that of his victim. The author of this account, Roland Wild, produced two notable volumes, which can still be found in second hand shops: *Crimes and Cases of 1933* and *Crimes and Cases of 1934*. The story of the Furnace manhunt is from the former.

On the second of January 1933 Samuel James Furnace, a builder living in Chalk Farm, rose late, after a New Year's Day party with his wife and three children, and went to work. He had not far to go. From Crogsland Road he walked to Hawley Crescent, Chalk Farm Road, and entered his yard. There he set his employees to work, and after attending to some details in the office walked to a café in Camden Road to meet friends.

Among them was Walter Spatchett, a rate-collector and former colleague of Furnace in the firm of Westacott & Sons, of Camden Road. Eighteen months before, Furnace had left the firm to work on his own, but the friendship continued, and the two men often met in the café or played billiards together in local saloons.

They drank coffee. They talked of the New Year festivities. They parted, Furnace to return home to lunch,

Walter Spatchett to continue his round of rent-collecting. He was in the local bank before closing time to deposit the £60 collected that morning. He made his usual call on a builder at five o'clock, where he made up his accounts. He counted £35.

"Have a cup of tea?" invited the builder.

"No, thank you," replied Spatchett. "I have one more call to make."

He went out, pocketing the £35, and walked to the shed which was Furnace's office.

The workmen had gone home. The yard was silent.

And some time during that period when Spatchett was in the office Furnace shot his friend in the back. Nobody heard the shot. Spatchett died instantly.

Furnace went out into the cool night air to reassure himself that nobody was about. Then he returned, bundled the still-warm body under the desk, and locked up the office.

He went home, saw his children to bed, listened to a broadcast of "Jane Eyre," and went to bed early.

He was up in good time. He made his wife a cup of tea, and hurried to the workshop. He sent the men away on various jobs. Then he sat down and reviewed the position.

Already the parents of Walter Spatchett were anxious at the non-arrival of their son. Old Mr. Spatchett, a chauffeur living in Dartmouth Park Road, was particularly worried, as his son regularly came home between six and six-fifteen. Furnace knew that the police would soon institute a search and inquire into the movements of the missing man.

Furnace also considered his own position. At forty, he was in somewhat grave circumstances. He had three children to provide for, an overdraft at the bank, and debts amounting to nearly £100. He employed four men and a boy, but work was scarce in spite of his energetic attempts to find commissions. He had always assured his wife of his progress, but secretly he was worried. He had already been pressed to pay various amounts.

Among his debts was one for a considerable sum to Spatchett.

Then, as he sifted the facts, he recalled the insurance policy taken out on his own life. The policy had been taken out with the Britannic Assurance Company for £1,000 at death and £100 a year for twenty years from the inception of the policy. He had paid the premium of £28 odd the month before.

There was a clause in the agreement that rendered the policy void if the assured person committed suicide within twelve months of its inception. That day, January 3rd, the policy was one year and three days old. And in addition Furnace had another policy for £100 with profits to be paid in twenty years or at death.

He walked home to lunch. Then he called on the firm of Westgate & Sons, and asked if there was any work for him to do. Then he went back to the shed.

That morning he had been lucky in concealing the body from the eyes of his workmen, who occasionally came into the office. The body was hidden with an overcoat, and unless someone was openly searching, it would remain undiscovered. But his thoughts ranged always over the insurance policy. With this in mind he drew towards him a piece of paper and a pencil and wrote: "Good-bye to all. No work, no money. Sam S. J. Furnace."

He walked out of the shed just before four o'clock and stood looking at it. A workman spoke to him.

"What are you doing, Mr. Furnace?"

"Just having a stroll round," he said.

He went back into the shed, pulled out the body, now rigid, and propped it into the straight-backed wooden chair. He pulled a bag of money out of the pockets of the dead man, took the silver from the trousers pockets and the gold watch from the wrist.

He took down the hanging lamp and poured the oil on to the body. He found tins of paint in a corner of the shed, and poured their contents on to the floor and on to the body. He found waste paper and shavings, dry and combustible.

These he stacked round the chair. Finally he pinned the note signed by his own hand on to a table in the outer office, and lit a candle. By seven o'clock he was ready. He lit the pile of shavings, locked the doors, inner and outer, and saw the flames licking up to the chair before he left the shed, taking a bag of tools with him.

But within a few minutes of his leaving the fire was discovered.

A small child, going into the yard where Furnace's shed was situated, saw the flames. By half-past seven the fire brigade had been called. Already civilians were doing their best to quell the flames, and had broken open the outer door.

Throwing water on the fire, they were able to force the inner door, which was held with an automatic lock. And shining an electric torch through the smoke, they were able to see the dim outline of a body in the chair against the desk. With the arrival of the brigade the fire was quenched sufficiently for the helpers to drag out the body. The features were indistinguishable, the clothes scorched and frail, and the flesh destroyed.

But while the police were taking the body to the mortuary a workman employed by Furnace made another discovery. Walking into the outer shed, he came upon the note written by Furnace.

That night the police, after an interview with Mrs. Furnace, informed her that the body was that of her husband. She related that her husband had that morning about £47 in his pocket, and was to pay the workmen that day before banking the remainder.

Meanwhile Furnace went to a lodging-house in Princes Road, merely a walk from the charred scene of the murder. He booked a room under the name of Roy Rogers. The next morning he slung the bag of tools on his back and took a train to Wembley, threw away the revolver into the canal at Camden Road, flung away the revolver holster at Dagenham, and returned again to the Princes Road apartment-house.

But during the day, unknown to him, there had begun the

greatest man-hunt that England has ever known, involving the watch of 20,000 men of the police force, every available detective from Scotland Yard and the big provincial cities, the B.B.C., the dock police, the shipping companies, and the newspapers. For the fire that Furnace had lit in the little office-shed had been put out a few minutes too soon for his purposes by the fire brigade, and the flames had failed to destroy vital evidence which Furnace had thought hidden for ever.

If the little girl who had warned her father of the fire had been ten minutes later in discovering the flames, Furnace would have been free to make his life anew. During the first few minutes of the doctor's examination it was proved beyond doubt that the body was not that of Furnace. By a simple process of elimination it was discovered to be that of Spatchett. There were laundry marks on the collar of the shirt. Fragments of the shirt itself were identified by Spatchett's parents. There were the remains of a pocket-wallet, and a portion of a girl's photograph, which Spatchett always carried with him. Although Mr. W. Abbott, who lived in the same house as Furnace, definitely identified the body as that of Furnace, conclusive evidence was given by a dentist, who was able to say that he recognised the teeth as those of his former patient Spatchett. But if the fire had continued for ten minutes longer, clothes, pocket-wallet, and all the other evidence would have disappeared, and the police would have been forced to base their conclusions on the farewell note signed by Samuel Furnace.

Now, with the case reversed so dramatically, that note was to bear a very different and ominous part in the situation. Furnace must have written it; it was in his handwriting. Furnace wished, then, to lead the police into believing that he was the victim of the fire.

Where was Furnace?

That whisper, spoken at the inquest at St. Pancras, among the grim relics of the fire, grew into an everswelling thunder of inquiry. It was asked in millions of homes over the radio, asked by hundreds of police-officers making systematic house-to-house searches at midnight in suspected areas. It was asked by cordons of police strung across the roads of England and checking the occupants of every car, examining the driver and the passengers. It was asked in the captain's cabins of little tramp steamers at the ports, in the stokeholds of cargo-boats which had signed on crews at Tilbury and Liverpool. The question was flashed across the ocean to ships labouring in the January storms. Where was Furnace?

Before considering the drama of the greatest manhunt in history it is as well to consider at this stage the possibility that Furnace was the innocent victim of circumstances. When, a fortnight later, he was to die without being proved guilty of the crime of murder, it was suggested that there was a faint possibility that he had run away from the consequences, not of his guilt, but of an accident.

His own statement to the police was to the effect that he and Spatchett were examining a service revolver in the shed when "the gun went off" He thereupon lost his head, according to his own version, and made a bid for escape.

Both these statements are upset by common-sense consideration. Furnace was not a nervous man or untutored with firearms. He had served through the whole of the War, and had later joined the "Black and Tans" in the Irish troubles. It was unlikely that he would at any time behave foolishly with a revolver. The experienced man never points a gun, even by accident. In a statement made to a friend on the day of his arrest he is reported to have said, "Spatchett was in the office – you know what a box of a place it was – and saw the revolver lying in a case at the side. He took it up, fiddled with the trigger, and tried the grip. That frightened me. 'Hold hard, boy,' I warned him. 'It's loaded.' With that he handed the gun to me, saying, 'You know more about it than I do.' He was ready to go home then. I had the gun in my left hand as he jerked the office door wide open. There was a shot then, and down he went in a heap. What happened was that the door hit my hand as he flung it open, and the revolver went off. I was staggered, dumbfounded, scared stiff . . ."

But the man who was "dumbfounded, scared stiff" was able to calm his fears sufficiently to bundle the body under the desk, sit quietly at home that evening, lie to his employees about the "bag of cement" under the desk the next morning, plan the fire, and cover his tracks sufficiently to outwit the police forces of the whole country for a fortnight afterwards.

Would he have stood a chance of safety if he had reported the "accident" to the police there and then?

It is true that he owed money to Spatchett. The shooting would have appeared an easy way out of debt. On the other hand, he could have enlisted many of his friends to speak well of him – as a good husband and father, as an honest and conscientious workman. He could have pointed to his foresight in paying the premium for his life insurance, in order to protect his wife and children in case of accident. He could have enlisted the support of Mr. MacDonald Smith, the Britannic Assurance manager, who said in court, even when Furnace was a sought-for murder-suspect, that "he was a man with a heart of gold – the kind of man who would help anyone who was down and out; anyone who asked for a pound got it."

Or Sydney Furnace, his brother, would have said that "he was devoted to his wife and three children; he had no vices, was a rigid teetotaller from birth, loved his home, spent his life between his work and his home. When he was at sea Sam saved all his wages and gave the money to his mother."

It is true that he was financially embarrassed. Who is not? Many small contractors are content to continue with more difficulties than faced Samuel Furnace. Most certainly he had a case to support his plea of innocence if he had at the time informed the police of the "accident."

There is a further suggestion that the murder and the burning were carefully planned days or weeks or months before the second day of January. That theory is also unsupported by evidence. Furnace is said to have been influenced, long before that fateful evening of January 2nd, by stories of Rouse and other burning crimes. It was suggested that he had planned to stage his fake suicide as soon as possible after the New Year, when the clause in his insurance policy regarding suicide became out of date. This theory is quite incredible. It is inconceivable that Furnace would delay twenty-four hours after the shooting before escaping. With Spatchett missing from home, and in all probability traced to his shed, Furnace could not have run the risk of being questioned about his friend's disappearance. As it happened, he was not questioned, but sooner or later the distracted parents of the missing young man, who knew his regular habits, would have come to Furnace for information. And there was always the risk of his own workmen blundering into the office and inquiring into the strange bundle under the desk.

One of them, indeed, did notice it, even when Furnace was sitting in front of the desk.

"What have you been buying?" he asked.

"Only some cement," replied Furnace.

It is only reasonable that if Furnace had shot Spatchett according to plan he would have found some other and safer hiding-place for the body.

Further, a man who is carefully planning a fake suicide does not take the first opportunity after the lapse of a prohibitive clause. He waits some time, weeks or months. Would Furnace have planned the crime for only two days after that clause had lapsed?

There is another point connected with the insurance policy. Furnace did not himself take steps to insure his own life. The insurance was the suggestion of Mr. Macdonald Smith. Furnace had been paying insurance premiums on property but had sold the property and had no more need of the policy. Mr. Smith then suggested that he should take out a policy on his life. This Furnace agreed to.

The Furnace we are asked to believe in now, if this

premeditation theory is correct, is a systematic and careful criminal. He would surely have taken every step necessary for his safety. If he had wanted a body to burn, and invest the charred remains with his own identity, would he have taken a neighbour and friend? It must be remembered that he would not have taken into great account the money he owed Spatchett – about £60. It may be said that he wanted to kill two birds with one stone, choosing Spatchett for the victim firstly for the insurance money on his own death, and secondly to get rid of his creditor. But that would have been arrant folly. The debt owed by Furnace could not have been levied on his wife, and with the thought of £1,000 coming to his wife he would surely have scorned to consider a matter of £60.

No, if Furnace had planned a fake suicide, and only murdered in order to get a body for the burning, he would not have chosen a friend and neighbour. There are other methods of obtaining unknown men to walk into the death-house, particularly in these days when the unemployed will walk twenty miles in a day for a chance of a job. A man in the position of Furnace could easily have manœuvred a strange man into his office, at whatever time and on whatever day he liked, on the promise of a job, and with quite a possibility of the man never being traced or reported missing. After the Rouse case there will remain always the sombre reminder that there are men in this small island unknown, unremembered, friendless, and unnoticed when they have disappeared for ever . . .

The conclusion must be that Furnace would have made some preparations if he had planned the shooting of Spatchett. When Spatchett came to the shed, therefore, Furnace had no intention of shooting him. What happened during that unknown period, before the shooting, that made him press the gun to the back of his friend and pull the trigger?

Anger? A sudden quarrel?

Spatchett might well have resolved, with the beginning of a New Year, that his friend had owed him money long enough. It must have taken some pluck for the young man to press the older and experienced man of 40 for the money. Perhaps he was tactless in his demands. Perhaps he provided, on that evening, the last irritation that was to make Furnace desperate. Nobody will ever know why and how Furness came to the last desperate resolve of the murderer.

He knew Spatchett had money on him. Perhaps he expected that it would be more. But he had money in his pocket; he usually had. The presence of money, however insignificant and disproportionate an amount, has before now pressed a desperate man to an act which in less impulsive moments he would never have considered.

Now, in considering the probability of a sudden impulse being the cause of Furnace's crime, the same arguments which dispose of the accident theory can be used in support. He was a man familiar with fire-arms. He had seen death and violence. If rage had driven him, he would not have been repelled at the last by the grim physical action of pointing the gun and pulling the trigger.

Impulse, then, is the only possible cause of the shooting. It is established that before Spatchett's visit to the shed Furnace did not contemplate murder, burning, disappearance, or the fake suicide. Some time after he had bundled the body under the desk, and had gone home to his wife for the night, the thought must have come to him of ensuring his safety by the fake suicide.

Remember, that only the month before he had been reminded of his life insurance. He had paid the £28 16s. 6d. annual premium during December. The payment must have been difficult, but with the foresight of a careful man he knew that regular payment was more personally important than the debts which he had contracted among his business acquaintances. He must have thought a great deal about that insurance. The payment extended his overdraft at the bank too far for him to pay and forget. And it is probable that during the last month, when paying the premium, he had looked at his policy and been reminded of the suicide clause which would become void during January.

There was another detail which may have shown him the way to what appeared to be safe disappearance. On the morning of Tuesday, after the murder, he woke early and hurried down to the shed to send his workmen away. He may, however, have chanced to look at the newspaper that morning. One of the most startling sensations of the morning's news was an account of a fire tragedy at Hordean, Hampshire. A bungalow had been burned, and two bodies were found in the charred wreckage. And it had been found impossible to identify either of the bodies . . .

There had, of course, been other cases. The Rouse case was not unique. Sidney Fox, who strangled his mother in a Margate hotel for the sake of the insurance money, set fire to the bedroom and was only accidentally discovered in his crime. Lindsay Marshall, a Bedfordshire farmer, tried by setting his car on fire to hide the evidence of the murder of his wife and his own suicide. And on that morning when Furnace decided on a fire at his office-shed, there was evidence before him in the day's newspaper of the obliterating efficiency of fire as an aid to crime.

Despair turned him, during the course of that day, from a home-loving and work-loving family man into a fugitive. He was willing to forget family love and fatherhood in his fear. Probably he now considered it too late to contemplate throwing himself on the charity of the law and chancing a protestation that this had been an accident. He was willing to pit his cleverness against the law.

In support of the theory that he had planned the whole crime months before it had been suggested that Furnace had for years led a double life. It was said that he had consorted with women in London, and had regarded his marriage and his home-ties as a burden. It was said that he spent considerable sums of money in West End restaurants, entertaining women, and that he owed his indebtedness to this extravagance. Indeed, a woman came forward during the search for Furnace and stated that the wanted man had been a frequent companion of hers for months past, and that she had known him under another name. It was also stated that Furnace had for months used the second name of "Roy Rogers" under which he engaged rooms after the crime.

Generally, however, little hard fact came to light supporting this reputation that had been given to Furnace. It was never proved that he had been regularly leading a double life. All his intimates described him as a faithful husband and father. The reputation of a gay adventurer and a spendthrift Casanova is easily fitted to notorieties. It is supposed to invest them with a greater public interest.

Furnace was also represented as a smart man-about-town, *habitué* of West End bars and restaurants. It was said that his clothes were expensive and his taste in women worthy of a rich idler. These improvisations provided human interest, but did not contribute to the truthful story of Furnace and his crime.

These suggestions can be discounted, and leave Furnace, on the day when he was faced with the necessity of disposing of the body of his friend, as a man resolved to sacrifice the happiness of his home and his obligations in a desperate bid for freedom. And with this thought in mind he bid good-bye to his wife and children with a nonchalance that he could not have felt.

Certainly, some support for the theory that Furnace had long ago contemplated a new life is given by the account of a former companion in arms during the Irish trouble. This man told how Furnace had, during the last weeks of 1932, questioned him closely as to the best way of getting to Ireland. He had asked what was the rate of pay in the Free State and Republican Armies, and seemed vitally interested in the question of whether he could enlist.

His friend laughed, but Furnace said, "Don't laugh; just look at this." And he showed him his old discharge, and, pointing to the name, explained how easily the initial "J" could be so changed so that his name appeared to be "Samuel O'Furnace."

"And there's another thing," Furnace said to his friend. "Supposing a man could get to Dublin, it would be easy to tramp to the west side and hide up in Mayo or Connemara. None of the natives have learned to read up there, and if anybody went after him from England they would hinder them rather than help. So that's where I might be going one day – to Mayo or Connemara."

And later he said, "Supposing a fellow couldn't get to Ireland, what about Canada or America? How would he manage that?"

At the end of the conversation Furnace wrote down in a note-book the address, given him by the friend, where the return halves of tickets to America could be bought cheaply.

There is no doubt that this evidence caused the police to concentrate a search on the ports, particularly at Liverpool; but the arguments against Furnace having contemplated a disappearance were strong enough to dismiss this conversation as a coincidence. Many are the men who "talk travel" in these days, particularly when they have at some time in their lives enjoyed a varied and thrilling existence. The context for such a conversation is not given. It may have been theoretical enough to reduce the whole incident to a mere love of conversation. In any case, the evidence to the contrary is strong enough to dispose of it as unimportant.

We have, therefore, Furnace in the position of a man deciding to fake his own suicide, with the possibility of his wife benefiting from the insurance money, himself financially secure, for the moment at any rate, and the body reduced to a heap of ashes which nobody could identify. He himself could vanish. Perhaps, even, it was fortunate that he had no contacts with boarding-house keepers or women under an assumed name. It should be easy for a man to disappear and lie low for a while . . .

The note, written as if by an intending suicide, was perhaps an unnecessary detail. He scorned to remove the wallet in the dead man's pocket, or any of the clothes. The fire would remove any trace of identity better than he could.

And now that man-hunt, started as a result of the inquest findings on the day after Furnace had walked away from the burning shed in full confidence, was driving him desperately.

At first the official information issued by the police was to the effect that Furnace was "wanted to be interviewed" by Scotland Yard regarding the fire in his office-shed. A description was given: "Height, five feet ten and a half inches; fair complexion; fair hair, thin in front; hazel eyes, full face, and a square jaw. One of Furnace's teeth is missing in the front of the upper jaw. He has marks of gunshot wounds on the left leg and both arms, and on the right bicep has a long scar showing the marks of thirteen stitches. When last seen he was wearing a navy blue suit; a new light blue shirt and collar to match, a lightish brown overcoat fully belted; a grey trilby hat with a black band and straight brim; light brown socks and black shoes.

"It is known," continued the statement, "that Furnace has been a ship's steward, and has served in the Rifle Brigade and the Black and Tans. He may endeavour to obtain employment in the decorating trade as a clerk or in the mercantile marine. He may also endeavour to leave the country."

Photographs of the missing man were issued to the newspapers. But it is not surprising that from this commonplace description the police for the next week were deluged with reports from all over the country to the effect that Furnace had been seen. When, also, Furnace was eventually captured, it was admitted by the detectives that the official photographs, of which many thousands were printed for distribution in country police offices, would not have led anybody to recognise the wanted man.

Superintendent Cornish and Chief Detective Inspector Yandell were put in charge of the case, and worked unceasingly for a week, when the former collapsed with influenza, then raging throughout England. They personally followed every clue which seemed at all hopeful, and daily widened the scope of the investigations being made all over the country.

It became known to the police, and through them to the public, that Furnace had been in London on Tuesday, January 5th, two days after the burning. An acquaintance saw him in Leicester Square, and informed the police. A squad of men converged on a café, but drew a blank. But that was only one of the disappointments that were to be the lot of the searchers.

On that day Furnace had made his way down to Southend, by a method not known. It is probable, however, that he walked all through the night, or at any rate slept on the way, for in the only account he gave of the period during which he was a fugitive he omitted to mention where he had spent the night. During the sixth day, however, the police received a report that a telegram had been received by the manageress of a Camden Town lodging-house. It was dated from Southend and signed "Rogers." This was enough to send flying-squad cars to Southend to organise a beat of the whole town, and a siege of the main roads leading out of the seaside town. The detectives drew blank. So far as is known, Furnace did not stay the night of the 5th at any lodging-house, and according to his own statement did not book rooms in Southend till the night of the 6th. And by that evening he would have found it very difficult to move about by ordinary methods in England.

Southend police were watching railway stations and motor-coach stations. Every Board of Trade official at the ports had been given a picture of the wanted man. Captains of every ship at sea which had sailed from an English port since the crime were asked to compare new members of their crews with the descriptions wirelessed to them. On the evening of the 7th Scotland Yard disclosed that every detective engaged on the search for Furnace had been armed "as a matter of precaution." Another important description of Furnace was given. The police had traced every detail of the purchases made by him during his visit to London on the 5th. "He may now be wearing a brown check cap and carrying a dark brown leather kit-bag, with two handles, such as is used by bank messengers." Just before his arrest, Furnace told a friend that he was terrified reading the details of his "disguise" in the newspapers, and dare not enter a shop to buy a change of clothes.

On Sunday the 8th, and the fourth day of the search, the police took the unprecedented step of stopping every car on the main roads leading from the capital to the south coast. A special conference at Scotland Yard, presided over by Lord Trenchard, decided to mobilise every available wireless car in the Force for the search, to comb out every lodging-house in Camden Town, where Furnace was now believed to be, and to concentrate men in other centres where Furnace might be found. By that time 200 reports had been received from various parts of the country. Information came from almost every large city in England. One of the apparently hopeful reports was from a docker at Liverpool, who stated that he had seen a man attempting to board a ship. Police formed a cordon round the docks, but with no result.

All England was keyed up to the scent. There was not a newspaper reader in the country who was not in possession of a theory. The fact may be regrettable, but it remains true that a man-hunt, and all the grim details of an organised search for a criminal, holds a terrible fascination for the public. In view of this nation-wide interest in the hunt it is not surprising that the police were hindered on all sides by the reports of amateur detectives. A prominent Northampton business man, for instance, was stopped three times by the police while on a journey from his native city to Leicester and required to give proof of his identity. He had, it was said, a faint superficial resemblance to Furnace.

The climax of drama was to follow, for on the evening of Monday, January 9th, the B.B.C. announced that Furnace was "wanted for murder." It was the first time since the

Crippen case, in 1910, that the police had appealed for a murderer in this way, and it was the first time that a broadcast "S.O.S." had been issued for this purpose. A warning was also given to landladies.

"It is earnestly requested," ran the appeal, "that any one prepared to take male lodgers, particularly at quiet apartment-houses, will keep a look-out for this man, and, if he is seen, communicate immediately with the nearest police station. Furnace takes his room in a false name. He is believed to be in possession of a Service revolver, without the holster, and he may endeavour to board a ship."

During that Monday night a train travelling from Southend to London was held up and every passenger examined. During the night more than 2,000 police, beginning at eleven p.m., carried out a house-to-house search for Furnace on the Essex side of London. The majority of the small boarding-houses in an area housing 300,000 people were visited, the owners knocked up, and questioned about their visitors. Other inquiries were made at cafés and in Soho, Euston, and Paddington.

Meanwhile, how was Furnace managing to evade the watchful eyes of every police-officer and landlady, every shopkeeper and passer-by in the streets?

He stayed only two nights in the boarding-house of Mrs. Lilley, in Hartington Road, where he had first engaged a room. On the second morning the newspapers were full of his description. Paying his bill, he walked out of the house, and the police were only a few hours behind him. But he moved, perhaps with infinite cunning, only two streets away, into another boarding-house kept by Mrs. Shaw in Whitegate Road, near Southend station.

Furnace told Mrs. Shaw that he had 'flu, and went to bed in a back room on the first floor. After one night, he said he "wanted to know what was going on" and changed to a room on the ground floor, in the front of the house. Mrs. Shaw looked after him well, and he satisfied her inquiries as to why he did not go out by saying that he was feeling too unwell. The public imagined a haunted fugitive constantly changing his bolt-hole, sleeping in huts on waste ground, running the gauntlet of prying eyes day after day, or perhaps hanging round the docks on the chance of sneaking on board a ship. In actual fact, however, the wanted man was lying in bed all day, reading detective thrillers and the newspapers containing accounts of the search. He planned to stay in the room until a friend had brought him a change of clothes, in which he could venture out in a dash for permanent liberty in another country.

The search continued unabated. On the night of the 10th, the greatest comb-out in police history took place in London. Altogether an area of 800 square miles was covered. Late tram-cars and omnibuses were stopped and searched. Cinemas were watched. There was no result.

On the 11th, reports were received that Furnace had been seen, *inter alia*, at Kettering, Guildford, and Hastings. In Kettering he was supposed to have been seen in a cinema. Police locked the doors, turned on the lights, and scrutinised every patron. On the 12th, Canvey Island, offering shelter for a fugitive in various unoccupied bungalows, was searched. Reports still came in to Scotland Yard at the rate of eighty a day. On the 14th, Saturday, Scotland Yard admitted that they had no knowledge of the whereabouts of Furnace, and had not had a workable clue since the Southend landlady, Mrs. Lilley of Hartington Road, had reported his staying there on the nights of the 6th and 7th.

But on the same day, Saturday January 14th, a week after he had been seen for the last time, the police gained the information which led swiftly and easily to the arrest of Samuel Furnace.

A letter fell through the letter-box of Mr. Charles Tuckfield, a brother-in-law of Furnace, into the hall of his home at Harringay Park. It was stamped Southend, January 14th, and had evidently been posted late the night before and caught the early post to London. The letter was in pencil. It read:

"*Dear Charlie,*

"Just a line to you in hope that I shall be able to see a friend before I end it all.

"I am writing to you because I know they will watch May [Mrs. Furnace] for a long time.

"I am at Southend, quite near the station, making out I have been ill with the 'flu, so have been able to stay in all the week.

"I am far from well through want of sleep. I don't think I have slept one hour since the accident happened. I will tell you all about it when I see you.

"Now what I want you to do is not for me, but for May and the kiddies. My days are numbered. I want you to come down Sunday, on your own, please. Catch the 10.35 from Harringay Park; that gets you down in Southend at 12.8. Come out of the station, walk straight across the road, and down the opposite road; walk down on the left side.

"I will see you. I am not giving my address in case you are followed. Just walk slowly down.

"If you come will you bring me 15½ shirt and two collars – any colour will do. Also one pair of socks, dark ones, and one comb. I think that is all now. Don't let anyone know, only Nell [Mrs. Tuckfield]. If possible say you have to work or something.

"Best of luck. Mine is gone.

"*H. Farmer.*"

It was from Furnace.

Charles Tuckfield took the letter to the police. They advised him to follow the instructions to the detail. The next day he went down to Southend, walked down the road indicated, and looked for a sign. Suddenly, at a ground-floor front window, he saw a piece of paper thrust to the glass. On it was printed in large letters: "S-A-M." The door opened as he came to it, and he walked into the front room with Samuel Furnace, white-faced and twitching with fear.

The story of that talk, between the man for whom all England was looking and the brother-in-law who knew that the house in which they were sitting was surrounded by a force of police, appeared in the *News of the World* under the signature of Charles Tuckfield, and is the only indication of Furnace's thoughts and actions during the whole of the time during which he was a fugitive from the police. It is true that in a brief statement to the police after his arrest he stated that the shooting affair was an accident, but to Charles Tuckfield he related in dramatic fashion all the incidents of his hiding.

It has already been described how he explained the cause of the accident. Furnace also told his friend that he was going to give himself up to the police on several occasions after the murder and the fire. "But my nerve failed me," he said. "Now my number is up. It's only a matter of hours now. The 'tec's are round me like a swarm of bees. But if I could get in touch with someone who would bring me some different clothes I could get out of this fix."

Soon after lunch Charles Tuckfield left him. At the end of the road the detectives and uniformed police were waiting. Police constables had entered neighbouring houses and made their way to the back of Mrs. Shaw's boarding-house. The road was blocked both ends. There were police on the roof. A detective disguised as a street violinist was on duty near the house watching the front door. Then Superintendent Cornish walked into the room, followed by two other Scotland Yard men, rushed at an unresisting and calm Samuel Furnace, and held his hands.

The twelve-day search was over, and the greatest fugitive in English police history had betrayed himself by a letter to a relative.

He was taken to London in a police car within a few hours, after being searched and charged at Southend Police Station. He helped the police by pointing out to them the spot in the

Camden Road canal where he had thrown his revolver. He made a short statement, was searched again in his cell at Kentish Town, and locked up for the night. During the night he was under constant observation by police constables, who watched him through a wicket gate in the cell door.

At seven in the morning, after the prisoner had paced his cell ceaselessly all through the night, Constable Partridge looked through the wicket gate into No. 3 cell. He saw Furnace's hand come suddenly from behind his back with a medicine bottle. Before the constable, rushing in, could take it from his hand, he had swallowed some of the contents. Furnace collapsed, and in spite of constant care throughout the day and the following night at St. Pancras Hospital died at seven a.m. on the morning of January 17th. Morphia eased his pain, but the spirits of salts which he had swallowed from the bottle killed him after terrible agony in the usual period of twenty-four hours. His wife and brother kept watch at his bedside with the detectives, but the only words he was heard to mutter were, "My wife, my wife . . ."

Thus Furnace provided in death yet another thrill for the crowds of people who had waited in the pouring rain outside Marylebone Police Court to see the fugitive of the generation appear before the magistrates on a charge of murder. They were disappointed.

"Charge No. 22, your worship," said the court jailer. "Samuel James Furnace. Reported ill, sir."

Two poison specialists were even then in attendance on him. They could do no more than try to relieve the pain.

There remained only the inquests on the two bodies in this swiftly moving tragedy which had shown so many facets of the criminal mind.

On the next day Superintendent Cornish stated at the inquest on Furnace that the dead man's pockets and clothing were properly searched, but that there was afterwards found to be a slit in the bottom of the trench-coat which Furnace was still wearing in the cell. He took the four-ounce bottle from the lining in the few seconds' interval between the changing of the guard. The jury quickly returned a verdict of suicide. "The deceased had well prepared for suicide," said the foreman.

At the inquest on Spatchett the Coroner stated: "One would have thought that if the shooting had been an accident the incident would have upset Furnace considerably. Yet you find him perfectly rational telling an entirely fictitious story to a landlady an hour later." The jury returned a verdict of "Murder" against Furnace.

When the body of Samuel Furnace was taken to St. Pancreas Cemetery, East Finchley, excited women held up the cortège, a street musician played jazz music during the passing of the procession, and the police cordon was broken by hilarious onlookers. A short service was held in a Nonconformist chapel, and the voice of the chaplain at the graveside was drowned in the chatter of onlookers. A wreath in the form of a heart was dropped on the grave. It bore the words: "From his heart-broken wife and babies." Another bore the inscription: "To err is human, to forgive divine."

There were two later echoes of the case which during the first month of the year had filled the newspapers. One was the decision of the Britannic Assurance Company that the claim made upon them by Mrs. Furnace was untenable, since the coroner's verdict on Furnace was *felo de se*. The company, however, had decided to make a generous grant to Mrs. Furnace. "The law of the land being that no person can benefit himself or his estate by a felonious act, the policy is, therefore, void, and the company is in no way liable thereto."

Later, Scotland Yard pursued an inquiry into the circumstances in which Furnace was able to conceal in his coat a bottle of poison in spite of being searched on two occasions.

In all the concentrated and swiftly-marching thrills of the man-hunt and dramatic end of the principal character, the name of Spatchett was only in the background of the public memory.

Roland Wild

Georges Sarret: The Acid Bath Killer

For the modern reader, the acid bath murderer is John George Haigh, the swindler who, between 1944 and 1949, dissolved six victims in sulphuric acid in his rented factory at Crawley. But Haigh had a French predecessor, Maitre Georges Sarret, who was also, in his way, a criminal genius. This account of Sarret and his two mistresses is again taken from Roland Wild's Crimes and Cases of 1933.

A woman was walking alone in the squalid streets of Marseilles. Suddenly she was recognised by an old friend. That sudden recognition led to the revealing of a series of crimes, and the exposure of a monster comparable in infamy to the famous Landru.

The case which has become known as "The Acid Bath Murders" takes its place among the most gruesome trials of criminal history. The details which came to light during the proceedings at the little provincial town of Aix-en-Provence grew more forbidding as time went on, culminating in the most rigorous sentence being passed by the jury on the chief actor.

Georges Sarret, once a lawyer, and described during the proceedings as "The High Priest of Murder," was accused of systematic and diabolical murder in company with two Bavarian sisters, over whom he was said to have exercised a powerful and malignant influence.

Katherine Schmidt and Philomene Schmidt were also charged with murder and with extensive insurance frauds at the bidding of the master-mind Sarret.

The little town presented a strange appearance, accustomed as it had always been to the serenity and peace of provincial France. The indignation of the populace reached such limits, long before the first day of the trial, that it was thought wise to guard the court with troops, the road to the assize court being lined with gleaming bayonets. The whole of the *gendarmerie* of the district, and mobile guards from Marseilles, were also brought to form an avenue of steel, along which there marched the principal figures in this sensational and horrifying exposure of a clever man's greed and the cruelty of his two dupes.

Further interest was added for English observers by the fact that, during the proceedings, the name of a distinguished Englishwoman, Lady Arnould, the aged widow of Sir Joseph Arnould, Chief Justice of Bombay, cropped up from time to time.

The public indignation was evident by the crowds which clamoured for entry, so that even counsel had difficulty in gaining admittance to the court, and were seriously incommoded throughout the trial. The formidable indictment was read during the first day and the details of the crime alleged against the chief character caused universal horror. But there were others also accused, in company with Georges Sarret, of the extensive insurance frauds in which this Landru the Second seems to have specialised.

It was a fantastic story that the black-robed lawyer unfolded on that first chilly morning in October. The court was deathly silent. The peasants and shopkeepers, who had waited outside from an early hour, felt their eyes drawn towards the dock. In addition to Sarret and the two sisters, there stood a certain Doctor Maurice Guy, a former Deputy-Mayor of Marseilles; Andrée Sarret, daughter of the ex-lawyer; a frightened cook, Calixte Lufeaux; and two insurance agents, Antoine Siotis, and Marie Nicolas Brun.

At strategic points in the court stood armed *gendarmes* and soldiers. It was difficult to breathe, and the atmosphere seemed charged with tension. Into that tense assembly the Public Prosecutor, in a still, small voice, poured chapter by chapter a story of human cruelty and greed more sensational than any fiction.

The indictment covered ninety pages, and no more was heard in the court that day than the methodical and unemotional voice of the lawyer reading from its gruesome pages. Only once or twice did his voice reveal that he himself was conscious of the drama he unfolded. For the most part he spoke in a monotone. But the contents of the indictment were, to be sure, sensational enough to shock without the aid of human histrionics.

Georges Sarret had been born in Trieste, of Greek parents, in 1880. He looked, however, more than his fifty-three years, and though for many years he had lived in France and had become a naturalised Frenchman early in life, his cold composure and lack of emotion seemed to indicate that here was no Frenchman, but a creature of more Eastern phlegm.

Of his early life in France little is known, but the first relevant date on which the police had bent their attention was in 1924. It was then that he had met the two sisters, who had up till that date been teaching in France for a period of seven years, and had on many occasions taken position as governesses in some illustrious families. Lady Arnould, indeed, had lived with the two women in 1922, and it was while she was at their house that she died. This fact was only mentioned in passing, and although Georges Sarret, treacherous as a snake even to his friends, had accused the two sisters of being concerned in her death, the police had made investigations, and early in the proceedings directed that the death of Lady Arnould was quite irrelevant, and that the sisters were guiltless of any wrong-doing in that instance.

It seems that from the first meeting Sarret was able to

exercise his baneful influence over them. He dominated them and was the prime mover in the terrible list of crimes which now came to light. In 1924 Philomene married a man named Villette, and Sarret was best man at the wedding. Perhaps it was even while he was at the altar that the idea came to him of practising frauds on insurance companies by causing the death of a man who had been persuaded to marry his accomplice. Soon afterwards, at any rate, he persuaded the other sister, Katharine, to marry a man named Deltreuil. The most significant thing to be noticed about this union was that, whereas the woman under his control was comparatively young and beautiful, the husband was twenty-four years her senior and in failing health. It is perhaps not surprising to learn that the husband Deltreuil was forthwith insured in the sum of a hundred thousand francs.

The prosecutor was warming up, and when he proceeded to give further details of the daring and criminal scheme evolved by Sarret, he was rewarded with a ripple of excitement that ran round the court.

It had been obvious to Sarret that considerable difficulty would be encountered in insuring an invalid like Deltreuil. But this difficulty meant little to the man whose greed dictated his every move. He had already met an unfrocked priest, named Chambon, and had noted his strong appearance and the likelihood of impressing any insurance company. Without any hesitation, Sarret persuaded Chambon to impersonate the sick Deltreuil for the insurance examination, and when Deltreuil died some months afterwards, the company paid and Sarret pocketed the sum of a hundred thousand francs as first earnings in his new life of crime.

It seems that at that period Katharine Schmidt was not in the conspiracy, for she evidently protested to Sarret, asking him where he had gained his sudden riches. To this Sarret, never without an answer, said that a friend had left him a legacy.

Some time after that, however, the two women seemed to have become willing to co-operate with Sarret even in the most nefarious of his misdeeds. They made no objection when he informed them that he must get rid of Chambon, because, he said, Chambon was blackmailing him. Katharine and Philomene even helped him actively in the preparations for the deed. What he required was a secluded villa, and it was the women who made a thorough search through the lists of estate agents until they found, in the "Hermitage," near the town of Aix, what they required.

That villa was to become notorious in the history of crime, and is still regarded to-day as a place of evil omen, from which its walls and picturesque thatched roof will never be rid.

If Sarret only told the sisters that he had to get rid of Chambon, in the recesses of his evil mind he had a far more dastardly idea. For Chambon had a mistress named Ballandreaux, and it was with that thought at the back of his mind that he bade his helpers prepare the villa for habitation. His second order was far more significant. He told them to buy, as unobtrusively as possible, an old bath. When he himself went shopping it was to buy a hundred litres of sulphuric acid; soon the stage was set for the carrying out of his idea.

It was in the summer of 1925 that he contrived to meet Chambon, as if by chance, in the streets of Marseilles, and after a friendly conversation, he invited him to look over the villa. The prosecution's story had a weak link in the chain at this point, for, whereas some believed that Sarret brought his victim back to the villa, other opinions were that Katharine Schmidt, by now a fully-fledged member of the conspiracy, lured him in a taxi-cab to her home.

But the prosecution's story was decided at any rate in regard to the next act in the drama. As Chambon and Katharine walked upstairs to view the first floor, a single shot rang out, and Chambon fell dead.

Whether Katharine was surprised or not is not known,

but on turning round she saw emerge from behind a screen the bland and self-assured figure of Sarret.

Something of the coolness of his nature is revealed by his unemotional comment as he surveyed the body. He merely said: "I am going to Marseilles to arrange this thing." Two hours later he had gone, and that night returned to the villa with the mistress of the dead man.

The sisters were by now certainly in the plot. According to the prosecution's story, Katharine helped her lord and master in the performance of his second evil deed for the day. Acting on instructions, she went out into the yard and started the engine of a particularly noisy motor-cycle, which may or may not have been bought for the purpose. As the engine spurted into life it drowned the noise of another shot, and the woman Ballandreaux fell, shot in almost the exact spot as Chambon had been a few hours earlier.

It was then that the cunning and cleverness of Sarret was fully revealed. Perhaps up to that moment neither sister had realised the purpose of Sarret's strange purchases. They were soon to know. The next morning the sulphuric acid was poured into the bath until it was half full, and the bodies dragged into the cellar and flung into the acid.

His plan went off without a hitch. In a few days nothing recognisable remained of the two bodies, and he was able to distribute the remains over the garden without incurring suspicion. Sarret and the two women thereupon left the villa, and for some time after that lived in comparative luxury in Marseilles. It seems strange that not a breath of suspicion was directed to the owner of the villa owing to the disappearance of the unfrocked priest and his mistress, but perhaps a man of his history and circumstances might well have lived for years without inviting friendship. Nobody missed him, at any rate, and though Sarret undoubtedly passed through a few days of anxiety when he learnt that a villager had reported to the police the presence of acid in the villa garden, the subsequent investigations came to nothing, and for many years the crime was never brought home to this new Landru.

It was no doubt the ease with which Sarret had accomplished his crime that led him to contemplate further essays in the art of murder. He was living in luxury, and though, so far, he had had funds enough to keep him in comfortable style, he realised that his bank balance would need to be further augmented from one source or another.

Since murder was so easy, why not insurance? He must have devoted many hours of thought to the problem before he acted, and it was not, in fact, until 1931 that he perpetrated a fraud on the insurance companies with the aid of Katharine and Philomene. Even so, caution was necessary, and with real patience and forethought the two sisters prepared the ground before the coup. They became fervent "lovers of the poor" and charitable workers in the sordid slums of Marseilles, and in a few months were well known for their sweetness of character and their widespread benevolence. Particularly kind were they to women who were obviously destined to spend but a few more years in this world, and, if the truth were known, they kept a sharp look-out for those suffering in the advanced stages of consumption.

Not till the end of the year did they reveal their hands, and it may be presumed that not till then had they found the perfect subject for the furtherance of their criminal intention. It was Philomene who recognised in a woman named Lorenzi, then dying in hospital from tuberculosis, the perfect ally. Philomene gave her money lavishly, and together with many other promises, guaranteed to find her husband and help him. But she protested that she would be helpless unless Lorenzi supplied her with all the personal papers of identification with which the French people are always equipped.

It was not surprising that Mme Lorenzi handed over the papers to her benefactress, and Sarret soon had them in his hands, later handing them over, the prosecution alleged, to

Lufeaux, the strong and healthy cook. Lufeaux forthwith took out an insurance policy in the name of Lorenzi in the sum of two hundred thousand francs. The fact that Sarret was now aiming at double the reward was no doubt due to his having introduced other confederates to the plot. But after consideration he was not even content with the prospect of that large sum of money, and within a few months a man known to the insurance companies as Lorenzi was insured for the sum of no less than a million francs.

But a great disappointment was in store for Sarret. He had expected that the real Lorenzi would die within a year or two, and he was willing to wait for that event, armed as he was with his papers. Lorenzi however, died almost immediately, and when an insurance agent expressed surprise and seemed likely to institute uncomfortable inquiries, Sarret was suddenly panic-stricken. He knew that none of his dealings would bear investigation. He decided to cut his losses on the instant. "The widow renounces all her claims," he said briefly. It must have been a bitter blow, but he realised that accidents will happen even in the best regulated crimes.

A considerable sum of money had been put down in this attempt, and it was unlikely that Sarret would be long in re-entering the business which seemed so certain to bring in vast profits. His next exploit seemed more foolproof, and Sarret became even more ambitious with the expectation of netting nearly two million francs. The method was almost the same, and there was still the same risk of the insured person dying too early to avoid the inquisitiveness of the insurance companies. But that risk had to be run, and the prize was sufficiently tempting for a man of the character of Georges Sarret, by now completely in command of the morals of the Schmidt sisters, and himself unperturbed by conscience.

Katharine Schmidt was this time to fill the rôle for the benefit of the insurance company while Philomene was to find a young girl who might soon be expected to die. The girl was easily found by Philomene during her benevolent visits to the Marseilles hospitals. Magali Herbin, aged only twenty-four, but already in an advanced stage of consumption, seemed to be ideal for the purpose. As it happened, the choice was not a happy one from the point of view of the conspirators, but there was nothing to indicate then that she would not fall a victim to the disease in the space of a year at the most. And having obtained her papers of identity, Katharine Schmidt called on the insurance companies, showed the papers giving her age as twenty-four, and arranged for insurance for the sum of one million seven hundred thousand francs, this being, she explained for the benefit of her aged mother in Germany.

Magali Herbin was taken from the hospital by the kind sister who had so often befriended her, and told that she was now going to live in the country where she would be given treatment under the supervision of a qualified doctor . . .

All these incidents in the deliberate campaign were recounted by the Public Prosecutor on that first day of the trial in the packed and expectant court in Aix-en-Provence. Now, for a moment, the lawyer allowed himself to make a dramatic gesture. The whole assembly was waiting on his words. Describing the promises made to the sick girl and the assurance that she would be in charge of a doctor, he turned and waved an arm towards the dock.

"She had strange fare for a consumptive!" declared the prosecutor. "They took her out at night, gave her cocktails and ice-drinks, and generally treated her to a high life."

There was no doctor to look after her. The intention of the benevolent sisters was soon evident. Although she did not realise it herself, Magali Herbin had been taken under their care to hasten her death. But strange as it may seem she lived on, and becoming desperate with impatience, the monster Sarret had to make a chance in his plans. One night he brought home two bottles of champagne, for a continuance of that "high life" which had failed to end her life. But he brought home also a packet of phosphate of zinc.

Two days later the girl was dead.

The prosecution allegation was that Dr. Maurice Guy, who now stood in the dock, had given a burial certificate in the name of Katharine Schmidt. He was, however, acquitted of the charge. A certificate was obtained and presented to the insurance companies by Philomene, now posing as her own mother, and the huge sum of money was paid over without demur. Sarret had every cause to be well pleased with the success of his plan. There was now no hint of suspicion from the insurance company, so well had Katharine and Philomene performed their tasks. It seemed as if there would be no flaw in similar operations to be carried out whenever the sinister trio were short of money.

And it is undoubted that similar atrocities would have been attempted had it not been for the folly of Katharine Schmidt. After lying low for a time the lure of Marseilles was too much for her good sense, and she took to visiting her old haunts from time to time. Apparently she did not even trouble to move in new circles or find new friends. The inevitable happened. An old acquaintance, shocked at seeing one day the familiar face and figure of the Katharine Schmidt she had believed dead, mentioned her astonishment to a friend. Word got round that the reports of Katharine Schmidt's death were untrue. An insurance agent heard the whisper. Mere inquisitiveness led to serious inquiry. The police arrived suddenly at the Sarret *ménage* and arrested Katharine. She could not stand up to the fierce hail of questions put to her by the police, and confessed, not only to the impersonation of the sick girl but to her part in the whole of Sarret's series of intrigues. Her sister Philomene, terrified out of her wits, gave herself up to the police. Sarret's arrest followed immediately, and, according to the Prosecution's story, confessed himself a murderer . . .

The Public Prosecutor sat down. He left the stuffy court in a fervour of speculation as to when Sarret would give evidence. All eyes turned suddenly to the principal figure in the dock, the grey-haired and intelligent-looking man who was now given the opportunity of answering a few formal questions put to him by the judge. He admitted having been twice divorced, and the judge's comment was that he was known to possess a most immoral reputation.

That same day the judge also disposed of the suggestion, first made by Sarret, that Philomene Schmidt had poisoned Lady Arnould. Philomene broke down when told of Sarret's allegation, and declared that she had been most devoted to Lady Arnould during the latter's illness.

On that note the day's proceedings ended, and an indignant and horrified crowd of spectators left the court and walked through the lane of dark-skinned soldiers to their cottages in the little town which had become so suddenly notorious.

During the week-end further facts came to light of the lives of the three principals. Sarret, it seems, had started life in France as an hotel clerk, and was later a street-trader, becoming a lawyer after the War. The Schmidt sisters were daughters of a Bavarian police-officer, having had a good education and coming to Paris in 1912, where they entered the service of a count. They made such a good impression on their employer that he was able to keep them out of an internment camp during the War, though the police at one time suspected that they had been engaged in spying activities. It was further revealed that Lady Arnould had left them a legacy of several thousand pounds, and they were still in possession of some of their money when they first met Sarret. It was on Sarret's advice that they married Frenchmen in order to attain French nationality, though in the case of Katharine her husband was a consumptive sailor who performed the act of marrying her for a few pounds, and was then turned adrift. When they were arrested the body of Lady Arnould was exhumed, but Sarret's allegation that they had poisoned their benefactress was scotched by the analyst who examined the body for traces.

By Monday morning, when the trial was resumed, the

public indignation was at fever heat, and if those who crowded the court were looking for sensation, they were soon satisfied.

Sarret was not long to remain the calm personality which he had seemed on the opening day. There was a stir in court when it became known that the prosecution were going to cross-examine his daughter. Sarret lost his nerve, bowed his head, and sobbed brokenly. Questions were flung at Mademoiselle Andrée Sarret regarding the period when she had acted as secretary to her father in his capacity of lawyer.

"Did you know what business was being conducted in your father's office?" she was asked.

"If I had known," she replied, "I would not have remained an hour with him."

One after the other her answers piled up the weight of evidence against her father, until, with his face suddenly purple, he thumped his fist on the ledge of the dock and yelled: "Sarret! Sarret! You talk of nothing but Sarret! I am getting tired of all this!"

But at other times he was enigmatic. Right at the beginning of the proceedings a storm was caused by the judge saying to Sarret: "You have been a lawyer, and therefore you can present your case without being questioned."

Two barristers jumped up at once to protest, one of them shouting:

"That man has never worn our robes; he is not a member of the Bar!"

Sarret was therefore questioned, and put forward an entirely new and fantastic explanation. The gist of his defence was that he shot Chambon accidentally after he had been told that Chambon had killed Mme Ballandreaux.

The Public Prosecutor jumped up immediately. "I have never heard such impudence!" he shouted. "This is the first time that such a version of the crime has been given!"

Throughout the next few minutes there was a tumult of shouting in the court, the judge, the Public Prosecutor, the lawyers and the chief prisoner all contributing to the uproar. It was Sarret's voice which dominated, however. He went on imperturbably: "These women have been telling lies about me. It is time for me to defend myself. I upbraided Chambon for what he had done as he stood there with a revolver in his hand. I tried to disarm him, but the revolver went off and he fell dead."

Asked why he did not tell the police, he said that he was frightened of them, and in explanation of his purchase of sulphuric acid, he answered lamely that he thought he might need it some time.

Philomene Schmidt repeatedly interrupted the examination, shouting: "My sister and I were his slaves. He kept us prisoners and threatened us with arrest."

She shook her clenched fist at Sarret and exclaimed: "You are a monster, the worst monster the world has ever seen!"

Evidence was given regarding Philomene's inspired acting when she took the part of the mother of Magali Herbin. It was stated that she wept profusely in the insurance company's office when collecting the money, and enlisted the sympathies of the whole staff.

At other times Sarret was calm and impressive; his steady voice dominated the court, and with one hand smoothing his grey hair, he blandly offered an innocent version of the whole affair while the Schmidt sisters trembled in the dock with fury, Katharine tearing her handkerchief with her teeth. When he put forward his new explanation of Chambon's death, never heard previously since inquiries began two and a half years before, the court was dumbfounded, the Public Prosecutor himself exclaiming: "Ah!" as if his breath had been taken away.

Whereas, in sharp contrast to his calm demeanour, Philomene provided a series of outbursts, at one time shouting: "He lies, he lies; you must believe me! You can imprison me all my life, I have suffered less during two years in prison than when I was free under the domination of Sarret!"

All eyes turned on the Greek: he was the most composed man in the court. But he seemed as if he were paying no attention. Only after hours of damning evidence given against him did he once more show any emotion, and that was when Philomene entered the box and gave evidence about the death of Magali Herbin. Philomene seemed determined to take revenge on Sarret. Both she and her sister sobbed continuously and frequently referred to the time when they were prisoners in his house and under his control.

Katharine said that she had been "buried alive in Sarret's house in Nice," and said that for many months after the death of Magali Herbin she had been forbidden to leave the house owing to Sarret's fear that she would be recognised.

As Katharine made further incriminating statements she rubbed her hands together as if she was enjoying herself. Sarret was obviously fighting his own emotion, but eventually his patience wore out and the court was treated to the amazing spectacle of witness and prisoner shaking their fists at each other and engaging in a shouting match, each protesting the untruthfulness of the other.

There was a long duel between Sarret and the Public Prosecutor.

"I implore you to tell the truth," said the prosecutor. But when Sarret began speaking his counsel jumped up and shouted: "Stop speaking, Sarret!" Suddenly there was renewed turmoil. The prosecutor protested that this was contempt of court, to which Sarret's counsel replied: "This man is fighting for his head! He owes nobody respect!"

Before that day's hearing was concluded the principal actors in this strange drama had cast aside all pretence, and were displaying the most primitive emotions.

The whole country was by now following the "Acid Bath Trial" with intense interest. The Paris newspapers were devoting more columns a day to the description of every passage in court than they had to the famous Landru trial.

For here was every factor which makes a *cause célèbre*. There was the dominating personality of Sarret himself, a clever man who might have prospered in any occupation he had taken up. There were the full-blooded personalities of the two sisters who had come under his influence. There was excitement in plenty, and when Philomene or Katharine was giving evidence the court could always be certain of the spectacle of women under the guidance of strong emotion, of which vengeance seemed always to be in the ascendancy.

The next day even laughter was added to the other ingredients of the drama. A seventy-eight-year-old accountant, M. Caracal, an important witness, was giving evidence. Before, however, he consented to speak, he made a spirited protest to the judge. It will be recalled that at that time the French Government was undergoing one of its periods of re-shuffling. The day before, in fact, the Government had resigned. M. Caracal complained that he had been kept waiting four days to give evidence.

"If I have to wait any longer," he declared, "I shall lose my job. In that case I shall sue the Government."

"Which Government?" asked the Judge blandly; "we have not got one."

The whole court exploded with laughter, Sarret himself joining in.

But if for a moment or two the atmosphere had changed from grave to gay, later on the court was to be reminded that this was a serious occasion. The prosecutor began fiercely to attack Sarret's version of the death of Chambon.

He said that Sarret, giving his version of the Chambon affair, had made statements which in every case were impossible to confirm, since the people he spoke of were dead.

"Sarret," he said, "you are surrounded by corpses! All your clients of yesterday are dead to-day! A curious coincidence!"

The opposing counsel were frequently unable to control their anger, and on many occasions abuse was thrown about the court. When, for instance, the prosecutor objected to an argument made by Sarret's lawyer, he sprang to his feet, saying: "It is a pity that you are to-day at the Bar!"

Immediately there was pandemonium. Every lawyer in court was on his feet in a second. "Leave the court" they shouted, and the public joined in the demonstration. On one occasion the court was suspended for half an hour to allow tempers to cool down, and, in fact, the judge adjourned the court early in the afternoon in the hope that a night's sleep might tend to obliterate memories of bitter scenes.

With truly Gallic resignation, however, the lawyers later shook hands and recriminations were forgotten.

The bad atmosphere, however, was not helped by a letter produced in court which a witness stated had been forged by a lawyer in order to removed from Sarret's shoulders the responsibility of having purchased the fateful bath. Allegations were freely made that a lawyer had arranged for a false witness to appear in court, and for a large part of the day the squabbles of the legal luminaries completely obscured the main issue. Meanwhile Georges Sarret looked down sardonically on the protagonists.

He smiled when Maître Roche, defending Sarret, admitted that he had given his client a certain document. Maître Moro-Giafferi, "the Marshall-Hall of France," who was appearing for Katharine Schmidt, protested against the insult to the Bar and, followed by all the other lawyers, gathered up his cloak and swept out of the room with great dignity. Nor was farce absent from these buffooneries. Sarret, smiling once more, rose in the dock and making a movement as if to leave said: "I am clearing out too." The court rocked with laughter.

During that day too a change of heart was apparent in Katharine Schmidt. She seemed now to be making desperate efforts to shield Sarret, who, it was proved, had undoubtedly been her lover. She was unmoved when Maître Moro-Giafferi implored her to remember her own dangerous position.

"I appeal to you, Katharine!" he cried, wringing his hands. "Now is the time to tell the truth!"

But Katharine would not budge from her quixotic position. She shook her head emphatically, repeating her previous statement, while her lawyer hung his head and swung his arms in the air, so that the voluminous sleeves of his black robe gave him the appearance of a huge bat, and once more he turned to his client with a hopeless gesture of despair. But she was still defiant, refusing to save herself if it meant incriminating the man, who it seemed, still exerted over her the old power and the old influence.

Sarret was now definitely at bay. It was considered inevitable that his version of the shooting had been privately ridiculed by the jury. The excited mobs which besieged the court every day, as this week of sensations grew to an end, were often violent and demonstrative when Sarret was driven to the court. The Senegalese troops sometimes had considerable difficulty in keeping them in order, and day by day there was additional trouble in keeping the fortunate ones who had gained admittance in proper order.

But although ridiculed at one stage, Sarret now produced an even more daring defence. Briefly, he challenged the court to continue with the prosecution of Katharine Schmidt, as, he explained, she was legally dead, for the consumptive Magali Herbin had been insured and buried in Katharine's name.

Though sometimes both sisters united in defending Sarret, at others they were most helpful to the prosecution. It seemed as if the sisters did not know their own minds themselves. Often enough they refused to compromise Sarret, but during his own evidence they frequently sprang to their feet, abusing and reviling him.

Sarret was next confronted by two of his former wives. The first of these collapsed in the witnessbox and could not give evidence, but the second wife, Mlle Airaud, disclosed that Sarret married her after he and his first wife had been divorced.

"But I was never considered a legitimate wife," she stated.

"His first wife was the only one who counted, and after a time he became completely reconciled to her."

She also revealed a curious side to the man's heartless nature. She had been pleased, she said, to find he was so lavish with presents for the home – furniture, ornaments, and even bed-linen. It was only later that she discovered the origin of these gifts. They had been the property of Chambon and his mistress . . .

Another defence attempt was the theory that Sarret intended to open a chemical business with the sisters Schmidt, thus accounting for the last purchase of sulphuric acid. In the ensuing tumult, when lawyers were on their feet shouting abuse at each other, while the judge was vainly appealing for order in this most extraordinary court, Sarret's voice could be heard above the others, his livid face turned towards the sisters, angry words on his lips.

"It is you who have brought us here, you two idiots of women!" he shouted, "and yet I am glad to be here instead of still living that disgusting life!"

The vitriolic abuse in reply from the sisters brought the court to its senses, and order was once more restored.

The hospital matron who had entrusted the consumptive girl to the care of Sarret was an interesting witness.

"Katharine came to me with the story that a fond relative had asked her to make pleasant the last years of a dying girl," she recounted. "Then Philomene told how Magali Herbin had died in Nice with a nun by her bedside. She had actually died in Marseilles."

"You see how you lied!" remarked the judge.

"We had to lie!" shouted the sisters; "we had to lie at his orders!" And both pointed at Sarret.

Another witness was the undertaker who buried Magali Herbin.

"Sarret," he said, "was the only mourner, and seemed desolated as he rode in the funeral procession." Sarret had told him that he wanted the funeral carried out as quickly as possible, and the driver of the hearse proceeded at a trot. "It was a modest funeral," concluded the undertaker sorrowfully.

"Yes," the judge commented dryly, "it was a modest funeral; but it brought him over one million francs."

The next day new evidence was forthcoming. This was in support of Sarrat's oft-repeated statement that it was Chambon who bought the sulphuric acid. He had frequently declared that it was Chambon who killed his mistress, Mme Ballandreaux, and now put into court two documents which seemed to show, to the great excitement of the court, that Chambon had certainly had a hand in these damning purchases.

The prosecution openly called these documents forgeries, and intimated that they would be subjected to the examination of Dr. Beraud, the famous handwriting expert, who thereupon set to work and promised to report on them by the next day. The defence lawyer naturally exhibited these documents with a flourish and was not at all perturbed when the judge turned to Sarret and asked why he had not produced these documents before. But before he could reply his counsel shouted that Sarret had nothing to do with the direction of the defence.

Thus one more line of defence was revealed at the eleventh hour. Sarret, after at first being defiant, had produced several theories to account for his actions, none of which could be substantiated. The latest attempt had at any rate the virtue of novelty, and when the court adjourned that day the town was in a fervour of excitement to know the fate of this last argument on behalf of a man who might already be feeling the steel of "Madame Guillotine" on his neck.

That day's sensation, however, and the results which the two documents might be expected to bring, were eclipsed the next day when the Public Prosecutor rose to outline the case against Sarret, and to demand the supreme penalty. The two documents were never heard of again, a fate perhaps which they deserved. At any rate, the speeches for the prosecution, and later for the defence, seldom had any relation to facts, and in the main were composed of high flights of rhetoric, and sometimes abuse.

The prosecutor spoke for four hours, his magnificent voice emphasising every outstanding point, continuing sometimes in a low key and sometimes dying out altogether while he permitted a lengthy silence to make his artistic performance more impressive. He had a good case and he enjoyed it. For a time he contented himself with a recital of the curious circumstances of Sarret's life, later he turned to the chief occupant of the dock, and reviled him with sonorous phrases, spitting out epithets and insults.

He told a story of the crime in eight episodes. The court followed him intently as he described Sarret persuading Chambon and his mistress to stay in the villa; Sarret and Katharine arranging the bath; the careful search for a suitable villa; the ruse of the motor-cycle to cover the sound of the shot; the absurdity of a bath in a house where there was insufficient water; Sarret obtaining a shooting permit when he was no sportsman; Sarret ordering the sulphuric acid; and lastly, Sarret hiding behind the screen and shooting his victims.

He concluded on a high note: "This monster," he said, "deserves no pity. I demand the supreme penalty. You had ordered sulphuric acid previously in 1923! That proves, Sarret, that you have other corpses on your conscience! You are an indescribable criminal and the whole world turns from you in disgust!"

No fewer than 197 questions were presented to the jury by the defence. These singled out the discrepancies in the prosecution's story, and made much of the best side of Sarret's character. In his own family, apparently, he had been well loved, and it was recalled that the only time he had manifested any emotion during the trial was when his daughter had given evidence against him. One of his sisters had stuck to him gallantly during the two and a half years of the police investigation, and if she ever suspected the truth of the allegations, she had never shown it. One of the minor tragedies of this amazing trial was that the agony of suspense killed her just before Sarret's first appearance in the dock.

When the time came for the defence of the sisters to be opened there was a pathetic incident. Just as Maître Moro-Giafferi was about to begin his speech on behalf of Katharine Schmidt, the woman who had struck every one in court by her beauty, bent down, took hold of his hand and kissed it. Both lawyers defending the sisters placed the entire blame for their crimes on Sarret. It was stated that they were completely under his power, and that they had paid bribes to the police totalling over £600 in a vain attempt to call off the hunt.

It was revealed at this stage that Sarret's legal knowledge had enabled him to delay the trial for two years, on the strength of his argument that Katharine Schmidt was legally dead, and that no action could lie against her.

The judge was exhausted when making his final speech to the jury, and had to pause in the middle of reading the long list of questions. By the evening, however, of a day entirely given up to counsel's speeches, he had finished. Nobody doubted that Sarret would receive the death penalty, and the public paid greater attention to the question of the sentences to be meted out to the two sisters.

In expectation of the increased public excitement still more troops were drafted into the town, and all preparations were made for an organised defence of the prisoners if the crowd became out of hand. Such was the public indignation, indeed, that the fear of a lynching of Sarret was well justified. The crowd outside the court had become ominously larger day by day, and it was observed that their temper was at a dangerous heat. It was decided to conclude the whole case that evening if possible. The jury retired to consider the verdict, and without being absent from court very long gave the expected reply.

Sarret was found guilty of murder of Chambon, Mme

Ballandreaux, and the consumptive girl Magali Herbin. He was sentenced to death.

Every eye in the court was turned upon him, and it was astonishing to observe that over his lips there played a charming smile. Perhaps it was no shock to him, since after the collapse of his various defences he could have expected no other penalty. But there was another reason for the smile. Coupled with the jury's supreme penalty was the recommendation that he should be fined. And the sum which he was thought to owe to the police authorities was sixteen shillings.

Soon after the case was over it was announced that his execution would take place in public. This was due to his having been convicted of murder without any extenuating circumstances, and this detail also precluded him from the privilege of appeal. Nominally, of course, all executions in France are held in public according to the Napoleonic code, but during the past sixty years the custom has been to exclude the public except those officials provided with special official passports. It was announced, however, that in the case of Sarret there would be no bar to the public approaching as near as they wished to the actual scaffold.

The two sisters received sentences of ten years solitary confinement and ten years banishment from the locality. It was a revelation of human character to observe their passive lack of interest on receiving their sentences, for, whereas they faced bravely enough their judges, Sarret himself, who was said to have been the dominating personality, was a pitiful wreck of humanity.

But the reserve of the sisters gave way when the tension broke and the jailers came to remove them to the cells. Katharine swayed, and with her platinum-blonde hair falling in disarray over her beautiful ashen face, was carried in a fainting condition below. For one moment Sarret looked up, and his old self-confidence was seen in a cynical smile.

Thus ended one of the most terrible criminal stories ever revealed in a French court of law. No adjectives or epithets were too strong to be used against the principal character. Press and public combined in reviling him and in suggesting that here was a monster in human form.

Some of the secrets of his astonishing life of crime were revealed after his conviction. It was fully expected that he would confess in the condemned cell, and indeed it was said that before he was taken from the dock he leant over to his counsel and whispered in a matter-of-fact tone of voice: "I have something to say to you. Come and see me some time."

But there were others who said that he would follow the example of that other monster to whom he had been so often compared. Landru never confessed, although for years after his death there were rumours that a written explanation of his crimes was in existence.

The character of Sarret was such that he might quite feasibly have boasted about his many crimes and might have made some reference to other feats of corruption and violence. The cryptic words of the Public Prosecutor were not forgotten. The world wanted to know what lay beyond that official's belief, impossible to prove, that Sarret had in the past caused many people to disappear for his own convenience. Though known at home as an honest, mild-tempered, and kindly man, he had revealed himself as callous and heartless where money was at stake, and it was not unlikely that such a man would revel in his ability to shock the world. One curious side-line of his personal character was his mania for tidiness. Every man has his own weakness. Sarret could not bear to see a paper or a book out of place, and it was said that he could never refrain from brushing away a speck of dust from the coat of a visitor.

The two sisters, who had been acquitted of murder, and were sentenced only for their part in the insurance swindles, were driven away from Aix separately from Georges Sarret, a last glimpse of whom they had obtained in the dock. The crowds gathered outside were ignorant of their departure, but a mistake led to Sarret's carriage being recognised, and the ranks of black troops had a considerable task in keeping the crowds in check. "To death! To death!" shouted the populace, and for a time it seemed as if human desire for vengeance would cheat the guillotine of its victim.

Roland Wild

The Cleveland Torso Killer

The Cleveland Torso killer has some claim to be regarded as the American equivalent of Jack the Ripper. The crimes are, in some ways, more horrific than those of the Whitechapel murderer. The author of this present account is my son Damon, who wrote it for our second *Encyclopedia of Unsolved Mysteries*, although the present version is, in fact, a longer account that he wrote for magazine publication.

On a warm September afternoon in 1935, two boys on their way home from school walked along a dusty, sooty gulley called Kingsbury Run, in the heart of Cleveland, Ohio. On a weed-covered slope known as Jackass Hill, one challenged the other to a race, and they hurtled sixty feet down the slope to the bottom. Sixteen year old James Wagner was the winner, and as he halted, panting, he noticed something white in the bushes a few yards away. A closer look revealed that it was a naked body, and that it was headless.

The two police patrolmen who arrived minutes later found the body of a young white male clad only in black socks; the genitals had been removed. It lay on its back, with the legs stretched out and the arms neatly by the sides, as if laid out for a funeral. Thirty feet away, also hidden among the weeds, the policemen found another body, lying in the same position; it was of an older man, and had also been decapitated and emasculated. The decomposition of the second body made it clear that it had been there some time longer than the first.

When Assistant Police Chief Emmet J. Potts arrived at the scene, he found it swarming with policemen, and the heights above crowded with spectators. The desolate gulley known as Kingsbury Run was used by the locals as a rubbish dump; railway tracks ran along its floor to join the industrial valley known as the Flats, with its factories and warehouses. In the remote past, a stream had flowed through Kingsbury Run to join the Cuyahoga River which had created the flats. After dark, the whole area was crowded with hobos amd vagrants – for this was the height of the American Depression – and Potts made a shrewd guess that the two corpses belonged to this fraternity of transients.

The first thing that struck Potts, as he viewed the remains, was the absence of bloodstains, either on the ground or on the bodies themselves. The obvious conclusion was that they had been killed and decapitated elsewhere, allowed to drain of blood, and then washed before being taken to Kingsbury Run.

By that time, the missing heads had also been found; hair sticking out of the ground had revealed one of them buried a few yards away; the second proved to be buried nearby. Moreover, both sets of genitals were also found lying nearby, as if casually discarded by the killer. Potts ordered the removal of the bodies to the police morgue.

That evening, Coroner Arthur Pearse performed the autopsies. The younger corpse was that of a good-looking young man, and he had been dead for two or three days. The rope marks on the wrists, and the torn skin, made it clear that he had struggled violently. But for Dr. Pearse, the most chilling observation was that the muscles of the neck were retracted. That could mean only one thing: that the man had been beheaded while he was alive and conscious. The decapitation had been done smoothly and cleanly with a few strokes of a very sharp knife.

The second body was more puzzling. Although decomposition had destroyed the fingerprints, the skin itself was of a curious red tinge, and had the texture of leather. Pearse was inclined to speculate that some unknown chemical preservative had been used on it. The man's age was about 45, and he had been dead for about two weeks. Decomposition made it impossible to tell whether he had also been decapitated while still alive.

The investigators felt more cheerful when the first of the two bodies was identified by the fingerprints. He was 28 year old Edward Andrassy, and he had a minor police record for carrying a concealed weapon. Andrassy had lived quietly at home with respectable parents. But he apparently lived a double life. At night he liked to frequent the sleazy brothel quarter that adjoined Kingsbury Run; rumour had it that he was a pimp. It seemed that he had recently stabbed an Italian in a fight, and that the man's friends were looking for him. Mafia killings often involved mutilation of the genitals. And when a witness claimed to have seen two Italians in Kingsbury Run shortly before the bodies were found, it began to look as if the case was nearing a solution.

Newspaper reports of the finds made many Clevelanders feel queasy at breakfast time the next day. But Cleveland's new Public Safety Director, Eliot Ness, had a stronger stomach. At the age of thirty two, Ness had an enviable record as a crime fighter. In Chicago, as a Prohibition agent, he had been largely responsible for the downfall of Al Capone. After this he had moved to another "city of sin", Cincinatti, Ohio, to clean up its bootlegging rackets. And when, in 1934, the Cleveland authorities decided that their city had become a cesspool of racketeering and gambling, Ness was invited to come and clean up its "mobs." His main problem here, as in Chicago, was that there was so much corruption in the police department and the D.A's office that he had to operate with a very small group of people he could trust absolutely – his "Untouchables", who were forced to remain strictly anonymous. With corrupt lawmen to worry about, not to mention the Mayfield Road Mob and the Lonardo Gang, Ness had little time or inclination to brood on the psychopath who had killed two vagrants.

That attitude seemed to be justified as the rest of 1935 passed without incident. Admittedly, the Italian mobster theory of the double murders led nowhere. But when the investigators learned that Andrassy had been bisexual, they switched their attention to the possibility of a love triangle, in which both men had been murdered by a jealous third party.

On January 26, the homosexual theory was dramatically challenged. That snowy Sunday morning, the howling of dog finally drove a black resident of East Twentieth Street – on the edge of the Flats – to go and investigate. She found the dog straining at its leash to get at a basket that had been left against a factory wall. A glance under the burlap bag that covered it convinced her that it was full of raw butcher's meat. As she walked away, she told a neighbouring butcher that the basket contained hams. Wondering if they might have been stolen from his own shop, he lifted the burlap and removed one of the "hams." It proved to be a severed human arm. The police who rushed to the scene found that the basket contained the dismembered remains of a woman. One of the thighs was wrapped in a newspaper dating from the previous day. Some parts of the body were still missing – including the head.

Fingerprints identified her as a 41 year old prostitute named Florence Polillo, a dumpy little woman who had a police record for soliciting and bar-room brawling. She had last been seen alive two days before her body was found. The police were inclined to dismiss the notion that she might have been the victim of Edward Andrassy's killer. But one ominous detail seemed to contradict them. The muscles of the neck were still retracted, as if she had been alive when decapitated.

More pieces of Flo Polillo were found in the backyard of an empty house, although these did not include the head.

(It was never recovered.) The most promising lead was the description of an Italian with whom she had been seen recently; he sounded like one of the Italians the police wanted to interview about Andrassy's murder. But he was never traced.

This latest murder presented Sergeant James T. Hogan., the new head of Homicide, with a troublesome question. If she *was* another victim of the "Head Hunter of Kingsbury Run" (as some journalist had christened the killer), then the theory of a homicidal triangle would have to be discounted. This man was not a jealous lover, but a perverted psychopath with an obsession about decapitation and dismemberment. And that in turn raised another disturbing question. Eighteen months ago, on September 5, 1934, the lower half of a female torso had been found on Cleveland's Euclid Beach; it had been severed at the waist and at the knees. The upper part was found some miles away – minus the head and arms. Coroner Pearse estimated the age of the woman as in her mid to late thirties. The curious feature of the case was the leathery texture of the skin. At first Pearse speculated that there had been an attempt to destroy the body by burning – then concluded that it had been preserved in chloride of lime. The head was never found and the woman – who became known as "the Lady of the Lake" – remained identified.

No one had thought to connect this victim with the "Head Hunter", even though the body of Andrassy's unknown companion had also been "preserved" in some chemical. Now the Polillo case suggested that the police should be looking for a psychopathic killer who had already claimed four victims, and who might now be looking for more.

Cleveland's Public Safety Director was still more concerned with police corruption than with the "Head Hunter." In May 1936 Ness brought a police captain to trial on bribery charges and had the satisfaction of seeing him convicted. A month later, he was chiefly concerned with organising safety precautions at the forthcoming Republican Convention, which was to be held in Cleveland.

Three days before the Convention was due to open, the Head Hunter reminded the police that he was still at large. On June 5, two black children walking through Kingsbury Run found a severed head wrapped in a pair of trousers. The following day the rest of the corpse was found a quarter of a mile away. The body proved to be that of a tall, good-looking young man in his mid-twenties, with a number of tattoos. Retracted neck muscles again indicated that he had been beheaded while alive, although it was not clear how the killer had restrained him, since there were no rope marks on the wrists. The coroner theorised that the killer had cut his throat with a single sweep while the victim was asleep, then allowed him to bleed to death before continuing the decapitation. He had been dead about forty eight hours.

It looked as if he was a vagrant, or a man looking for work, who had been killed as he slept in Kingsbury Run. Yet the most careful search of the area failed to reveal the kind of bloodstains that would indicate the spot. And the absence of blood on the body suggested an alternative theory – that he had been killed indoors and carefully washed before he was disposed of.

The body was still unidentified when, on July 22, 1936, a 17 year old female hiker in woods to the south of the city saw a naked and headless body lying in a gully. It was badly decomposed, and it became clear that the victim had been killed before the tattooed young man who had been found in June. Blood that had soaked into the ground indicated that he had been killed where he lay. No identification was possible. The cheap clothing found near the body suggested that he was a vagrant, and the presence of a disused hobo camp nearby supported that theory. Again, it looked as if the head hunter had found his victim lying asleep, and had killed him with one stroke of a large and very sharp knife.

Fortunately, Clevelanders had other things to think about. A Great Lakes Exposition was packing in the visitors, with everything from an exhibition of scientific wonders to Hollywood film stars. With his natural flair for publicity, Ness had organised an exhibition on the history of criminology. This included a plaster cast of the head of Victim No. 4 – the tattooed man – with a note asking for information about his identity. But no one came forward.

The head hunter returned to Kingsbury Run to dispose of his next victim. On September 10, 1936, a hobo about to jump on to a slow moving goods train tripped over a headless and armless torso. He raised the alarm, and the police soon discovered the lower part of the body – minus the legs – nearby. Both parts had been washed from a nearby sewer which flowed into a foul-looking pool. Fragments of flesh on the side of the pool indicated that the rest of the body might be in its depths. Using grappling hooks, the police succeeded in recovering the legs.

The coroner determined that the latest victim was a young man in his mid-twenties. Since the head and the arms were missing, identification was impossible. But a hat found near the body – together with some bloodtained clothing – led the police to a hat shop in nearby Bellevue, and eventually to a housewife who had given the hat to a young tramp two weeks earlier.

Ness decided that one way to thwart the killer was to deprive him of potential victims; he sent police officers in to Kingsbury Run with instructions to order the vagrants to move on. He also had railway police search trains entering Cleveland; one of these contained no less than two hundred tramps. A hobo ejected from Kingsbury Run had an interesting story to tell. As he was sitting in the darkness on the edge of the hobo camp, a man dressed in black had approached him; when he saw a big carving knife in the man's hand, the tramp had not stayed to find out what he wanted . . .

It was clear to Ness that he had to direct some of his attention to catching this psychopath before bad publicity about the murders swamped the increasing amount of good publicity about his war against organised crime. A meeting held on the evening of Monday September 14 included pathologists and police chiefs. The conclusions they reached were that the head hunter possessed a certain anatomical knowledge, that he was big and strong enough to carry corpses around, that, like London's Jack the Ripper, he preyed on "down and outs", and that he probably possessed a "laboratory" somewhere near Kingsbury Run where he could murdered and dismember his victims without fear of interruption. It also seemed to be a reasonable assumption that he owned a car.

A "hot line" was set up at City Hall, and two detectives, Peter Merylo and Martin Zalewski, assigned to full time work on the case. One interesting lead was about a man known in brothels as "the Chicken Freak", a powerfully-built man who entered brothels with a chicken under each arm. Naked prostitutes had to behead the chickens with a butcher's knife while the man looked on; if this failed to bring about the desired result, a prostitute had to rub the bloody knife against his throat until he climaxed. After a search that lasted weeks, Merylo and Zalewski arrested a truck driver who admitted to satisfying his sadistic impulses on chickens. But when shown photographs of the head hunter's victims he was so obviously nauseated that the police let him go.

The unknown tramp was the last victim of 1936. And as the months went by without further gruesome discoveries, Clevelanders began to hope they had heard the last of the Head Hunter – or the "Mad Butcher", as other newspapers preferred to call him. That hope was dashed on February 23, 1937, when another female torso was cast up from Lake Erie close to the spot where the "Lady of the Lake" had been found nearly three years earlier. The head and arms had been removed with the same ferocious skill as in the other cases. The only major difference was that this woman had been dead before her head was removed. She was apparently in her mid-twenties and had borne children. But an extensive search failed to reveal any other parts of the body, and the victim remained unidentified.

Ness begged his friends in the press to tone down their coverage of the case – the headlines about head-hunting maniacs were beginning to cause panic. Merylo and Zalewski redoubled their efforts, and tracked down half a dozen possible suspects – alcoholics with a penchant for carrying concealed knives or razors. All were released after questioning.

The Cuyahoga River, not far from Kingsbury Run, was the site of the next discovery. A teenager discovered a skull under the Lorain-Carnegie Bridge on June 6, 1937; nearby, police found fragments of a female skeleton inside the remains of a burlap bag. A piece of newspaper in the sack dated from June of the previous year confirmed the coroner's view that this unknown victim had been killed before the tattooed man. Black hair found on the skull enabled him to say that the victim had been a black woman of about thirty five. It seemed that the possibility of identifying her was remote. But since the pathologist had the skull to work on, dentists were circulated with a description of the teeth. This long-shot paid off; a dentist was able to identify work he had done on a woman called Rose Wallace, a prostitute who had vanished in the previous August. She had last been seen in a car with three white men, on her way to a party. Moreover, she had lived close to Flo Pollilo – in fact, they had even shared a lover. But the trail ended there.

But since this victim belonged to the previous year, the police had every reason to expect another victim around the time Rose Wallace was identified. The Mad Butcher seemed to kill about once every four months. And on July 3, when Ness's attention was taken up with a strike in the Flats – which often led to violent encounters between strikers and strike-breakers – a factory guard saw a white object floating in the Cuyahoga River below West Third Street bridge, and recognised it as a legless lower torso. The upper half was found floating in a burlap bag – minus, inevitably, the head. The legs, also separated into halves, were found nearby; so eventually, were the arms and feet. Only the head was never found. This victim, number 9, had been a man in his thirties, and death was again due to decapitation. And, more ominously, he had also been disembowelled, and the heart removed. The compulsions of the Mad Butcher were becoming increasingly sadistic.

That same afternoon, a drunken man who was heard boasting that he "knew all about the torso murders" was swiftly arrested, but proved to be an ambulance driver who was able to prove his innocence.

A few months later, Merylo and Zalewski became convinced that they had caught the Head Hunter. Examining the effects of one of the first victims, Edward Andrassy, they found some undeveloped photographs showing Andrassy in a bedroom with flowered wallpaper. This, they speculated, might be the "laboratory" in which the killer dismembered the bodies. The picture was published in newspapers and recognised; in fact, to Merylo's embarrassment, it turned out to be a bedroom he had entered at one point in the investigation. It was the room of a middle aged homosexual, who proved to possess a trunk containing a butcher's knife and bloodstained clothing. The man was jailed on a sodomy charge, and Merylo and Zalewski prayed fervently that they had heard the last of the torso killer . . .

They were disappointed. On April 8, 1938, the lower part of a leg was discovered caught in a tree root on the Cuyahoga River. The new County Coroner, Samuel Gerber, pronounced it to be that of a woman in her late twenties or early thirties. Four weeks later, on May 2, two burlap bags were pulled out of the river, and proved to contain more parts of the same body – minus the head. No identification was possible.

The new coroner was convinced that the Head Hunter was a man who had had medical training, and that he probably drugged his victims before killing them. Traces of drugs in the latest victim seemed to confirm his theory.

And when Ness heard about an ex-hobo in Chicago who claimed to have seen the killer, he had him brought to Cleveland. The man had a strange story to tell – of how he had been invited to the office of a man who claimed to be a doctor – he described him as short, with ginger hair. There, as he ate a meal, he felt he was losing his senses, and realised he had been drugged; he lurched to his feet and managed to escape. But this had been before the first two victims had been found in Kingsbury Run, three years ago. The "doctor's" office had been in East Fifty Fifth Street, near Kingsbury Run. But the police were too late; only a local bartender seemed to recall the short doctor, and he had not seen him for two years. One detective pointed out that the doctor's description matched that of Victim No. 9, which suggested he was victim rather than killer.

Press criticism of Ness was mounting. Why was he not personally engaged in the hunt? There were two answers: first, that Ness had no idea of what to do, and second, that he felt he had more important things to do anyway. In his own eyes, one of his most successful schemes was to organise youth recreation programmes in slum areas with a high rate of teenage crime; the result was a remarkable fall in juvenile delinquency. But Clevelanders were not interested in this type of achievement; they wanted to see the Head Hunter behind bars.

Criticism reached a climax when two more bodies were found on the same day. A group of blacks scouring a rubbish dump near the City Hall found a female torso wrapped in an old quilt. Nearby, police found the head wrapped in brown paper, and the arms and legs in a cardboard box. Not far away, human bones were found half-buried. A tin box proved to contain a man's head.

The woman had been in her mid-thirties, and the hardening of the flesh suggested that she had been kept in a refrigerator. But although the whole body had been recovered, identification proved impossible. The set of bones proved even less revealing. A reconstruction of the face indicated that he had a broken nose. A detective recalled that Victim No. 1, Edward Andrassy, had been seen around with a man named Eddie, who had a broken nose, and who seemed to be about the same build as the skeleton. But all attempts to trace "Eddie" were a failure.

Although these latest remains clearly pre-dated those of the woman found in the Cuyahoga River, Ness felt that it was time he took swift and drastic action. There were still no clues to the identity of the killer. But there could be no possible doubt that most – if not all – of the victims were down-and outs. If they could not catch the killer, at least they could deprive him of victims. The cardboard box containing "Eddie's" skull had been traced back to the Central Market, in the Flats. This area housed the largest of the hobo "shantytowns", thirty home-made shacks.

On the day after the discovery of the two bodies, Ness co-ordinated his plans. Shortly after midnight, police and fire engines surrounded the shantytown. Floodlights were switched on and the raid commenced. Sleepy tramps were dragged out into the warm August night and taken to the Central Police Station. Another camp near the Lorain-Carnegie Bridge was the next target; ten more tramps were detained for questioning. Finally, the police poured into the camp in Kingsbury Run, and arrested fifteen men. Back at the station, these were made to identify themselves. Eleven out of sixty three hobos had criminal records and were kept in custody. The others were sent to the workhouse. The following day, all three shantytowns were burned to the ground.

Ness received harsher criticism than usual for his summary treatment of the vagrants. But his method worked. Deprived of victims, the Head Hunter went out of business. He had killed twelve people in three years – thirteen if the Lady in the Lake was counted. And at the end of that time, the police still lacked the slightest clue to his identity.

But although the Torso murders were over, no one yet realised it, and police activity was more frantic than ever.

The crimes had reached foreign newspapers. In Germany, Dr. Goebbels himself had unfavourable things to say about America's decadent civilisation, and Mussolini's newspapers were equally scathing. But as no more dismembered corpses were found, the fever slowly abated.

By the following spring, Merylo was one of the few policemen still working full-time on the case. The sheriff's department had also hired a private detective named Lawrence J. Lyons, known as Pat. And it was Pat Lyons who unearthed what seemed the most significant clue so far. He learned that three of the victims – Edward Andrassy, Flo Polillo and Rose Wallace – had frequented the same tavern on East Twentieth Street and Central Avenue. There Lyons heard tales of a man called Frank, who boasted that he was an expert with knives. When he learned that Flo Polillo had lived with Frank at one point, Lyons felt he had a prime suspect for the murders.

"Frank" proved to be a squat, middle aged immigrant bricklayer named Frank Dolezal. Further investigation revealed that he had been seen with Rose Wallace, and a man who resembled Andrassy. Moreover, Dolezal was bisexual, and had often been seen accosting strangers near the Central Market shantytown.

Detectives gained entrance to Dolezal's four room apartment on Central Avenue. On the bathroom floor they found ominous stains. Scrapings were taken and sent for analysis to Lyons' brother, who was a chemist; he declared them to be blood.

The sheriff's office was excited by the breakthrough; it would be a triumph if they could solve the case that had baffled Ness and the Police Department. But when he heard that Merylo was asking questions about Dolezal, Sheriff O'Donnell decided it was time to arrest their suspect. On July 5, 1939, Dolezal was picked up and taken in for questioning.

Two days later, O'Donnell called in the newspapermen. "Boys, Frank Dolezal has confessed to the Polillo murder."

Dolezal had signed a confession describing how he had quarrelled with Flo Polillo two days before her remains were found, and had killed her accidentally by knocking her against the bath tub. Then he had dismembered her and disposed of part of the body, throwing some – including the head – into Lake Erie.

It certainly looked like the solution. Ness was generous in his congratulations. Yet when the "bloodstains" in the bathroom were re-examined by a pathologist, he declared positively that they were *not* blood. Discrepancies were also noted in Dolezal's statement. He claimed to have thrown the arms and legs into Lake Erie, yet they had been discovered with the body in the basket. When Dolezal was finally accused of manslaughter, interest in him waned.

On August 24, 1939, four weeks after his arrest, Frank Dolezal was found hanging from a hook in the ceiling of his cell. An autopsy performed by Coroner Gerber revealed that six of his ribs were cracked, and that this injury dated back to soon after his arrest – supporting Dolezal's complaint that his confession had been obtained by force.

Nevertheless, as far as Clevelanders were concerned, Dolezal's death was the end of the story of the Head Hunter of Kingsbury Run. Cleveland's Safety Director held other views – which, for the moment, he kept to himself.

Sadly, the last decade of Elliot Ness's life – he died in 1957, at the age of 54 – was full of poverty and disappointment. He resigned as Cleveland's Safety Director in April 1941, after a scandal involving a hit-and-run accident. In 1947 he was heavily defeated when he ran for the post of mayor of Cleveland. A year later he was even turned down for a sixty dollar a week job. "He simply ran out of gas," said one friend. In 1953, after five years of obscurity and poverty, he became involved with a paper-making company which tottered on the verge of bankruptcy. But it was through a friend in the company that Ness met a journalist called Oscar Fraley, and began telling him the story of his anti-bootlegging days. And in the course of their conversations, Ness told Fraley that he was reasonably certain that he knew the identity of the Torso killer, and that he had driven him out of Cleveland.

What Ness told Fraley was as follows. He had reasoned that the killer was a man who had a house of his own in which to dismember the bodies, and a car in which to transport them. The skill of the mutilations suggested medical training, or at least a certain medical knowledge. The fact that some of the victims had been strong men suggested that the Butcher had to be big and powerful – a conclusion supported by a size 12 footprint near one of the bodies.

Ness set three of his top agents, Virginia Allen, Barney Davis and Jim Manski, to make enquiries among the upper levels of Cleveland society. Virginia was a sophisticated girl with contacts among Cleveland socialites. And it was she who learned about a man who sounded like the ideal suspect. Ness was to call him "Gaylord Sundheim" – a big man from a well-to-do family, who had a history of psychiatric problems. He had also studied medicine. When the three "Untouchables" called on him, he leered sarcastically at Virginia and closed the door in their faces. Ness invited him – pressingly – to lunch, and he came under protest. Sundheim refused to either admit or deny the murders. Ness persuaded him to take a Lie Detector test, and Sundheim's answers to questions about the murders were registered by the stylus as lies. When Ness finally told him he believed he was the Torso killer – hoping that shock tactics might trigger a confession – Sundheim sneered: "Prove it."

Soon after this, Sundheim had himself committed to a mental institution. Ness knew *he* was now "untouchable", for even if Ness could prove his guilt, he could plead insanity.

During the next two years Ness received a series of jeering postcards, some signed "Your paranoid nemesis." They ceased abruptly when "Sundheim" died in the mental institution.

Ness went on to collaborate with Fraley on a book called *The Untouchables*. It came out in 1957, and was an immense success, becoming a bestseller and leading to a famous TV series. But Ness never knew about its success; he had died of a heart attack on May 16, 1957, six months before *The Untouchables* was published.

Damon Wilson

The Rattlesnake Murder

The Rattlesnake Murder case was partly responsible for my decision to produce an encyclopedia of murder in 1959. I was introduced to Sunday Express journalist Robert Pitman by the novelist John Braine, and was delighted to discover that his wife Pat shared my interest in murder. We began to discuss cases that fascinated us – Jack the Ripper, Sylvestre Matuska, ("the man who wrecked trains"), and Kreuger and von Arbin, who disposed of an unwanted business partner by placing a bomb in his taxi. And, inevitably, the name of Robert James was mentioned. It was Pat who wrote up the case in *An Encyclopedia of Murder*, indulging her macabre sense of humour: "The obliging Hope (he said afterwards that James had 'hypnotized' him) went the round of local snake vendors, but his purchases were puny specimens; James, getting progressively more furious, would test their lethal efficiency on hordes of rabbits and chickens, who seemed to thrive on snake bites."

Pat's article is too short to include here, but the account by lawyer Eugene D. Williams (in *Los Angeles Murders*) is a minor classic in its own right.

You ask if I remember the rattlesnake murder case – that fantastic, almost unbelievable nightmare of torture and death. I remember it. The word "rattlesnake" brings a kaleidoscope of memories. The picture of the D.A., a small crew of detectives and myself deciding to "go to work" on the death of Mary James – the days and nights at the dictagraph, listening to James' southern drawl, his love making – the arrest – Hope's bizarre confession – in the morgue looking at the body of Mary James, taken from the grave – days and nights of work, work, work. Then the trial, Judge Charles W. Fricke, calm and competent – the jury, intent and interested – "Wild Bill" Clark, Russ Parsons and Sam Silverman, ably and forcefully fighting for their client – the crowded court room – the press row – special writers – Gene Markey, Carey Wilson, Bradley King, Bartlett Cormack, Tod Browning, Florabel Muir, Walter Winchell who dropped by to listen for a half-day session, Peter Lorre, the character actor studying abnormal psychology at first hand.

I remember the murderer's impassive face and beady eyes as he watched the witnesses and later on the witness stand as he lied and lied, and finally lied himself into a noose. I remember the "experts," herpetologists who told us about the Crotalus Atrox and a dozen other varieties of rattlesnakes and about snake venom and its effect – the rattlesnakes brought into the court room – the long days and weeks of trial – the tension, the snap decisions as to whether to ask or not to ask a certain question, to call or not to call a certain witness, always with John Barnes at my side bearing his share in the smooth team work which we had learned by experience and by which we fitted piece by piece the jigsaw puzzle which showed "beyond a reasonable doubt and to a moral certainty" the guilt of the defendant.

I remember the arguments – Johnnie Barnes, cool and logical, putting the case together bit by bit – Bill Clark and Russ Parsons, dramatic, forceful, emotional – and dangerous. And then my job of pulling all the loose ends together, pulling the jury up to the task of doing its hard and solemn duty, asking the death penalty, in a packed court room still as death itself – the judge's instructions. The jury goes out – God, how tired I am – weighted with the responsibility, wondering whether some mistake, some error of judgment, some lack of tact, on my part, might let a guilty man loose again to prey on defenseless women. The jury comes back quietly. The stir in the court room is hushed.

"Mr. Clerk, read the verdict."

"We, the jury . . . guilty of murder . . . first degree."

Silence. No recommendation for life imprisonment. That means death.

The stir – movement – excitement – relief – congratulations! – pats on the back – headlines – but God, am I tired!

The long drawn-out appeals – the Supreme Court of California: "Judgment affirmed." Then the arguments before the Supreme Court of the United States – the kind but stern white-bearded Chief Justice – the keen and searching questions by the Associate Justices: "Affirmed."

I remember the weighted rope hanging all alone in the little room adjoining the death cell at San Quentin. The guard said:

"Did you ever hear of the rattlesnake murder?" I had. "We're saving this one for him – he's the last one – we're going to gas 'em after this."

I remember when they hanged him. I wasn't there, I'm no ghoul, but I remember –

Robert S. James was born on a little cotton patch in Alabama. He wasn't christened "Robert S. James." His folks gave him the colorful name of "Major Raymond Lisenba." When and why he abandoned his true name and adopted "Robert S. James" is unknown, but at a certain time "Lisenba" disappeared and "James" sprang into existence.

He had a hard youth. At eight he was working in the cotton mills. He got very little schooling, perhaps three or four years. One of his older sisters married a kind, upstanding man who was a master barber. He took James into Birmingham, sent him to barber school and gave him a job. James became a good barber – but he got into trouble (with a girl, rumor has it) and left Birmingham between suns.

Years of adventure followed – hazy years, but always there was a woman. Marriage, affairs, another marriage, one half-told tale of a wife who returned with him from a rowboat ride on the lake one night dripping with water, fearful, who left him then and there. Apparently he was a good barber, but always women were his first and foremost interest.

He was always after a new woman. He liked to spend money, be a "big shot" for their benefit. Men didn't care much for him, nor he for them – but certain types of women did! He had a sallow complexion, wavy red hair carefully oiled, a suave, pleading "Southern" voice – and a way with women. One woman, after enjoying his masculine charms, effusively confided to him that he was the "most nutritious man I ever knew."

Being a good barber, working in high-class shops, he learned about good clothes from observing his customers. He was doing all right for himself – but it takes a lot of money to impress a lot of women.

His mother died. She had been carrying a small insurance policy payable to him. This opened his eyes. Then a nephew was killed in an automobile accident. He had an insurance policy and James was the beneficiary. Twice death paid benefits to James. That set him thinking.

In 1932 in Los Angeles, he met and married Winona Wallace. She had had for a long time a thousand-dollar insurance policy payable to her sister. James got her to make him the beneficiary. He also induced her to take out other policies payable to him, each paying double in case of accidental death. In case of her accidental death he would receive about $14,000. The first quarterly premiums on these policies safely paid, but with little money in his pockets, he took his bride on a honeymoon trip.

Late one night he appeared at the office of the toll-road

company at Glen Cove, near Pike's Peak, Colorado, and told the superintendent and others that his wife had been driving their car, had lost control and gone over the edge of the road. He had jumped. She was undoubtedly dead. The superintendent looked at him. "You jumped?"

"Yes."

"How far down?"

"About fifty feet."

The superintendent eyed James' natty, well-creased blue suit. "You must have made a perfect landing," he muttered. He was suspicious and he observed everything carefully.

They went to the site of the wreck. Luck had been against James. About one hundred fifty feet down the hill a big boulder set solidly in the ground had stopped the car. Except for this boulder it would have ended in a twisted mass of wreckage hundreds of feet below. Winona was lying on the ground at the right side of the car, unconscious but not dead.

In the hospital at Colorado Springs skilful surgeons saved her life. She had no memory of what had happened. Soon James took her from the hospital and went to a lonely cabin in a summer resort at Manitou, which at that fall period of the year was practically unoccupied. Their cabin was remote and they were to all practical purposes alone.

James was in bad shape financially. He had had to borrow some money from Winona's father, who had come to see her in the hospital, and then he had to borrow some money on Winona's old thousand-dollar life insurance policy. His first effort to collect death benefits on the insurance had failed and he needed money badly. Winona was getting well. In a short time they would have to move on. James, watching Winona with his beady eyes, gave thought to the subject. That thought resulted in action.

One day he took the stage to Colorado Springs. He dropped in to see his acquaintances, the hotel proprietor and others. At each place in response to questions about Winona's condition he said he was worried about her; that her head was still bad; that she kept insisting on washing her hair, although the doctor told her she shouldn't. He said she was having dizzy spells. This seed implanted in fertile soil, James returned to the cabin.

Shortly thereafter he appeared at the store at Manitou, said he was just back from Colorado Springs and that he was tired, and asked that the delivery boy take him and some groceries he bought up to his cabin. This was the first time that any such arrangement had been made, but the boy went with him. James asked him to carry the groceries into the house. As the boy was putting the groceries on the sinkboard, James came into the kitchen, having been around in the bedroom part of the house, walked from the kitchen into the bathroom, and then called the boy and showed him Winona's nude body lying on its back in a tub of warm, soapy water. She was dead from drowning. The tub was small and Winona's position, lying with her feet over the end of the tub and on her back, was such that it appeared almost impossible for her to have gotten into that position or to have drowned without "help." However, no one seemed interested, so no official investigation of Winona's death was made at that time.

James collected for accidental death by drowning, complicated by injuries received in the automobile accident, a sum of over $14,000. And then he went to town! He bought himself a new Pierce Arrow convertible coupe. He bought a lot of clothes and expensive luggage. He took a trip back to Birmingham, Alabama, and visited his relatives. He splurged all over town, bought himself some fighting game cocks and entered into the life of the sporting fraternity in Birmingham. He bought presents for his sisters and other relatives.

There he met for the first time his pretty little eighteen-year-old niece, Lois, daughter of the master barber who had befriended him. The details of her seduction are unpleasant and not necessary to this story. It is sufficient to say that when he left Birmingham, she left with him, traveling toward California as "man and wife."

After arriving at Los Angeles, James purchased a barber shop in a good downtown location. He had several barbers and a manicurist working for him. He sent his niece to beauty school and had her learn the manicuring trade. At times she worked in his barber shop as a manicurist.

By the time he was well settled in Los Angeles, although he was making good money as a barber, he began to feel the need of more money. He was carrying on affairs with various women. On one drunken spree he married one of them who later sought to have the marriage annulled. Before the annulment was effected, however, he met Mary Busch. She went to work for him as a manicurist. He talked her into marriage, and at the same time made all of the preliminary arrangements and got her to take out $10,000 worth of life insurance payable to him with double indemnity in case of accidental death. He was still a married man, as his annulment had not been completed. But Mary was insistent, and he was described as her husband in the policies which were about to be issued.

Under the circumstances, he hired a friend to act as minister and had a mock marriage ceremony performed. Of course, Mary thought it was legitimate. They then went to live in a small bungalow which James had rented in a section of Southern California lying at the foot of the Sierra Madre mountains known as La Canada.

This place was well adapted for James' purposes. The house was set amid a grove of trees, well concealed from the road and from the neighbors by luxuriant shrubbery, and was sufficiently distant from all other houses so that very little noise, if any, could be heard by the neighbors. On one side of the house, entirely surrounded by a thicket of shrubs and bamboo, was a fish pond.

Well settled in this "love nest," James started his plans.

On Monday, August 5, 1935, James made arrangements by telephone to take two friends of Mary's out to his house for dinner. He explained to them that Mary would prepare the vegetables but that he would buy the meat and they would have steaks. They arrived at the house about dark. There were no lights, no sign of Mary. James procured flashlights. He started one way, one of the friends started another way around the grounds looking for Mary.

The friend found her body in the fish pond. James came, very agitated, helped get her body out of the pond, and wept over his dead wife. The police were called. James played the bereaved husband to perfection.

The coroner pronounced it death by accident. Notwithstanding the suspicion which arose from the fact that Mary was heavily insured (far beyond the normal insurance for a person of her means), and that James had had the fortunate coincidence of having another heavily insured wife die by accident, the investigation was dropped.

In the meantime, however, James, not content, spent an evening with a woman acquaintance of his. He made love to her, talked of marriage, and then told her that the police were trying to frame him for the death of his wife, which he said was a "lot of bunk." But he said, "You know I worked at my shop all day Monday, and if you would testify that you drove by my house about ten o'clock Monday morning and saw Mary sitting on the porch, I could call you as a surprise witness. That would knock out any effort to frame me. If you'll do this, I'll pay you two thousand dollars." The woman half-heartedly agreed.

No further action was taken by the authorities. James proceeded to try to collect the insurance. One of the insurance companies asserted some defects in the policy and succeeded in settling with him for $3500 on its $10,000 liability. The other company refused to pay. The case was brought to court and tried, and judgment rendered in favor of the insurance company and against James on the ground of a defect in the application for insurance.

James now purchased a small bungalow in the southwest part of Los Angeles and moved in with his young niece, Lois. The furor about Mary's death had been forgotten, all was quiet, and he was proceeding on the even tenor of his ways. He hadn't done so well, but he felt safe. He had his niece and other women. He was again seriously considering marriage – and insurance. Then all hell broke loose.

In March, 1936, some seven months after Mary's death, a crew of detectives of the D.A.'s office, working under my direction, had just completed an extensive murder investigation which resulted in the conviction of a woman for having killed her husband eight years before. We were temporarily free, and we felt that the James case deserved investigation. We knew that James had insured his wife, Winona, and later, Mary, for sums greatly in excess of what would normally be carried by wives in their station of life, that Winona had died as a result of what appeared to be an accident and that he had collected her insurance, that Mary was dead, apparently by accident, and efforts had been made to collect her insurance. We felt it was unlikely that within three years after one such fortunate accident for James, a similar accident, equally fortunate for him, should happen to another wife, likewise heavily insured.

It was known that in the celebrated bathtub murder case in England, the defendant, George Joseph Smith, had had three wives die from drowning in bathtubs, and in each case had collected substantial sums from their estates and insurance. We were aware of the fact that in that case the eminent British jurist who presided had advised the jury:

> "If you think that the prisoner has a system of obtaining money from women by going through the form of marriage with them and then getting the money either by robbery or murder, you may use the evidence of the other deaths for that purpose.
>
> "Now, I want to give you one or two illustrations of that sort of thing, in order that you may exactly understand for what purpose you may use

these other deaths. Let us get away from crime for a moment. You are playing cards for money with three men; suddenly in the pocket of one of them is found a card of the pack you are playing with. Possibly your first view could be – it would depend a good deal on what sort of a card it was; if it was a 'two' of one of the suits that was not trumps you would not think very much of it. Cards do sometimes tumble into odd places. If it happened to be the ace of trumps in the game you were playing at that time you might regard the matter with more suspicion, and, perhaps, in view of the fact that cards do tumble about, you might say that in that one case only, you could not form any opinion about it. But supposing on your mentioning it to someone else it turned out that on five previous occasions of playing for money the gentleman had had the fortunate accident of finding the ace of trumps in his coat pocket, what would you think then?

"What the law says you may think is that that series of fortunate accidents does not usually happen to the same person so many times, and that you may draw from that series of fortunate accidents the inference that it was not an accident at all, but that it was designed. That illustrates the way in which you may use, in dealing with a criminal case, the occurrence, the repeated occurrence, of the same accident to a person who benefits by the accident each time."

With this in mind, we investigated the circumstances of the insurance of both Winona and Mary, getting all the details. We learned that James, in both cases, had initiated the applications for insurance, had secured the cheapest insurance which would pay double for accidental death, had paid but one quarter's premium. We located a witness who testified that as early as January, 1935, James had stated that he expected a large sum of money from an estate. Investigation disclosed that he had no relatives who had any large estates, so we connected that in our thought with his subsequent effort to collect the large sum of insurance on Mary.

We then rented a furnished house next door to where James was living with his young niece. We installed microphones connected with a dictagraph, and set a twenty-four hour watch on James. We heard and recorded everything that was done and said in that house. We were there for almost a month.

To our disappointment there was not one word said about the death of Mary James. Our suspicion that perhaps the niece had been party to the murder found no support in anything we heard. But we did learn that James was having sexual relations with this niece (as well as with a number of other women). These relations with the niece constituted the crime of incest, a felony under the laws of California, so at a certain time in the course of the investigation, having become convinced that nothing further could be learned by means of the dictagraph, I instructed the investigators to go into James' house the next time he committed an act of incest with his niece, and arrest him in the act.

Locks on certain windows were "jimmied," screens loosened and the men waited for the right time. That time came on April 19, 1936, and James was placed under arrest. After questioning, it was determined that he would admit nothing in reference to the crime of murder. He tried to laugh off the crime of incest by asserting there wasn't any such crime. However, he was booked in the county jail. The newspapers played up the arrest. The story of the untimely deaths of his wives was again revived, and the thing happened which very frequently happens in the investigation of crime: somebody started to talk.

It is a sad commentary on human nature but nevertheless true, that men (and women, too) like to kick people when they are down. It happens very frequently when a criminal is under arrest, definitely in trouble, that people who know things about his crimes will start to talk. That is well known to experienced prosecutors and investigators. As anticipated, it happened in this case.

The owner of a liquor store spoke to a lawyer friend. He said that he knew something about this fellow James, and he didn't think that a fellow who would treat his little niece the way James had was entitled to any protection. The lawyer agreed. The liquor man said he didn't want to get mixed up with the police or D.A. in any way or come to the fore in the matter, but if the lawyer thought it was all right and could keep his name out of it, he could give some interesting information. The lawyer assured him he thought it was all right and suggested that a friend of his, "Pat" Foley, a reporter for the *Los Angeles Herald-Express*, could carry the information to the D.A.'s office. They arranged to meet.

The liquor man's "information" was that he knew a fellow named Hope. That on a certain day in August of the previous year, Hope had appeared at his liquor store in an obviously nervous, jittery condition. He babbled about going around the country buying rattlesnakes, about a woman having been bitten by a rattlesnake, about a murder and a woman's body in a pool. The liquor man had thought that Hope was on the verge of d.t.'s and ordered him out of the store and had given him a bottle of wine to "sober up" on. He had regarded the fantastic story as a "wino's dream." But the next day he had read in the newspaper of Mary James' body having been found in a fish pond. Upon reflection he had come to the conclusion that Hope perhaps really knew something of that murder.

Pat Foley conveyed this information to me. There was one added item: Hope owned a certain make of automobile. Within hours our investigators had got the name and address of every person named Hope in the State of California who owned an automobile, and had ascertained that the only one of that make had been registered to Charles Hope, Los

Angeles. They also learned that he had disposed of that car and had purchased another. From the latter license they got an address. They located Mrs. Hope. She told them that "Chuck" was working as a cook in a hamburger stand at Hermosa Beach.

Within an hour Hope was under arrest. In another hour he was in the D.A.'s office. Two hours later he had told me of the drowning of Mary James. He had said nothing about rattlesnakes. I wasn't satisfied. I ordered him placed in jail over night.

Before he left I said, "Chuck, you've told us part of this story; you haven't told it all yet. You are trying to protect yourself. There's something about rattlesnakes. As long as you're going to confess, I think you should tell the whole truth. Go to bed, have a good rest and tomorrow morning we'll talk it over some more."

The next morning Hope was taken to the scene of the crime. In the bathroom of the cottage he turned white and shaky – and told the whole gruesome story.

About June of 1935, Hope had dropped into James' barber shop. He was broke and he asked James for some barber work on credit. James agreed, and while he was barbering Hope he asked him if he knew anything about rattlesnakes. Hope said he didn't. James said, "Well, there's a chance for you to make a hundred bucks. I have a friend whose wife has been bothering him and he wants a couple of snakes to use to bite her."

Hope thought that James was kidding, but James said he really wanted the snakes, and Hope undertook to buy them. He finally located and purchased some snakes from a man running a little side show on the Pike at Long Beach. The snakes cost but a few dollars. James told Hope to have some boxes made in which to put the snakes, which Hope in due time delivered to James at his home in La Canada. The hundred dollars was paid. James experimented with the snakes by putting some chickens in the boxes with them.

The snakes didn't kill the chickens. James then complained to Hope that the snakes were no good and urged him to buy others.

James had heard that there was an exhibit of rattlesnakes in a side show at Ocean Park. He and Hope, after having a few drinks, drove down to Ocean Park and visited the side show. They were both drunk and a little noisy and attracted some attention by arguing with the proprietor as to whether the snakes were "hot." The proprietor offered to bet money that they were. After leaving the side show James arranged for Hope to go back alone and buy one of the snakes. This was done. The snake was put in a box with a rabbit. The next morning the rabbit was still hopping about, but the snake was dead.

Again James put it up to Hope to get a "hot" snake, and Hope made some investigation which finally resulted in his purchasing from "Snake Joe" Houtenbrink, a snake dealer, for the sum of six dollars, two guaranteed "hot" Crotalus Atrox rattlesnakes gathered in the Colorado desert. These snakes, upon being tested with live chickens, killed the chickens promptly. Thereafter, they were kept in boxes in James' garage for future use.

In the meantime, James was somewhat worried as to the legality of his marriage to Mary. He was fearful that upon investigation it would be found to be no marriage, and that his status as a beneficiary of the policies of insurance would be weak. Soon, however, his annulment decree was entered and he took Mary on a little trip down into one of the adjoining counties and there they were legally married. He made sure, by questioning one of the insurance agents, that the fact that he was legally married after and not before the policies had been issued would not invalidate the insurance. He was then prepared for the final steps in the drama to be enacted.

Mary was pregnant. She was very anxious to have a baby. James tried to persuade her to have an abortion performed. After weeks of persuasion she agreed. James told her that

Hope, whom she had met, was a doctor or medical student competent to perform an abortion, and that he would do the job. Mary agreed to this. James then explained to her that it would be necessary to strap her on the kitchen table, blindfold her and seal her lips with adhesive tape because, as he explained, there must be no noise, and Hope insisted that she not see him so that she would never be able to testify against him.

On Sunday morning, August 4, 1935, Hope met James in the garage of James' home. James then told Hope that he intended to use the rattlesnakes to kill his wife, Mary. He offered to split the insurance money with Hope. He said, "You're in this as deep as I am. You've been going all over Southern California buying rattlesnakes. It's too late for you to back out now. Bring one of the snakes and come into the house."

Hope seized a box with a sliding glass cover, containing one of the proven rattlesnakes, and followed James into the house through the back door. Mary, scantily dressed, lay strapped to the table in the kitchen. Her mouth had been taped shut and her eyes were covered with adhesive. James ordered Hope to place the box near Mary's foot. The lid was slipped back. James seized Mary's leg and thrust it into the box with the rattling, vibrant snake. It struck. Hope pulled the box away, the cover slid back, and James motioned him to take it out of the house. Later that day Hope, using James' car, took the two snakes back to "Snake Joe" and sold them back at half price. He then threw the boxes into a field as he was passing, and returned to James' home.

All that happened in the James house that day is not known. But it is known that Mary must have suffered the tortures of the damned. Her leg was swollen to almost double its normal size and was black and blue. Her suffering must have been excruciating. Much whisky must have been fed her.

Whether from drunkenness or pain or threats, or a combination of all, she was induced to write a letter in an almost illegible scrawl (although she usually wrote very well), in which she told that she was "pretty sick," that "my leg is all swollen, something bit me – I cut my toe," and how much she loved and relied upon her "daddy" – "He takes good care of me." This letter, addressed to her sister, was found in the James' home after Mary's death. It was an important bit of evidence in James' plan to lead the authorities to believe that Mary had met her death by accident.

Notwithstanding that the snake's venom was gradually working up Mary's leg, thigh and hip, and toward her vital organs, notwithstanding the disintegration of the cells that was taking place and the horrible pain, Mary continued to live. Hope stayed out in the garage. Late that Sunday night he and James were out there drinking. James was worried – Mary wasn't dying fast enough. He said, "Hell, she's not going to die; the damned snake didn't work." Hope suggested, "Let's call a doctor."

James replied, "Hell, no. They'd string us higher than a kite. She'd squeal."

They had another drink. Silence. James was thinking. Perhaps a vision of Winona, dead in the bathtub at Manitou, came to him. Finally he arose. "I'm going in and drown her." And into the house he went. He was gone for a long time, while Hope sat in the garage and drank more whisky.

Finally James returned. He looked at Hope. "That's that," he said. He went into the house again. About six-thirty in the morning he came back. He said, "She's been dead since four o'clock. I've got everything cleaned up. You come in and help me carry her out."

They went into the house. In the hallway just outside the bathroom lay the dead body of Mary. She was dressed in fresh lounging pajamas. Except for some moisture in her hair, she appeared to be dry.

On direction from James, Hope took Mary's feet. James took her shoulders and they carried her out through the kitchen into the back yard, around to the side of the house by the fish pond. At this point Hope refused to go farther. The body was placed at the side of the fish pond. James then dragged it so that it lay with the head and shoulders in the fish pond, face down, in such position as to indicate that Mary had fallen from the path headfirst into the pond. They then gathered the wet towels, clothing, blankets, the pieces of adhesive tape and rope with which Mary had been tied. By that time it was daylight on Monday morning.

James drove Hope to his home in Los Angeles. Hope took the towels, clothes and blankets, bits of rope and tape, to dispose of them. James then went for a ride out Wilshire Boulevard, so timing himself that he came back to his barber shop in time to open it. Hope disposed of the towels, clothing, rope and tape by burning them in an incinerator. The blankets he kept and took to the cleaner.

James stayed in jail for eleven days and then one morning he was taken into the chaplain's room, where he was confronted by his accomplice, Hope. The story of the murder was recited to him. He was asked what statement, if any, he had to make. He said, "Nothing." Then he was taken out to the murder house. He saw the officers in company with Hope. He saw pictures taken. He saw the investigative process at work. He was taken back to the D.A.'s office. He was again questioned about his participation in the death of Mary James. He was asked about the death of Winona up in Colorado. He refused to make any statement or any admission.

Finally, as he sat there, he saw that the authorities believed Hope's story. He thought that Hope might get out and put it all on him. A dull but deadly anger stirred him. He called one of the officers to his side. He said, "Let's go out and get something to eat. I'll tell you the story."

James, accompanied by three officers and a young lady (fiancée of one of the officers) went to a cafe, had a steak dinner, accepted a cigar, lighted it and sat back. One of the officers said, "Do you want to tell the story now or shall we go back to the D.A.'s office?" He said, "We might as well do it here." And then, in that public place, he recited his version of what had happened.

He admitted he had insured Mary. He admitted he had agreed with Hope to murder Mary and divide the insurance money, but he claimed that Hope had devised the idea of the rattlesnakes, had urged the unwilling James to agree to the murder. He asserted that he, James, had backed out at the last minute ("I couldn't kill her; she'd been too good to me") and that Hope, under a pretext of committing an abortion on Mary, had probably killed her. He denied any knowledge of the exact details of the killing. While inadvertently and unknowingly admitting sufficient participation in the crime to render himself guilty as a principal in the murder, he viciously tried to throw the greater burden and onus of the conception and carrying out of the murder upon Hope's shoulders.

Detectives were sent out and in a short time the various persons from whom rattlesnakes had been purchased, the individual who had built the boxes for the snakes, and all of the other witnesses were brought in. Mary's body was exhumed. The mark of the snake bite, the swollen and discolored limb, testified all too clearly to the truth of Hope's confession.

Hope was taken up into the chaplain's room of the jail and there confronted James with his story of the murder. James failed to deny the accusation. Then another "break" came. The woman who had been asked by James to testify falsely to having seen Mary alive on the Monday following her death approached her lawyer and she came to the D.A.'s office and told her story. The tentacles of the law were wrapping themselves around James.

In the midst of all of the flurry of local investigation, it was decided that at this time it would be well to inquire further into Winona's death. Jack Southard, ace investigator, was sent to Colorado. He interviewed the superintendent of the Pike's Peak Toll Road Company, who told him what he had observed about James and about his examination of the footprints at the scene of the "accident," the blood-smeared hammer, the blood on the upholstery of the coupe back of the right seat. The surgeon who had treated Winona testified as to the character and type of the injuries to her head. The boy who had helped discover her body and other witnesses were interviewed, pictures and diagrams obtained, and in five days Southard returned with proof that Winona had been murdered.

Hope pleaded guilty to first-degree murder and received a life sentence. He prepared to testify against James. A mass of detailed corroborative evidence was gathered. We had, as you know, James' admission of participation in the murder of Mary. The investigation was completed. We were ready for trial.

Under the law, as indicated by the reference which I have already made to the famous English case of Rex v. George Joseph Smith, it is permissible upon a prosecution for murder to establish the facts relating to prior similar death for the purpose of showing intent, design, identity of the murderer and the fact that the death was intended and not accidental. Under that rule, evidence of the murder of Winona was admissible in our California prosecution for the murder of Mary.

The sum total of our evidence demonstrated that James had engaged upon a career of marrying, insuring and murdering women. At the very time of our investigation we learned over the microphone that he had become engaged to still another woman, was intending to marry her and was talking to her about the advisability of insuring their mutual future by carrying insurance for each other's benefit.

I have not the slightest doubt that if we had not solved the prior murders and convicted James when we did, there would have been a third and perhaps a fourth to add to his list. After his success in collecting the insurance on Winona, he became convinced that he was smarter than the insurance companies and smarter than the "law." This egotism carried him on to further efforts. He had absolutely no compunction, no thought of the suffering of his victims, no emotion other than an egotistical desire to satisfy his own perverted tastes. Even at the time we were questioning him about the murder of Mary, he said, "I don't see why you are so worried about her. Why all this investigation? She was nothing but a damned whore when I married her."

A few months later James was on trial. Five weeks later he was convicted of murder in the first degree with the death penalty. After long-drawn-out appeals, he was finally "hanged by the neck until dead" in San Quentin penitentiary, the last person to die by the rope in the state of California.

Eugene D. Williams

Jerome Braun von Selz: The Laughing Killer

Herewith another strange and little-known murder case, this time from the San Francisco area – it concludes the volume *San Francisco Murders*, edited by Joseph H. Jackson and published in 1947. It is an odd little affair, involving a man abundantly endowed with charm combined with a dangerous criminal streak. It is difficult to know whether the "Laughing Killer" was insane or feeble minded, or whether he killed one or three people. The key to von Selz seems to be an over-developed craving for "fame", which led to his arrest.

In *The Encyclopedia of World Crime*, Jay Robert Nash concludes his short entry on von Selz by recording that in 1962, he again escaped, this time from the San Luis Obispo prison, but was recaptured within three days. Finally released in 1966, he was back again within a year on charges of welfare fraud. Nothing is known about his subsequent career. I find myself regretting that no one took sufficient interest in this oddly puzzling killer to write a book about him. I am sure he would have collaborated enthusiastically.

The poker murder of Mrs Ada French-Mengler-Rice was a suburban affair, and, as is well known to all connoisseurs and chroniclers of violence, not many metropolitan murders can approach the suburban slaying when it comes to stark and grisly appointments. In the city, a corpus delicti is ordinarily quick of establishment. A homicide there too often assumes the coziness of parlor, bedroom and bath, and if you must dig, it is usually in the cellar. For contrast, I recommend the setting of the Woodside Glens, where at night the hills lie dark and brooding, and wraiths of fog ride down on the lonesome wind from San Francisco's Skyline Boulevard.

Those were the hills that rang with the mirth of the mercurial young man who killed Mrs Rice. His confession was not easily obtained, but once started it was gleefully given. "Ha ha!" he roared when they showed him the long-buried body. "Hell of a looking thing, isn't it? Teeth? No – ha ha! – they don't look like her teeth. But, hell" – and another burst of laughter – "it must be her. I killed her and put her there!"

I met this young man before he killed. Later, I became involved, in the remote fashion of a news editor, in assembling and presenting the story of his crime, and his dubious and equally mirthful confession of having done away with a doubly dubious Bulgarian cavalry officer. And as I look back on the singularly fey characters then peopling the city room of the *San Francisco Chronicle*, I know this:

That pixilated place, and no other, was proper setting for an introduction to Slipton J. (for Just) Fell. Under its soundproofed ceiling, his hearty, booming laughter had no hollow echo, as it must have in San Quentin. And where else would he have gone to seek a couple of fellow adventurers named Upton Rose and Faran Wide?

Slipton Fell must have sensed these things when he wandered into the city room one afternoon early in the spring of 1935. To me, those were lighthearted days in which newspaper work was a delightful form of peonage; no uninformed visitor could have guessed that many of us were engaged in any serious enterprise. As I remember it, Mr Fell entered just as a hundred-pound Jap *yawara* instructor was paving the way for some publicity by throwing a two-hundred-pound reporter flat on his back before anybody could hiss "Excuse please." A copy boy was running hot dog and coffee errands in white tie and tails: he belonged to one of the Peninsula's most prominent families, and was going to a formal dinner when he got off work. The copy desk used to sing at its labors, and there was an ancient retainer in the Sunday department who emitted a series of nine tremendous sneezes – never any more, never any less – every hour and a half. A legend had sprung up around him – if he ever sneezed a tenth time, he would die.

In addition to these, we were currently busied in freeing a brilliant but erratic member of the staff, who loved to ensconce himself in a cab, bottle in hand, wave airily at the driver, and say, "Drive elsewhere, my man!" He usually ran up a bill of twenty or thirty dollars, was unable to pay, and landed in city prison. To complicate matters, he was extremely coy about giving his right name. I remember that on this occasion the day police reporter had to pick him out of the collection in the drunk tank, and convince authorities that he was not really "J. Hannegan, cook."

The personable young man calling himself Slipton J. Fell had no difficulty in attracting attention, despite these rival sideshows. He wanted a story in the paper. He was lately returned, he said, from Latin-American vagabondings, and somehow had become separated from Upton Rose and Faran Wide. He wanted to apprise them of his whereabouts.

There was about him the air of a soldier of fortune who had plotted a revolt that failed, and had just managed to conceal himself aboard the lugger in time to escape alive. He laughed, and his mirth was infectious. Anybody, we said, who would adopt the name of Slipton Fell was worth a story . . . and never mind his real name.

He got a story, with a picture. He went happily on his way, and when he had gone the city room seemed a quiet and sober place, and the managing editor decreed a more conservative make-up for the first street edition . . .

A short time later, the personnel department of a large oil company was pleased to note frequent letters commending the courtesy and efficiency of one of their employees, currently filling gas tanks and wiping windshields in a station at Woodside. This paragon of industry was Jerome Braun von Selz, twenty-six, born Ralph Jerome Selz in San Francisco (alias Ralph Sells, alias Charles Oliver, alias Slipton J. Fell). What the company did not know was that Selz had worked for them previously, in Oakland, and had been discharged there. Nor was it discovered until later that his adroit pen had produced the letters of recommendation which reinstated him in the company's employ at Woodside – as well as the letters from sundry customers, praising his work.

At the *Chronicle*, we were ignorant of a few facts, ourselves. We did not know that when Slipton J. Fell visited us, any Latin American adventurings he might have had were in the past, and that his last voyage was only from Alcatraz to the Army pier. He had been in the disciplinary barracks of more than one post, and had come to Alcatraz as an Army deserter.

He was six feet at this time, weighing two hundred and thirty pounds. He had slate-gray eyes, light brown hair, and a ruddy complexion; he talked volubly, and in a positive manner. He spoke Spanish, French and German, and was – as described years later in a statewide police bulletin – "restlessly active."

On April 6th, when everybody had forgotten Slipton Fell, the *Chronicle* city room was occupied in toning down a particularly gory bit of business for its breakfast-table audience. A girl variously described as Betty Coffman and Lena Coffin was found dead in her bed at the Bay Hotel on that date, with one of her breasts sliced off. There was no special class to the story; it had its day on the lips of newsboys, and died . . .

S omewhere around this time, Mrs Ada French-Mengler-Rice returned to her home in the Woodside Glens from Seattle, where her last marriage had gone on the rocks. Not too much is known about her, now, and some of the alleged facts brought to light in a later investigation, when she was no longer around, appear contradictory. She had neighbors, but was not friendly with them; they knew nothing of her movements. She had been a newspaper woman and a writer, and was traveled. August Mengler married her in 1930. In 1932, she became president of the Redwood City unit of the W.C.T.U. A newspaper clipping observed later that she was not remembered as a very good leader, although she had reportedly caused the home of a neighbor to be raided on suspicion that a still was being operated there.

In 1933, Mr Mengler sued for divorce, charging that his wife had become obsessed with social welfare work. Two days later, he dropped dead in a San Francisco hotel lobby.

The then Mrs Mengler later married Charles Freeman Rice, who was seventy-two, a Seattle contractor, and known as a former mayor of Nome. Newspaper files show that Mr Rice obtained his divorce on February 2, 1936. This also was at a time when Mrs Rice was no longer around, or interested, as will be presently revealed . . .

M rs Rice had been in Seattle a considerable period, and her sedan was standing in her Woodside Glens garage, blocks under the wheels. She went to a service station and asked that a man be sent out to pump up her tires and remove the blocks. The manager told her that one of his very best employees lived only a short distance from her home.

She went by the address given her, awoke Selz, took him

to her house, and gave him a glass of lemonade. Then, according to his story and that of officers – who obviously could have heard it only from Selz – she proposed that he move into her house.

This may be one of the contradictory elements. Mrs Rice was fifty-eight, and a former leader, remember, of the W.C.T.U. She lived alone in a square sort of house with a penthouse sunroom, where workmen remembered seeing her sunbathing.

But remember, too, the infectious, booming laugh of that personable young man. Whatever the arrangement, he moved in with his matchless mirth. And somewhere around the early part of June – the date has been fixed as June 13th – Mrs. Rice vanished.

Apparently she was not missed for several months. She had been in the habit of coming and going; the neighbors paid no attention. Meanwhile, however, Mr Rice went to the courts to seek his freedom, and the sheriff's office of San Mateo County began hunting her to serve the papers.

"Mrs Rice?" the neighbors said. "Oh, she went to Greece, or the Balkans, or somewhere over there. Took a job as a foreign correspondent for some paper . . ."

The thin shade of one Baronovich – Michael Baronovich of the Bulgarian cavalry – was beginning to stir vaguely in the wings, off stage.

Jerome Braun von Selz loved publicity; there is no telling how many clippings he had of that *Chronicle* story. His next appearance in the public prints, however, was, in a way, involuntary. It occurred in February of the following year – 1936 – when he reported that the service station where he now worked had been held up and robbed.

Von Selz was attending San Mateo Junior College, now. In describing the gunman, he exhibited a form of egoism that bordered on the psychopathic – he furnished police with a perfect description of himself.

The result was his arrest, a few days later, on a charge of having made a false robbery report, and his subsequent confession and restitution to the till of some twenty-eight dollars. He was sentenced to thirty days in jail.

That was the end of freedom, except for a stolen period years later, for Selz. Slipton Fell had done just that. He had been tripped by a misdemeanor, by, perhaps, his restless activity and his equally restless imagination. The oil company must have been shocked – it was still getting those neatly forged letters, all in varying chirography, telling what super service he gave . . .

On Leap Year Day, February 29th, 1936, Inspector George O'Leary of the San Francisco police department's auto detail, and M. L. "Jimmy" Britt of the National Auto Theft Bureau, went to the Redwood City jail to interview Selz on another matter. He had reported an auto stolen. The insurance had been paid. A finance company held title to the car; Selz had received eighteen dollars for his equity.

Deputy Sheriff Thomas F. Maloney, who probably deserves the major credit for solving the mystery of Mrs Rice's slaying, sat in on the questioning. Selz laughed, but after two and a half hours and a promise of no prosecution, he led the officers to a private garage in Burlingame, where the car was stored. It now bore stolen license plates, and Maloney and the others searched it.

They found a passport, bearing the name and photograph of Mrs Rice when she was Mrs Ada French. They found rope, adhesive tape, cotton, ammonia, and a blanket.

Jerome Braun von Selz – they were calling him Jerry, now – laughed jovially. Sure, he had been keeping those things in the car. He was looking for a couple of fellows who had done him harm.

Tom Maloney jumped out to the Woodside Glens.

"Who told you," he asked the neighbors, "that Mrs Rice went to the Balkans as a correspondent?"

"Why, the young man who lives in her place. He said she went away with a Bulgarian officer – what was his name? Something ending in 'itch.'"

That night, Maloney and the others searched the house. They found checks bearing Mrs Rice's signature, but written after she had disappeared. Maloney went to the bank in Palo Alto the next day, and saw a letter allegedly written by Mrs Rice from Coxsackie, N. Y. – but posted, it was revealed later, in Redwood City. The letter asked the bank to transfer a hundred and thirty-five dollars from her savings account to her checking account.

Further investigation revealed almost everything but the all-important body. Mrs Rice had deeded Selz her property in the Woodside Glens; he, in turn, had transferred to her certain mining property in Sierra County. It is interesting to note that the latter not only was found to be worthless, but that Selz owned only a part interest in it – and even that under another name.

Maloney and Britt began work in earnest. Selz laughed and laughed. They saw that they were dealing with a very strange young man, whose mental processes were best described by one of his own statements when he basked, later, in the light of notoriety.

"No one knows," he boasted then, "what is in my mind!"

Tom Maloney and Jimmy Britt didn't know, but they were finding out a few interesting things. That Selz hadn't been sleeping at the Woodside Glens place – not unless somebody else was there, too. He snatched sleep a couple of hours at a time, in the car he had reported stolen. He drove a lot at night. He was filled with a great and fearful respect for the Secret Service and the F.B.I.

He had tried to get men with whom he worked to move in with him. They refused. He picked up an itinerant marathon dancer on the highway – there was always some sort of curious attraction for the grotesque – and took her to live with him. She was there when he was arrested for making the false report. He had been going to see a girl in Oakland,

and when she went out with another man, he threatened her with a gun. She complained to police, but did not want to prosecute him, and the Oakland authorities merely warned him to stay away from that city.

He had been trying to trade the Woodside Glens property for a large and powerful cabin cruiser, and was going to take this girl on a tropical cruise. And just before his arrest, he had asked the Redwood City public library for a manual of toxicology. He simply had to have the book, he said, before March 25th.

Nobody knows what laughter might have been planned for March 25th. Fortunately, the book had to be requested from the state library, and before Selz could call for it, he was in jail . . .

Maloney and Britt began a campaign to win his confidence. They waged this mainly through the medium of food – steaks and chicken – because Selz, a big man, was a tremendous eater. They never put handcuffs on him; they laughed with him, and called him Jerry. Maloney drove the car, Britt asked the questions, Maloney listened and studied their man. He discovered that Selz' mind was very receptive: if an idea were planted in it, he adopted it as his own, and almost always brought out some version of it later.

Tom Maloney may be no student of psychology, but he has learned a lot of it in his years as a law enforcement officer. They could find no body – they knew there was one, somewhere. They could not break down the laugher – they knew he had a story to tell. It occurred to Maloney that if he were to plant the idea of accidental death, this might cause Selz to tell that story, and that it might be the stepping stone to the truth.

They took Selz to the Woodside Glens house. The ceiling was covered with blow flies, and he was afraid of them. Tom Maloney searched the attic for a body, and found none; he does not really know to this day why the flies were there. They drove the lonely roads that lead to Skyline Boulevard, and Maloney called attention to a shallow depression covered with the same sort of flies.

"This looks like a grave," he remarked. "And that canyon would be a fine place to throw a body – nobody would ever find it."

"Say," Jerry asked in jail the next day, "do you get premonitions?"

"No," Maloney said casually. "Why?"

Selz guffawed. "Well," he said, "yesterday up on the Skyline, you made a couple of remarks too close to suit me!"

Tom Maloney knew, then, that Mrs Rice was buried somewhere by Skyline Boulevard. But that is a long road, and lonely; the redwood canyons drop away from it by the hundreds, and restless fogs come in from the sea to enshroud it. On Skyline, but where?

They had photostatic copies made of the forged checks and the letter. They called Captain Thomas Foster of the U.S. Secret Service, and had him come from San Francisco to question Selz about misuse of the mails, about the fraudulent removal of funds from a national bank.

For the first time, Selz' laughter wavered and turned weak. Fear of the federal officer made him crack – just a little way, at first. He agreed to tell his story.

But the first account had nothing to do with the body. Britt said, "Jerry, we know there is a body up there, somewhere. If it were your sister or your mother, you'd want it brought in for a decent burial. If you – "

Selz had never lost his temper, but now he leaped to his feet. "I'll be God-damned if I'll confess to something I didn't do!" he screamed.

Tom Maloney sighed, and started all over again. He made Selz a friendly little speech, pointing out to him that events since June 13th of the previous year had encircled him like a boa constrictor. He reminded Selz that he couldn't sleep at the house when alone, that he was afraid to stay there, that he was haunted.

"You cry out in your sleep here in jail!" he said. "Why? Because there's something on your mind. You know Mrs Rice was killed. Maybe she fell and hit her head – perhaps it was an accident. But I figure it this way: she tried to burn the deed to the property, and there was a fight. She was killed in that fight."

Selz was silent for a space, and his chin sank to his chest. "There was a hell of a fight, all right," he said finally. "Give me time to think . . ."

The story broke in the newspapers. Selz responded to the rays of the spotlight: he roared with laughter again, and jested with reporters and cameramen. A lie detector test showed him guilty, and he ate another big steak, and autographed the white starched collar of the waitress who couldn't believe such a personable young man could possibly be suspected of murder. By this time, the newspapers had unofficially linked his name to the mutilation slaying of Betty Coffman.

They took him to the Woodside Glens house again, spiriting him there in a mad night dash to elude the reporters. Selz bathed and changed clothes and shaved.

Then he told his story.

It was an accident. He had come into the house at night. No lights were on, but he immediately sensed the presence of two other persons, who began fighting. In the darkness, he grabbed something – the fireplace poker, he thought – and swung. Somebody fell, and the other person rushed out the door. There was moonlight outside, and it glinted on a saber in the fugitive's hands.

That man, he said dramatically, was none other than the Bulgarian cavalry officer – Baronovich. Michael Baronovich. He had had a lot of trouble with Baronovich.

He left Mrs Rice's body in the living room all that next day. With nightfall, he put it in the sedan, drove down the Skyline, turned four miles on the road to Big Basin, and dumped the body in a canyon. He had stolen two sacks of lime from a warehouse. He went back the next night on a motorcycle, carrying a shovel. He dug what amounted to a foxhole, broke the shovel handle doing it, and couldn't make the grave very deep.

He buried Mrs Rice there, jackknife fashion, head down, hands behind her back, and poured the lime over her.

"What about Baronovich?"

Von Selz roared with laughter. Oh, he had killed the Bulgarian, too, some time later. A big man, Baronovich was, with husky hair. It was, Selz said, the survival of the fittest: Baronovich had attacked him. He had killed the Bulgarian, tied a large collection of iron plates to the body, and heaved it from the San Mateo Bay bridge . . .

He finally led them to the spot where he had buried Mrs Rice, and he made the canyons echo his mirth there while they dug her up. A couple of the newspapermen became ill, but Selz laughed all the harder. He posed and tapdanced. He enlarged upon his story of killing Baronovich – in self defense, of course – and shouted with mirth as he offered to toss Fred Glover, a newsman, into the Bay to show how it was done.

About this time, one Otto von Feldman came forward in Southern California, to say he had been the night porter at the hotel where Betty Coffman was killed, and to identify Selz as the man who had registered with her. Now the papers called Selz "triple murder suspect." They also called him "burly Lothario," "soldier of fortune," and "the Laughing Killer of the Woodside Glens."

He did not confess to the Coffman killing. He was having too much fun with Baronovich. They dragged the Bay at the spot he indicated, and brought up wire, and – once – something that might have been flesh.

But Selz was a mercurial sort, and when reporters asked him questions about his family, the publicity suddenly began to pall. He begged Tom Maloney to shield him from the newspapermen. He didn't want his family, or his lodge –

Maloney had found a lodge uniform in the house – brought into it.

Maloney hid the uniform, but a reporter found part of it, and reached a rather whimsical conclusion after they had dug up Mrs Rice's body, and were looking for that of Baronovich.

The reporter spread the word that Selz had the uniform of a grave digger from Holy Cross cemetery . . .

Selz agreed to plead guilty to murder in the first degree, after a dentist had identified Mrs Rice's remains, and after he had chortled at the sight. The trial set a record for brevity in San Mateo County murder cases, and one seldom equaled anywhere. It lasted fifty-five minutes, and on that same afternoon Jerome Braun von Selz became a number in San Quentin prison, serving a life sentence. That was on March 12, 1936.

He made a little speech to the reporters who followed him to the prison gates – a speech in which Tom Maloney had carefully rehearsed him. He stopped laughing, and said: "I'm going in to make good," after the fashion of a football player about to do or die for dear old alma mater.

And did he? Well, San Quentin heard his incredible laughter, and he made friends there, and became the strong man of the prison's tumbling team, as well as its champion weight lifter. He may have been responsible for the plea – quickly denied – that inmates be allowed to take up pole vaulting. He tried to enlist in the Army during the war, but was rejected by a psychiatrist as a "constitutional psychopathic inferior."

He laughed, and acquitted himself so well (although his plea for parole had been denied) that he was transferred to the California Institution for Men, at Chino, on May 23, 1944.

This is something of an honor institution, and Selz virtually advertised his intention to flee from it. He obtained and studied maps of Mexico. He shipped out his favorite possession – a mandolin. On the evening of May 3, 1945, he simply walked away.

But he didn't go to Mexico. He went to Minnesota, instead, and somehow managed to register there with a draft board – which fingerprinted him.

The master file of the F.B.I. did the rest. It took a little while, and by the time they caught up with him, Selz was in the Canadian Army – a corporal, known as Ralph Jerome "Tiny" Morgan, teaching physical education. He roared with laughter, and told how he had written back to San Francisco for his birth certificate.

They brought him back with extradition papers later that month, and his mirth is heard at San Quentin again, and may be for a long time to come. The confession of a merchant seaman cleared him, in 1940, of the "unofficial" charge of Betty Coffman's mutilation murder. Nobody has ever cleared him of his own charge that he disposed so gleefully of one Michael Baronovich . . .

But I think I know who Michael Baronovich was, and who Upton Rose and Faran Wide were, too. I think all three of them were none other than Slipton J. Fell.

Allan R. Bosworth

1937

An Axe for Frau Marek

The story of Martha Loewenstein seems to have been designed as a moral fable. It is the kind of tale that has fascinated our ancestors down the centuries. It is difficult to understand how an exceptionally beautiful girl turned into a multiple poisoner; most murderesses have been plain or downright ugly. Beauty, after all, gives a girl confidence, and confident girls usually develop a certain ability to cope with life. Even when things go wrong, they seldom resort to murder. I am inclined to believe that Martha's original "protector", Moritz Schmidt, whose mistress she became while still little more than a schoolgirl, was to blame. He accustomed her to luxury, and the idea of a return to poverty became intolerable. It seems appropriate that her lover probably became her first victim.

"An Axe for Frau Marek", by ex-Police Commissar Ignatz Peters, is again taken from Kurt Singer's remarkable collection *My Strangest Case*.

Luck, I am convinced, often can be misfortune in disguise, and if this were not true I should not now be telling you the story of Martha Löwenstein. She, of all people, had good reason to curse the day she thought she was lucky.

Many will remember her as a very beautiful girl, always stylishly dressed every day she took the electric car for Kirtnerstrasse, where she worked in a dress shop, from Ottakring, one of the shabbiest places in Vienna. It was a district of down-at-heel houses and depressed people, and Martha was one of the rare flowers that grew there. Men would put down their newspapers as soon as they saw her and always she had a bright smile for her fellow passengers.

She was well worth looking at, blonde, slim and with a fine complexion that certainly did not come from a box. Every day she wore something different and her elegance piqued the women to whom she was known by sight. They whispered that no girl from a poor neighbourhood could dress so expensively unless . . . well, that was what they said, but it was untrue. Martha was virtuous, and there was a simple explanation for everything.

She confided the truth to Moritz Fritsch, the owner of a large department store in Vienna and a wealthy and cultured man. He was in his sixties, but looked very much younger. He found an opportunity to speak to Martha one evening as she was on her way home. He told her that he had often seen and admired her and he complimented her on the way she dressed. Martha said she came from a very poor home and worked in a dress shop. Her employer had always been exceedingly kind, and treated her almost as a daughter.

"She likes to see me in good clothes," Martha said, "and says I am a splendid advertisement for her shop. But for her I should look as poor as do many girls who have to work for a living."

Herr Fritsch promptly offered to find her a well-paid job in his store, but the young girl would not hear of it. She was devoted to her employer and on no account would she leave her.

"I must say I admire your loyalty," said Fritsch. "But you will, of course, allow me to take you home?"

Martha stepped into the chauffeur-driven limousine, and on the way to Ottakring explained that she and her mother lived alone. Her father had emigrated to America many years before and they had not heard of him since.

Back at his villa at Mödling that evening, Moritz Fritsch

could not get the girl out of his mind. Her home was deplorable, and so, too, was her mother, a hulk of a woman, vulgar and tactless. She had told him all there was to know about the family, and it had turned out that Martha was, in fact, a love-child and her daughter by adoption only.

Fritsch was divorced and his two children were married. Except for his servants he lived alone, and that night he felt how empty his home had become. He was very rich and very lonely.

Shortly afterwards he took Martha out to dinner, and not only showed her a glimpse of luxury but suggested that she should become his ward. It would give her, he said, the right to everything her beauty deserved – clothes and jewels, education and travel and the company of intelligent people.

Martha did not need to be persuaded, and the fashionable villa in the suburbs became her home. Fritsch kept his word. He sent her to a school for young ladies and, for holidays, to France and England. At eighteen Martha was more lovely than ever and she had acquired poise and social polish.

When she returned to live at the villa her benefactor introduced her to his friends at parties and dinners. He never refused her anything and soon she possessed more jewels and clothes than she could ever have dreamed of. However, when the gilt had worn off a little Martha began to suffer from the moods that harry all unfulfilled young women. Whenever she was in a tantrum Fritsch would buy her some new piece of jewellery and he seems to have understood just why his fascinating ward behaved as she did.

Fritsch's devotion to the girl had, of course, long been the subject of gossip, particularly among the servants. A maid said she had seen him embracing his ward in the garden and in a manner that was hardly fatherly. On another occasion they were together in Martha's bedroom, both rather carefree and lively from the champagne they had drunk.

Three years went by, and towards the end began a period during which Martha could not be roused from her black moods, despite all the presents Fritsch gave her. The old man felt, as he told his friends, that he was, perhaps, demanding too much from her and was certain that she feared the day when he would no longer be alive to protect her.

Fritsch was probably right, for when he told Martha that he had made a new will in which she had not been forgotten, she cried a little and put her arms round the old man. It was the end of her unhappiness. Fritsch by law was bound to leave a third of his estate to his ex-wife and he had settled money, too, on his children. Martha was to have what was left, including the house.

A year after this arrangement was made Fritsch died at the age of seventy-four. Present at the bedside were Martha, the old man's family and Dr Pollack, his physician.

When the will was read Betty Fritsch was furious. "I do not understand it," she protested. "At the time of our divorce Moritz solemnly promised that the estate would be left to the family."

"I drew up the will according to Herr Fritsch's wishes," said the lawyer sharply.

But Betty was not to be persuaded. "My husband was old, but his health was good. I think this girl knows something about his death. There is only one way to find out. The body must be exhumed."

Everybody was horrified by the suggestion, particularly Fritsch's son and daughter. "Mother was always terribly jealous of Father's ward," said young Fritsch. "Under no circumstances must Father's body be disturbed."

There was no inquiry and Martha received her inheritance in due course, but got far less money than she had anticipated. Although she was not seen about much a handsome young man began to visit her at the villa, and three months after Fritsch's death it became known that she had married him. His name was Emil Marek and he was studying engineering. Martha had been meeting him secretly for over a year.

It was not until some time afterwards that I heard the name of Martha Löwenstein Marek for the first time, and it happened in this way. One day I got a telephone call from Herr Möller, the vice-president of an insurance company. He said he was at the Billroth Hospital and asked me if I would go at once to meet him there. Möller was waiting for me and we went into one of the smaller rooms of the hospital, where a man's leg, severed just below the knee, lay on a table. The shoe and sock had not even been removed.

Möller explained why he had called me at the *Polizei Dezernat*.

"The leg belongs, or rather belonged, to a young man named Emil Marek. He lives in a villa in the suburbs with his wife, and the maid telephoned me to say that he had injured himself badly while cutting down a tree in the garden. He was brought here and the surgeon who completed the amputation tells me the leg was hanging only by a sinew."

"Why were you telephoned about the accident, Herr Möller?"

"Because Marek is insured with us for a considerable sum of money."

Möller gave me the details. About a week before Marek had called on him to take out a policy by which he would be covered for £10,000 in the event of any serious accident. Marek told him he was studying engineering at the Vienna Technical Institute and not long ago had married a young woman who had money. The Government was interested in an electrification scheme for Burgenland which he had prepared, and he felt that it was only fair to his wife that he should be adequately insured against the possibility of an accident. He did not want to become a burden to her.

"I was dubious about the proposal," said Möller, "and refused to entertain it. All the same I was impressed by Marek. He seemed a very decent young man, honest and very intelligent. Later I wondered if I had done the right thing and made some inquiries. I found that he has a good name at the institute and I was able to confirm that he had told me the truth about the scheme he has put up to the Government. In fact, I became convinced that he was a good risk and made arrangements to issue the policy. He came back, signed the papers, and paid the premium."

We were still talking when Dr Rudolf Küster came into the room, and Möller introduced him to me. "Marek has had a very narrow squeak," said the surgeon, "and if his wife had not used several tourniquets he would have bled to death before anything could have been done for him. He is very shocked and has lost a lot of blood, but he is young and healthy and should get over it."

I asked the surgeon the angle of the wound and he looked at me curiously.

"It is rather puzzling," he said. "The cut is almost straight, and it is difficult to say exactly how it happened, but an accident can often show a freakish result."

"If it was an accident," said Möller.

It was asking a lot to believe that a person would hack off his leg to collect insurance, but then one can never tell. Marek was far too ill to be questioned, but Martha, too, was detained at the hospital, for she had collapsed as soon as her husband had been taken into the operating theatre.

She had been given a sedative, but was conscious and able to talk. She cried as she told us that her husband had been cutting down a tree when the axe slipped. She had heard his cries and so had the neighbours. They had found him in a great pool of blood, and everybody had helped with the tourniquets while awaiting the ambulance which had been telephoned for.

Despite her pallor and distress she looked very elfin and lovely as she lay in the hospital bed. She murmured that she would always love her husband, and soon she was sleeping like a tired child.

In the meantime I sent Detective Carl Huber to the villa to have a look around, and he came back with some surprising news. In the garden was a half-felled tree, a great patch of blood and a razor-sharp axe. "Somebody had wiped the axe clean," said Huber. "There was not a spot of blood on it, nor a fingerprint."

It was possible of course that the axe had been wiped innocently by a maid or someone, but it was not possible to explain away the expert evidence Möller and I heard the following morning at the Vienna Medical Institute, to which the leg had been sent for examination.

Removing his pince-nez, which he wore attached to a silk cord, Professor Meixner pointed to Exhibit A and said: "Gentlemen, there can be no question but that these wounds were inflicted deliberately. The partial amputation required three separate strokes of the axe, and the marks on the limb are plainly discernible, each going deeper than the previous one."

Quite involuntarily I exclaimed, "But that is incredible!" and then remembered that it is the incredible that gives the police their employment.

"What is credible," remarked Möller sagely, "is that Marek had help in mutilating himself."

"You mean his wife, I suppose?"

"Yes; I believe she can tell us what really happened."

There were many inquiries to be made before the Mareks could be arrested on a charge of attempted fraud, and, in any case, Emil Marek could not be moved from hospital for some time. I learned a lot about Martha and how she had become an old man's darling. The case was so unusual that it became the talk of Vienna, and Martha herself was astute enough to take part in the controversy.

Shortly after being released on bail she invited me to call

on her at the villa. A smart little maid opened the door and showed me into the drawing-room, where I found her lying – Recamier-like – on a chaise-longue surrounded by an audience. The room, beautifully furnished, and with many rare pieces, was full of reporters, and Martha offered me her hand to kiss as if I were a courtier instead of a police officer.

"You must pardon me for not rising, but I am still very weak. I have invited the reporters here in order to tell them that my husband and I are being prosecuted at the instigation of an insurance company which hopes to evade paying the money it owes us."

She paused and gave me a cool stare, and I could see that she had won the sympathy of everybody present. "You see," she went on, "I have received certain information of which I am sure the police cannot be aware. It was given to me by a person who works at the hospital and he tells me that he had seen Herr Möller talking very confidentially with one of the surgeons. Later, and I am assured of the truth of this, this witness saw this selfsame surgeon extending the area of the wound on poor Emil's amputated leg."

This was sensational "copy" for the newspapers, and one of the reporters asked: "Can you tell us the name and occupation of your witness?"

Martha smiled a little sadly. "No, I am not able to say who he is, for reasons I am sure you will understand. He was kind enough to volunteer this information, and that is all I can tell you for the time being."

I stayed behind, and it took me a long time to secure from Martha the name of the person who was supposed to have witnessed an act of collusion between Möller and a surgeon. It was a very ugly allegation and not for one moment did I think it was true.

The person in question was a hospital orderly named Karl Mraz. He was a frail creature and not very intelligent. He bore out Martha's story when first questioned, but he did not stand up to the interrogation and finally admitted that

Frau Marek had offered him 10,000 schillings if he would repeat the story she had concocted.

A further charge of attempting to obstruct the course of justice was added to the indictment when the two prisoners were tried, but they were not seriously inconvenienced.

Crime has an ugly face and nobody looked less like criminals than Emil Marek, a most handsome cripple, and Martha, his enchanting wife. They had the newspapers on their side too, and the charge of attempted fraud was dismissed for lack of sufficient evidence. On the second count they were found guilty and sentenced to four months' imprisonment, but it was ruled that since they had already spent a similar period in custody while awaiting trial the sentence had already been served.

Over coffee with Möller I could see he was very worried at the prospect of his company having to meet the Mareks' claim. Had I not been convinced that it was fraudulent I would not have offered him certain advice. I knew the history of Martha, and of the doubt in Betty Fritsch's mind that her husband had died a natural death, and advised him that Martha, quite literally, might not care to have her past dug up. I offered him this advice as a friend, and not as a police officer, and said that no doubt a little heart-to-heart talk with her might persuade her to accept a more modest settlement.

Möller dropped in at a party the Mareks gave to celebrate their freedom and he said enough to convince Martha that in the circumstances it would be wiser to settle for £3,000, which she did. After all the costs of the defence had been met Emil's amputated leg did not return much of a profit.

They had been very lucky to escape a long term of imprisonment, and it was because I felt so certain of their guilt that I kept an eye on them. The scandal of the trial ruined all prospects of Emil's electrification project, for the Government promptly withdrew its support and he could find nobody as a private backer. He tried to make money with a fleet of taxis he bought, but the venture was a costly failure and ended in the villa having to be mortgaged to meet his debts.

The Mareks disappeared for some time, and one of my detectives discovered they had gone to Algiers to manufacture radio sets for foreign markets. Labour was cheaper there and no doubt the couple regarded this move as a fresh start.

The next time I saw Martha I could hardly believe it was her. She was selling vegetables from a barrow on a street in one of the poorest sections of Vienna. She had not lost her looks entirely, but her face was drawn and angry. I stopped my car to speak to her.

"Yes," she said bitterly, "we're as poor as I look. Nothing has gone right for us. Emil's business failed in Algiers, and that meant the end of the villa, which was already mortgaged. This is what I have been reduced to. I escaped once from the filth and ugliness of poverty, but now I am a prisoner again."

Martha was wearing a soiled cotton dress and shoes that appeared too big for her. Her appearance would have horrified Moritz Fritsch. I realised how much she disliked me, but at least I was someone she could talk to. "We are really up against it. I have to do this to keep a bit of bread in our mouths. My husband is no longer able to work and we have a young daughter and a baby boy."

The Mareks had been knocked about pretty badly, but Martha was so viperish that it was difficult to feel any sympathy for her. I did not see her again for some time, but in July 1932 I read of Emil Marek's death in one of the newspapers. I got thinking about it and made some inquiries among neighbours. Emil, they said, had been ill for some time. There seemed to have been some paralysis, loss of vision and other painful symptoms. Martha, I was told, nursed him and did everything that was possible until neighbours made a collection among themselves and paid for an opinion by a specialist. Emil's illness was diagnosed as advanced tuberculosis and he was admitted to the charity ward of the Calvary Hospital, where he died soon afterwards.

These facts I was able to confirm, but I might not have been so convinced that Marek's death arose from natural causes had I known that a little over a month afterwards the death also occurred of his daughter, Ingeborg. In the rush of police work the event escaped my notice.

It was 1933 and Hitler already was in power and Europe's long night had begun. Five years of darkness and change went by, and in March 1938 the Nazis marched into my country, and nobody, not even those who welcomed the *anschluss*, could foretell what awaited them tomorrow. The past seemed completely wiped out and with it the record of one's own life and work. Perhaps that explains my feeling of astonishment when I again heard the name of Frau Marek.

She had, according to a report placed on my desk, been the victim of the theft of a number of valuable tapestries and paintings. She was living in Kuppelweisergasse, one of the better parts of the city, which was certainly an improvement on selling carrots, onions and potatoes to the underprivileged, as she had been doing when last I saw her.

I thought it would be interesting to call on her, and, at first, Martha did not recognise me. With a graceful gesture she indicated the bare walls of her large and handsome apartment. "They were stolen during the night," she said tersely. She looked at me a second time and with recognition. "Well, *how* very nice to see you again," she said, as if she actually meant it.

"You've had a change of luck," I said.

"Yes, indeed. This house was left to me by Mrs Löwenstein, a relative of my father. Please do your best to recover the stolen articles."

Martha had plenty of nerve, I had to admit to myself. I said to her: "I suppose you had the valuables insured?"

"Naturally. Herr Neumann, who incidentally is a tenant here, issued the policy."

It was my turn to be surprised, and I wondered if she had been up to her old tricks again. Surely, I thought, she must have learned her lesson, but frauds invariably repeat their offences, and I decided it would be worth my while to make a few calls. If the robbery had been faked, then Frau Marek must have had the tapestries and paintings removed, and eventually I found the removal firm who had done the job. Martha had arranged for the collection to be made at night-time and her valuables were in safe storage at the Omega repository in Ottakring.

For the second time I arrested Martha on a charge of attempted fraud. The newspapers had not forgotten her trial eleven years before, and, since she began once more to dominate the front pages, things began to happen. While the fraud case against her was pending a young man named Herbert Kittenberger called on me and told me he was convinced that Frau Marek had poisoned his mother. He wanted her body exhumed.

From what he told me, his mother, Felicitas Kittenberger, had rented a room in Martha's apartment house and had died there after a brief illness. Her son had not been told of her death until after the funeral.

"Why not?" I asked.

Herbert Kittenberger said he had not even known of his mother's illness. He admitted that he was often away looking for work, but asserted that Frau Marek could have got in touch with him had she wanted to. "I tried to get an explanation from her and she said she had tried to find me, but I am certain she was lying."

Although Frau Kittenberger's doctor maintained that his patient had died from natural causes I thought it advisable to apply for an order to exhume her body. During the last few years death, it seemed, had followed Martha around, and I sensed there was much to be explained. It meant a lot of work and a lot of back-tracking, but I found out that shortly after the death of her husband Martha had moved into the home in Kuppelweisergasse of her aged relative, Frau Susanne Löwenstein. In the neighbourhood there were still those who remembered the old woman's pretty companion. Martha had visited Frau Löwenstein to begin with, and had then persuaded her that she needed someone to look after her.

Once again Martha was able to escape from poverty. She was still young, just over thirty, and the old woman must have bought her some clothes, for she dressed well and had apparently saved a few of the jewels that Fritsch had bought her years before.

She did the cooking for Frau Löwenstein, read to her, and, according to a witness, when the old woman told her she intended leaving her all she possessed Martha had replied: "Everything I do for you is a labour of love. I do not do it for money."

Frau Löwenstein did not long survive, and in her final illness the symptoms were similar to those reported of Martha's late husband – numbness in her legs, dim vision and a difficulty in swallowing. When she died she left Martha the house and a substantial parcel of money.

One of the persons I talked to about Martha was Herr Neumann, her insurance agent, and the occupant of a couple of rooms at her house. He was garrulous but co-operative.

"I first met Frau Marek in 1935," he said. "One could not but be impressed by her – she was very good-looking and had superb manners. We saw a great deal of each other and she used to confide in me. She had been extravagant and had run through the money Frau Löwenstein had left her. The house in Kuppelweisergasse was expensive to keep up and she asked my advice.

"I suggested that she rent me a couple of rooms to help her out, and later Frau Kittenberger joined our little family. Frau Marek became very fond of her."

"Really?"

"Oh, yes. They were the best of friends. You can't believe a word that Herbert, Frau Kittenberger's son, says. He was a great trouble to her. I can assure you of that. He could not keep a job and money ran through his hands.

"Frau Kittenberger told Martha that the little money she had would go in no time if Herbert got hold of it, and there would certainly not be enough left to bury her. Martha consulted me about the problem and I worked out an insurance policy for Frau Kittenberger. The money was to go to Martha, and it was just as well the arrangement was made, for she was decently buried when her time came."

"What was the amount of the policy?" I inquired.

"It was very little, about three hundred pounds."

It appeared logical to assume that if Martha had indeed murdered Frau Kittenberger it was not the first occasion she had killed, and it became necessary therefore to open the graves of Emil Marek, Ingeborg, her daughter, and Frau Löwenstein.

While awaiting the medical findings of each of the four autopsies a question that had irked my subconscious mind for some time was suddenly liberated. What had happened to the other Marek child – the little boy? On their return from Algiers Marek and his wife had lived in Hitzing, and it was in this district of Vienna that detectives traced the child, Alfons, who was boarded out with neighbours. He was reported to be very ill.

The woman who looked after him told me that she feared little Alfons was suffering from tuberculosis, which she believed he had contracted from his father. The symptoms were greatly similar. Frau Marek, she said, was a constant visitor and often arrived in time to give him his evening meal. Frequently she brought him something special to eat.

"Frau Marek is a very brave woman," said my informant with tears in her eyes. "I heard her telling the little boy he would soon be with his father, and she herself looked just like an angel."

"Don't you ever read the papers?" I asked her.

"*Nein*, Herr Peters. We are very poor."

We got the little boy into hospital, and during the

trial of his mother doctors had to fight hard to save his life.

Martha was charged with the multiple murders of her husband and daughter and of those of Frau Löwenstein and Frau Kittenberger. All of them had died from one of the poisonous compounds of thallium, and a pharmacist in Florisdorf produced records of sale of the poison to Martha on a date prior to the death of each victim. There was other evidence that dovetailed and proved the guilt of the accused beyond all possible doubt.

White and tense, Martha heard the public prosecutor brand her as a creature more vile than Lucrezia Borgia herself. With the advent of Hitlerism the death penalty had been restored in Austria and Martha was sentenced to be beheaded.

On December 6th, 1938, she was taken from her cell to the execution block. Her hands tied behind her, she knelt down to receive the death-blow and her head was severed from her body in a single and fearful swing of the axe.

I am not able to say what were her thoughts during the short time she awaited the carrying out of the sentence. She may, of course, as she had every reason to, have thought of the days when her beauty attracted Moritz Fritsch and how lucky she had imagined herself to be for the golden chance of turning her back on poverty. Ultimately, though, it had brought her face to face with murder.

Perhaps even as a young girl she had possessed the instincts of a killer, but it is just possible that had she remained poor she might well have stayed alive.

Who can say?

A Mixed Bag

There are certain cases whose omission from a book on crimes of the 1930s would be absurd. The Lindbergh kidnapping is in many ways *the* crime of the 1930s, as the Jack the Ripper murders were of the 1880s. The story of Sylvestre Matuska is so bizarre that it surely ranks among the strangest cases of all time. The Jeannie Donald case deserves to be remembered for its brilliant forensic detection. The murder of Mona Tinsley is equally remarkable for its well-authenticated piece of "psychic detection". Finally, the Ruxton case shares with the Wallace mystery the distinction of being *the* British murder of the decade. I might have chosen longer accounts of each one of these, but space was running out. So the "mixed bag" of cases that concludes this book is selected from my own *Written in Blood*, with the exception of the Mona Tinsley case, which is from *The Psychic Detectives*.

THE MAN WHO LOVED TRAINS

The most extraordinary sexual criminal of the post-war years was undoubtedly the Hungarian sadist Sylvestre Matuska, the "man who played with trains".

On 8 August 1931, a bomb had exploded on the Basel-to-Berlin express near Jüterbog (not far from Potsdam) injuring 100 passengers, some of them seriously. On 30 January of

230

that year, there had been an unsuccessful attempt to derail a train near Anspach, in Lower Austria, and it seemed likely that both crimes had been committed by the same man – perhaps for political motives. On a telegraph pole there was a notice with swastikas and "Attack! Victory!"

Only a month after the Jüterbog attack, on 12 September 1931, a tremendous explosion shook the Budapest-Vienna express as it crossed a viaduct near the station of Torbagy, hurling five coaches into the depths below. Twenty-two people were killed, and many more injured. A 20-year-old reporter on the *Vienna Morning Post* named Hans Habe was asked to rush to the scene of the disaster. He found dozens of ambulances, stretchers taking away the injured, and wooden coffins beside the track. Some victims had been blown into pieces, and he saw two heads in one coffin and three legs in another. While Habe was talking to Superintendent Schweinitzer, who was in charge of the investigation, a short, well-built man with a military haircut came up to them. He introduced himself as Sylvestre Matuska, a Hungarian businessman who had been in one of the coaches. He seemed a lively, friendly man, and had apparently had a miraculous escape from one of the wrecked carriages that lay below the viaduct. Habe agreed to give him a lift back to Vienna. The next day, Habe met him by appointment in a café and found him describing the accident – complete with sketches – to a crowd of fascinated onlookers. "I saw one woman with her arm torn off . . ." Habe quoted him at length in his story, which brought the young journalist much favourable notice from colleagues.

But Superintendent Schweinitzer was suspicious. Matuska looked healthy and unshaken – quite unlike a man who had just survived a train wreck. He questioned all the surviving passengers on the train; none could recall seeing Matuska. Forensic examination had established that the train had been blown up by an "infernal machine" in a brown fibre suitcase – virtually a mine which had exploded by the weight of the train. A great deal of explosive must have been used, and explosive was not easy to come by. A few days after the explosion, a taxi-driver came to the Vienna police and told them that he had been hired by a short-haired man to take him on a long journey to two munitions factories, where he had bought sticks of dynamite. This raised the question of how the man had managed to obtain an explosives permit. The answer came a week later when a society woman name Anna Forgo-Hung went to the police with another piece of the jigsaw puzzle. Sylvestre Matuska had approached her about leasing some of her property, but had finally rented only a quarry, explaining that he wanted to do some blasting. This is how he had obtained his permit to buy explosives.

Matuska was arrested and charged with blowing up the Torbagy express. When Habe heard the news, he hastened to see Matuska's wife, a pretty blonde with an obviously gentle nature. Frau Matuska told him that her husband was undoubtedly innocent; he was travelling on the train himself, and she had seen his ticket. Yet her attitude convinced Habe that she herself had her suspicions; a wife who believes her husband incapable of a crime says so plainly, and does not talk about tickets and other "proofs" of his innocence.

In fact, Matuska soon confessed. He *had* been on the train from Budapest; but he had got off at the next station, hired a car, and drove to Torbagy in time for the explosion. Forensic examination of the trousers he was wearing at the time showed semen stains, and psychiatrists who examined Matuska verified that he was a sadist. He was also, like Bela Kiss, a man of insatiable sexual appetite, who slept with a different prostitute each night when he was away from home on business trips. Yet his gestures in courts – his trial began in Vienna on 15 June 1932 – were oddly effeminate. From the beginning, Matuska set out to give the impression that he was insane, declaring that he had been persuaded to wreck the train by a right-wing guru called Bergmann, who had tried to persuade Matuska to have intercourse with his incredibly beautiful wife – Matuska rolled the word "intercourse" round his tongue – and then persuaded him to help him found a religious sect. Matuska spoke of spiritualist seances, and claimed that he had been under the telepathic influence of an occultist called Leo since he was 14. But perhaps the most interesting piece of evidence was that he had bought his son an electric train set, then spent all his time playing with it.

The jury was unconvinced by all this talk of mysticism and occultism, and sentenced Matuska to life imprisonment – there was no capital punishment in Austria. He was retried in Budapest, and this time sentenced to death; but since the Viennese court had sentenced him to life imprisonment, the sentence was not carried out.

At the end of the Second World War, a reporter asked the Hungarian authorities what had become of Matuska, and learned – after many evasions – that the train-wrecker had been released.

In 1953, towards the end of the Korean War, an American patrol near Hong-Song captured some North Korean commandos who were about to blow up a bridge; they were led by a white man who seemed to be about 60. After long interrogation, during which he apparently failed to answer the questions, the man announced: "I am Sylvestre Matuska". His interrogator was obviously unimpressed, at which point the man explained with pride: "I am Matuska, the train-wrecker of Bia-Torbagy. You have made the most valuable capture of the war."

An American report of the incident stated that Matuska had been freed from his Hungarian prison by the Russians, and told them that he had wrecked the Jüterbog train on the orders of a Communist cell of which he was a member; this is how he came to be accepted as a volunteer on the side of the North Koreans. As a saboteur trained to blow up bridges, he must have felt as contented as a necrophile placed in charge of a morgue. Habe is of the opinion that Matuska betrayed Communist military secrets to the Americans, and was then released. What became of him after the Korean War is unknown.

THE LINDBERGH KIDNAPPING

March 1, 1932, was a rainy and windy day in Hopewell, New Jersey, and the family of the famous aviator Charles Lindbergh were all suffering from colds – which is why they had decided to delay their departure to the home of their in-laws by 24 hours. At 10 o'clock that evening, the nurse Betty Gow asked Ann Lindbergh if she had taken the baby from his cot. She said no, and they went to ask her husband if he had the baby. Then all three rushed up to the room where 19-month-old Charles jun. should have been asleep. On the windowsill was a note demanding $50,000 for the child's return.

There were few clues. Under the window the police found some smudged footprints; nearby there was a ladder in three sections and a chisel. The ladder, a crude home-made one, was broken where the top section joined the middle one. There were no fingerprints in the child's room.

The kidnapping caused a nation-wide sensation, and soon Hopewell was swarming with journalists – to Lindbergh's anger and embarrassment: he knew that the furore would make it more difficult for the kidnappers to make contact. Crooks all over the country had reason to curse the kidnappers as the police applied pressure. Meanwhile, the kidnappers were silent.

The note offered few clues. It had various spelling mistakes, like "anyding" for "anything", and a handwriting expert said that it had probably been written by a German with low educational qualifications. It was signed by two interlocking circles, one red, one blue.

A week after the kidnapping, a well-wisher named Dr. John F. Condon sent a letter to his local newspaper in the Bronx offering $1,000 of his own money for the return of his child. The result was a letter addressed to Condon signed with two circles – a detail that had not been released to the public. It asked him to act as a go-between, and to place an advertisement reading "Mony is Redy" when he was ready to hand it over.

Lindbergh was convinced by the evidence of the two circles; he instructed Condon to go ahead and place the advertisement. That evening, a man's deep voice spoke to Condon on the telephone – Condon could hear someone else speaking Italian in the background – and told him the gang would soon be in touch. A rendezvous was made at a cemetery; at the gates, a young man with a handkerchief over his face asked if Condon had brought the money; Condon said it was not yet ready. The man took fright and ran away; Condon caught up with him and assured him he could trust him. The man identified himself as "John", and suddenly asked a strange question: "Would I burn if the baby is dead?" Appalled, Condon asked: "Is the baby dead?" The man assured him that the baby was alive, and said that he was now on a "boad" (boat). As a token of good faith, he would send Condon the baby's sleeping suit. In fact, it arrived the following day, and the Lindberghs identified it as that of their son.

On 2 April 1932, Lindbergh himself accompanied Condon when he went to hand over the ransom money; he clearly heard the kidnapper's voice calling "Hey, doctor!" But the baby was not returned. Lindbergh flew to look for a boat near Elizabeth Island, but failed to find it. And on 12 May, the decomposing body of a baby was found in a shallow grave in the woods near the Lindbergh home; he had been killed by a blow on the head – apparently on the night of the kidnapping.

The police investigation made no headway. The maid Betty Gow was widely suspected by the police of being an accomplice, but the Lindberghs had no doubt of her innocence. Suspicion transferred to another maid, Violet Sharpe, when she committed suicide with poison, but again there was no evidence.

Meanwhile, a wood technologist named Arthur Koehler was continuing his investigations into the ladder. He had written to Lindbergh offering to trace its wood, using the laboratory of the Forest Service in Wisconsin. Slivers of wood from the ladder had been sent to him for identification soon after the kidnapping. Now he spent four days studying the ladder microscopically, labelling every separate part. Three rails were of North Carolina yellow pine, four of Douglas fir, and ten of Ponderosa pine. The yellow pine rails contained nail holes, indicating that these pieces had been taken from elsewhere, and "rail 16" had square nail holes, and differed from all the others in that it had obviously been planed down from something wider. The whole ladder was "of poor workmanship", showing poor selection of wood and little skill in the use of tools. The microscope showed that the yellow pine rails had tiny grooves, which indicated that the lumber mill that had processed them had a defective knife in the planer. Koehler was aware that this was virtually a fingerprint; if he could find that planing machine, he would stand a good chance of finding what happened to this shipment of wood.

The investigation that followed has been called (in *The Trial of Richard Hauptmann*) "one of the greatest feats of scientific detection of all time". Koehler discovered that there were 1,598 lumber mills that handled yellow pine, and sent duplicated letters of enquiry to each of them. It took several months, but eventually he identified the mill as the Dorn Lumber Company in South Carolina. Between September 1929 and March 1932, they had shipped 47 carloads of yellow pine to East Coast lumber yards; Koehler and Detective Lewis Bornmann spent 18 months visiting yard after yard, and finally had to admit defeat; most of them had long ago sold their consignments of yellow pine, and had no record of the customers. Yet for some reason, they decided to revisit the National Lumber and Millwork Company in the Bronx, and there found a wooden bin which had been constructed of some of the pine they were looking for, with its distinctive planing. Of course, that was no proof that the wood of the ladder had come from that particular lumber yard; it could have come from 29 others. But it was certainly a triumph of sheer persistence . . .

The ransom bills – which included "gold certificates" which could be exchanged for gold – had all been marked (without Lindbergh's knowledge). Now banks were asked to look out for any of the bills, and in 1933 they began to turn up, mostly in New York, although some as far away as Chicago. This seemed to indicate that the kidnappers lived in New York or thereabouts. In early September 1934, $10 gold certificates began to appear in northern New York and the Bronx. In May of that year, Roosevelt had abandoned the gold standard, and called in all gold certificates; but they continued to be accepted by banks – and, of course, shops.

On 15 September 1934, a dark-blue Dodge sedan drove into a garage in upper Manhattan, and the driver, who spoke with a German accent, paid for his fuel with a $10 gold certificate. Because these had ceased to be legal tender, the pump attendant noted the car's number on the back of the certificate. Four days later, a bank teller noticed that the certificate was part of the Lindbergh ransom money, and saw that it had a registration number on the back: 4U-13-41-NY. The police were informed. They quickly discovered that the vehicle was a dark-blue Dodge sedan belonging to Richard Bruno Hauptmann, a carpenter of 1279 East 222nd Street, the Bronx. It proved to be a small frame house, and that night, police surrounded it. The next morning, when a man stepped out of the door and drove off, police followed him and forced his car over to the kerb. Hauptmann, a lean, good-looking German in his mid-30s, made no resistance and was found to be unarmed. In his wallet, police found a $20 bill which proved to be from the ransom money. Concealed in his garage, they found a further hoard of Lindbergh money. Later, a further $860 of ransom money and a gun were found concealed in a plank in the garage.

The evidence seemed overwhelming – particularly when police discovered that Hauptmann bought his timber at the National Lumber Company in the Bronx located by Koehler and Bornmann. But Hauptmann protested his total innocence. The money, he explained, had been left in his care by a friend, Isidor Fisch, who had returned to Germany in December 1933, owing Hauptmann over $7,000, on a joint business deal. When Fisch had died of tuberculosis in March 1934, his friends in America – including Hauptmann – began looking into his business affairs, and realized that he had been a confidence trickster who had simply pocketed investments. Hauptmann and Fisch had been involved in a $20,000 deal in furs; now Hauptmann discovered that the warehouse did not even exist. In August 1934, said Hauptmann, he had noticed a shoe box which Fisch had given him for safe keeping before he left. It had been soaked by a leak, but proved to contain $14,600 in money and gold certificates. Feeling that at least half of it was his by right, Hauptmann dried it out and proceeded to spend it.

That was Hauptmann's story. It sounded too convenient to be true. And when Hauptmann's trial opened in Flemington, New Jersey, on 2 January 1935, it was clear that no one believed it. But the most important piece of evidence was the ladder. Not only was there a clear possibility that some of its timber had been purchased at the Bronx yard where Hauptmann bought his timber, but one of the rungs (16) had been traced to Hauptmann's own attic: Detective Bornmann had noticed a missing board, and found what remained of it, with the "rung" sawed out of it. The evidence could hardly have been more conclusive. Moreover, Condon's telephone number had been found pencilled on the back of a closet door in Hauptmann's house, together with the numbers of some bills.

It was true that there was nothing conclusive to connect Hauptmann with the kidnap itself. The footmarks found outside the child's bedroom window were not Hauptmann's size; none of Hauptmann's fingerprints were found on the ladder. But a man called Millard Whited, who lived near Lindbergh, identified Hauptmann as a man he had seen hanging around the Lindbergh home on two occasions. And Lindbergh himself declared in court that Hauptmann was the "John" whose voice he had heard at the cemetery. All this, together with the ladder evidence, left the jury in no doubt whatsoever that Hauptmann was the kidnapper, and on 13 February 1935, he was sentenced to death. By October, the Court of Appeals had denied his appeal. But when the prison governor, Harold Hoffmann, interviewed Hauptmann in his cell in December, he emerged a puzzled man, feeling that Hauptmann's pleas of innocence rang true, and that the case deserved further investigation. The truth was that Hauptmann could easily have been "framed". Soon after her husband's arrest, Anna Hauptmann had made the supreme mistake of moving out of the house, leaving it empty for police and reporters to examine. It was after this that Bornmann had discovered the missing board in the attic. But was it likely that a carpenter, with plenty of wood at his disposal, would prise up a board in his attic and plane it down to size? Even the ladder itself gave rise to suspicion; as Koehler pointed out, it was crudely made, and showed poor judgement. But Hauptmann was a skilled carpenter . . .

For Lindbergh, Governor Hoffmann's attempts to prove Hauptmann innocent were the last straw. He was totally convinced that Hauptmann was guilty, and he felt that Hoffmann was seeking publicity. He and his wife sailed for England, and did not return for many years. He went to Germany, was impressed by Hitler's revolution, and became a frequent guest of the Nazis; later he tried hard to prevent America entering the war on the side of the British.

But Hoffmann's efforts were of no avail, and on 3 April 1936, Richard Hauptmann was finally electrocuted, still protesting his innocence.

Is it conceivable that Hauptmann was innocent? According to one investigator, Ludovic Kennedy, it is almost a certainty. In the early 1980s, Kennedy took the trouble to interview all witnesses who were still available, and to look closely into the evidence – that which was presented in court and that which was not. His book *The Airman and the Carpenter* (1985) makes one thing very clear; that if all this evidence *had* been presented in court, Hauptmann would have been acquitted. Hauptmann came to America as a stowaway in 1924; he had a minor police record for burglary during the black days of inflation. But in America he prospered; he and his wife worked hard, and by 1926 he was in a position to lend money and to buy a lunchroom; the day after the Wall Street crash he withdrew $2,800 from his account and began buying stocks and shares at rock bottom prices. Hauptmann had no need to kidnap the Lindbergh baby; by modern standards, he was very comfortably off in 1932.

Kennedy's investigations revealed that Hauptmann's story about his friend Isidor Fisch was true. Fisch *was* a confidence swindler; he and Hauptmann were in the fur business together, and Fisch *did* owe Hauptmann over $7,000. His swindles were uncovered only after his death in Leipzig in 1934.

Then how did Hauptmann – or Fisch – come to be in possession of so much ransom money? The probable answer, Kennedy discovered, is that the Lindbergh ransom money was selling at a discount in New York's underworld – one convict bought some at 40 cents in the dollar. Nothing is more likely than that Fisch, with his underworld connections, bought a large quantity, and left it with Hauptmann when he sailed for Germany. Forensic examination of the money showed that it *had* been soaked and dried out, confirming Hauptmann's story that he had left it on a top shelf in a closet and forgotten about it.

But Kennedy's major discovery was that so much of the evidence against Hauptmann was fabricated. When arrested, he was asked to write out various sentences; the court was later told that Hauptmann's misspelling of various words had been exactly as in the ransom note. This was untrue; he had spelled correctly the first time, then been *told* to misspell various words – "singature" for signature, "were" for where, "gut" for good. The court was also assured that handwriting experts had identified Hauptmann's writing as that of the ransom notes; Kennedy submitted the samples to two modern experts, who both said they were *not* written by the same man. Kennedy's investigation revealed that Millard Whited, the farmhand who identified Hauptmann as a man he had seen hanging around the Lindbergh property, had earlier flatly denied seeing anyone suspicious; he was later offered generous "expenses", and changed his story. As to Lindbergh himself, he had been invited to sit quietly in a corner of the room in disguise when Hauptmann was brought in for questioning; he therefore knew him well when he identified him in court as "John". As to the writing in the closet, Kennedy established that it was made by a reporter, Tom Cassidy, who did it as a "joke". Hauptmann had no reason to write Condon's telephone number on the back of a door; he had no telephone, and in any case, the number was listed in the directory. The numbers of bills written on the door were not, in fact, those of Lindbergh ransom bills.

The most serious piece of evidence against Hauptmann was, of course, the ladder. This constituted the "greatest feat of scientific detection of all time". Examined closely, it is seen to be highly questionable. Koehler's efforts established that some of the yellow pine was sent to the Bronx timber yard, and it may have been from this consignment that the rungs of the ladder were made. But this was only one of thirty timber yards to which the same wood was sent; the man who made the ladder could have bought the wood at any of them. Hauptmann rightly pointed out in court that he was a skilled carpenter, and that the ladder was made by an amateur. If the jury registered this point, they may have felt that he had deliberately botched it to mislead investigators – for, after all, was there not the conclusive evidence of the sixteenth rung, whose wood was found in Hauptmann's attic? But, as Kennedy points out, this plank was "found" when Mrs. Hauptmann had abandoned the house to the investigators. Was it likely that Hauptmann would go to the trouble of tearing up his attic floor, sawing out a piece of wood from the plank, then planing it down to size, when it would have been simpler to get another piece of wood? He was, after all, a professional carpenter. Kennedy quite clearly believes that rung 16 was concocted by Detective Bornmann or one of the other investigators – he refers to the whole story as "Bornmann-in-Wonderland".

So in retrospect, it seems clear that the "greatest feat of scientific detection of all time" was based on false or suppressed evidence. The police firmly believed that Hauptmann was guilty, and they strengthened their case where necessary. Hauptmann may well have been guilty; but all the latest evidence points clearly to his innocence.

THE CASE OF JEANNIE DONALD

The murder trial of Jeannie Donald was rendered memorable by the brilliant forensic detective work that convicted her. The murder, of an eight-year-old girl named Helen Priestly, took place in a working class tenement in Aberdeen. On 20 April 1934, Helen failed to return from an errand; her body was found a few hours later in a sack under the stairs. The missing knickers and blood trickling from the vagina suggested a sex crime. But forensic examination revealed no traces of semen, and suggested that the injuries had been inflicted with some instrument like the handle of a pudding spoon. The body had been found close to the flat of a woman called Jeannie Donald, who was known to have a violent temper and to dislike Helen Priestly – the child liked to chant the nickname "Coconut" in her hearing. Jeannie Donald seemed to have a perfect alibi – she said she had been out shopping at the time of the murder – but when she named the prices she had paid for various items, it was noted that they were the prices charged the *previous* Friday.

Sydney Smith, Professor of Forensic Medicine at Edinburgh, was called in to see what he could make of the clues. A magnifying glass showed human and animal hairs in the sack in which the body had been found, and some washed cinders. Many people in the block re-used partly burnt cinders, but Jeannie Donald was the only one who washed them first to remove the ash. The human hair proved to be virtually identical to Jeannie Donald's, and the potato sack resembled others found in her flat (her brother was a farm worker who supplied the Donalds with vegetables). Blood spots found on a newspaper in Jeannie Donald's flat were type "O", the same as Helen Priestly's. But they could, of course, have been Jeannie Donald's. She refused to have a blood sample taken, but Smith was able to obtain one of her used sanitary towels from the prison; it proved to be of a different blood type. Finally, bloodstains found on a floorcloth in the flat were found to contain a rare type of bacterium, which was also found in Helen Priestly's intestines. It became clear that Helen had run past the Donald's flat chanting "Coconut", and that Jeannie Donald had grabbed her on the way back and dragged her inside. Her intention was probably to shake her violently by the throat, but Helen may have fainted. Then, assuming she had killed her, Jeannie Donald attempted to make it look like a sex crime, and placed the body in a sack.

The defence underestimated the strength of the scientific evidence, and decided to plead "Not Guilty". But Smith's performance in the witness box convinced the jury, who took only eighteen minutes to find Jeannie Donald guilty of murder She was sentenced to death, but it was later commuted to life imprisonment, of which she served ten years.

THE RUXTON CASE

September 29, 1935, was a cool autumn day; a young lady had paused in her afternoon walk to lean on the parapet of a bridge across a pretty stream called the Gardenholme Linn. As she stared at the narrow, rocky stream, she noticed some kind of bundle that had jammed against a boulder. Something that looked unpleasantly like a human arm was sticking out of it.

The police were on the scene by mid-afternoon, and had soon discovered two human heads on the bank of the Linn, as well as four bundles, each containing human remains – thigh bones, legs, pieces of flesh, and an armless torso. One piece of newspaper wrapped round two upper arms proved to be the *Sunday Graphic* for 15 September 1935.

When, the following day, Professor John Glaister – author of a classic *Medical Jurisprudence and Toxicology* – arrived with his colleague Dr. Gilbert Millar, he quickly realized that this killing was not the work of some terrified amateur; he had taken care to cover his tracks. He had not only dismembered the bodies, but removed the skin from the heads, to make the faces unrecognizable, and cut off the fingertips to make fingerprint identification impossible. He had made only one mistake: instead of tossing the remains into the River Annan, a few hundred yards downstream, he had tossed them into its tributary, the Linn, which had been swollen with heavy rains at the time. If the rain had continued, the parcels would have ended up in the Solway Firth. But there were a few days of fine weather; the stream dwindled to its usual trickle, and the parcels caught in the rocks.

The remains were sent to the Anatomy Department of the University of Edinburgh, and there treated with ether to prevent further decomposition and destroy maggots; then they were "pickled" in a formalin solution. Glaister and Millar found themselves confronted with a human jigsaw puzzle of 70 pieces.

The first task was to sort the pieces into two separate bodies, and this was made easier by the fact that one was six inches shorter than the other. And when it was finally done, Glaister and his team found that they had one almost complete body, the taller one, and one body minus a trunk. There was also an item that caused much bafflement – an enormous single eye, which certainly did not belong to either of the bodies; by some odd chance, this eye, probably from an animal, had also found its way into the Linn.

What could be deduced about the murderer? First, that he was almost certainly a medical man. He had used a knife, not a saw, to dismember the body, and a human body is almost impossible to dismember with a knife without detailed knowledge of the joints. He had also removed the teeth, recognizing that they could lead to identification by a dentist.

Fortunately, the murderer had either lost his nerve or been interrupted, for he had left some of the hair on the smaller body – which, at first, Glaister thought to be that of a man. And when more parcels were found in the river, Glaister found that he had a pair of hands that still had fingertips. After soaking them in hot water, he was able to get an excellent set of fingerprints. And the discovery that the assorted pieces of flesh included three breasts also made it clear that both bodies were of women.

The next problem was the age of the bodies. Glaister determined this by means of the skull sutures. Sutures are "joining lines" in the skull, and they seal themselves over the years; they are usually closed completely by the age of 40. In one of the two skulls, the smaller of the two, the sutures were unclosed; in the other, they were almost closed. This indicated that one body was that of a woman of about 40; the other was certainly under 30. X-rays of the jaw-bone

245

of the younger woman showed that the wisdom teeth had still not pushed through, which meant she was probably in her early 20s. The cartilage, the soft material of which bones are originally made, gradually changes into "caps", called "epiphyses", and the age can also be estimated from how far this change has taken place. The epiphyses of the smaller body confirmed that this was a girl of 20 or so; the other was of a woman approaching middle age.

As to the cause of death, this was fairly clear. The taller woman had five stab wounds in the chest, several broken bones, and many bruises. The hyoid bone in the neck was broken, indicating strangulation before the other injuries had been inflicted. The swollen and bruised tongue confirmed this inference. Glaister reasoned that a murderer who strangled and beat his victim before stabbing her would probably be in the grip of jealous rage. As to the other body, the signs were that she had been battered with some blunt instrument. It hardly needed a Sherlock Holmes to infer that she had been killed as an afterthought, probably to keep her silent. The fact that the murderer had taken less trouble to conceal her identity pointed to the same conclusion.

Meanwhile, the police were working on their own clues. The *Sunday Graphic* was a special local edition, printed for the Morecambe and Lancaster area. And the clothes in which some of the remains had been wrapped were also distinctive: the head of the younger woman had been wrapped in a pair of child's rompers, and another bundle had been wrapped in a blouse with a patch under the arm . . .

And in Lancaster, a Persian doctor named Buck Ruxton had already attracted the suspicions of the local police. Five days before the remains were found in the Linn, Ruxton – a small, rather good-looking man with a wildly excitable manner – had called on the police and mentioned that his wife had deserted him. The police were investigating the murder of a lady called Mrs. Smalley, whose body had been found a year earlier, and in the course of routine investigations, had questioned a domestic in Ruxton's household; he wanted to protest about this harassment. And when he spoke of his wife's disappearance, they were not in the least surprised; they knew that the relations between the two were stormy. Two years before, Mrs. Isabella Ruxton had come to the police station to protest that her husband was beating her, and Ruxton had made wild accusations of infidelity against her; however, he had calmed down, and 24 hours later the two were apparently again on the best of terms.

The parents of Mrs. Ruxton's maid, Mary Rogerson, were not only surprised but incredulous when Ruxton came and told them that their daughter had got herself pregnant by the laundry boy, and that his wife had taken her away for an abortion. Nothing was less likely; Mary was a plain girl, with a cast in one eye, who loved her home and her parents, and spent all her spare time with them; she was as unlikely to get herself pregnant as to rob a bank. In spite of Ruxton's feverish protests, they reported it to the police. On the evening of 9 October 1935, 10 days after the remains had been found in the Linn, Ruxton came to the police and burst into tears. People were saying that he had murdered his wife and thrown her into the Linn; they must help him find her. They soothed him and sent him away. But, in fact, Ruxton had been the chief suspect since earlier that day. The Scottish police had been to see the Rogersons, and had shown them the patched blouse. As soon as they saw it, they knew their daughter was dead; Mary had bought it at a jumble sale and patched it under the arm. They were unable to identify the rompers, but suggested that the police should try a Mrs. Holme, with whom Mary and the three Ruxton children had spent a holiday earlier that year. And Mrs. Holme recognized the rompers as a pair she had given to Mary for the children.

The police spoke to the Ruxtons' charlady, Mrs. Oxley. She told them that on the day Mrs. Ruxton and Mary

Rogerson had disappeared, Sunday 15 September 1935, Ruxton had arrived early at her house and explained that it was unnecessary for her to come to work that day – he was taking the children to Morecambe, and his wife had gone to Edinburgh. The following morning, she found the Ruxtons' house – at 2 Dalton Square – in a state of chaos, with carpets removed, the bath full of yellow stains, and a pile of burnt material in the yard. A neighbour told the police that Ruxton had persuaded her to come and clean up his house to prepare it for the decorators, claiming that he had cut his hand badly on a tin of peaches. She and her husband had obligingly scrubbed out the house. And Ruxton had given them some bloodstained carpets and a blue suit that was also stained with blood.

On 12 October, the police questioned Ruxton all night, and at 7.20 the next morning he was charged with the murder of Mary Rogerson.

In spite of Ruxton's attempts to cover his tracks, and to persuade various witnesses to offer him false alibis, the truth about the murders soon became plain. Ruxton was pathologically jealous, although there was no evidence that his "wife" – they were in fact unmarried – had ever been unfaithful. A week before the murder, Mrs. Ruxton had gone to Edinburgh, where she had a sister, with a family named Edmondson, who were close friends of the Ruxtons. The Edmondsons and Mrs. Ruxton had all booked into separate rooms; nevertheless, Ruxton was convinced that she had spent the night in the bed of Robert Edmondson, an assistant solicitor in the Town Hall. Ruxton had driven to Edinburgh to spy on them. The following Saturday, Isabella Ruxton had gone to spend the afternoon and evening with two of her sisters in Blackpool. Convinced that she was in a hotel room with a man, Ruxton had worked himself into a jealous frenzy, and when she came back far later than expected, he began to beat her – probably in an attempt to make

her confess her infidelities – then throttled her unconscious and stabbed her. Mary Rogerson had probably
heard the screams and come in to see what was happening; Ruxton believed she was his wife's confidante in
her infidelities, and killed her too. He had spent the next
day dismembering the bodies and packing them in straw;
that night, he made his first trip north to dispose of the
bodies . . .

Ruxton's counsel, Norman Birkett, must have known that
his client did not stand a ghost of a chance. His line of
defence was that the bodies found in the Linn were not
those of Isabella Ruxton and Mary Rogerson, but of some
other persons. But when the medical experts – Glaister,
Millar, and Professor Sydney Smith – gave their evidence,
it was obvious that the identity of the bodies had been
established beyond all possible doubt. One photograph,
which has subsequently been used in every account of
the case, superimposed the larger of the two skulls on a
photograph of Mrs. Ruxton. She had a rather long, horsy
face, and it was obvious that the two fitted together with
gruesome exactitude. Ruxton seemed determined to trap
himself in a web of lies and evasions. The result was a
unanimous verdict of guilty, arrived at in only one hour.
He was hanged at Strangeways jail, Manchester, on 12
May 1936.

Yet examination of the evidence – and of Glaister's
famous book *Medico-legal Aspects of the Ruxton Case*
(1937) – makes it clear that Ruxton came very close indeed
to getting away with murder. If he had taken the trouble
to remove Mary Rogerson's fingertips, and destroyed the
telltale breast tissue as well as the trunk (which was never
found), the evidence against him would have remained
purely circumstantial; and since British juries are unwilling
to convict on circumstantial evidence, he might well have
been given the benefit of the doubt. Glaister's forensic
skill and Ruxton's failure of nerve played an equal part
in bringing him to the gallows.

The Nancy Titterton Case

The case had all the makings of a classic murder mystery.

The body of Nancy Titterton was found by two furniture removal men; she was lying face downward in an empty bath, naked except for a pair of silk stockings, and for the pyjama jacket knotted round her throat. Torn underclothes on the bedroom floor indicated that the motive had been a sexual attack. When the two men had arrived at four o'clock on that Good Friday afternoon – returning a love seat that had been under repair – they found the front door of the apartment standing open. The elder of the two, Theodore Kruger, had called Mrs. Titterton's name, and then, hearing the sound of a shower, glanced in through the open bathroom door; moments later, his young assistant, Johnny Fiorenza, was telephoning the police.

Beekman Place, where the Tittertons lived, was traditionally the home of New York artists and intellectuals. Lewis Titterton was an executive at the National Broadcasting Company, and his 33-year-old wife was a writer of exceptional promise. They had been married for seven years, and were known to be devoted to each other. Most of their small circle of friends were, like themselves, interested in the arts and literature. Neither of them was fond of socializing – Nancy Titterton was shy and introverted. Yet she had opened her door to her killer and let him into the apartment, which argued that she knew him.

It was the kind of case that would have driven a nineteenth-century detective to despair; a preliminary search of the apartment revealed no clues. But this was 1936, and the New York police had an impressive armoury of scientific and forensic aids. At the beginning of the twentieth century, the great criminologist Edmond Locard had formulated the basic principle of scientific crime detection: "Every contact leaves a trace." The criminal *must*, of necessity, leave behind something at the scene of the crime, and take something away with him. A single fibre from his clothing could be identified under the microscope; so could dust or mud from his shoes. A new process involving silver nitrate could raise fingerprints on fabric. Even the rapist's blood grouping could be determined from his seminal stains. This is why, as he surveyed the Titterton's flat, Assistant Chief Inspector John A. Lyons was not unduly discouraged.

In fact, a clue came to light as soon as the body was lifted from the bath: a 13-inch length of cord, which had been severed by a sharp knife. Marks on Nancy Titterton's wrists indicated that the killer had bound them before he raped her. He had cut them free when she lay, face downward, in the bath, and taken the cord with him; but in his haste he had overlooked the short piece that slipped under the body. This suggested that he knew the cord could provide a clue to his identity. Lyons ordered his men to check with every manufacturer in the New York area, to try to trace its source.

The mud samples on the carpet were disappointing. Microscopic examination revealed minute traces of lint, such as is found in upholstery establishments; that meant it had been brought into the apartment on the shoes of the two men who delivered the love seat.

A minute smear of green paint on the counterpane suggested another lead. The building was in the process of being painted in that precise shade of green. It looked as if the killer had brushed against the wet paint and left some on the bed. It also suggested that he might be one of the four painters. But a check revealed that only one of them had been working there on the day of the murder, and the other tenants were able to confirm that he had been working on another floor between 11 o'clock and midday – estimated by the medical examiner as the time Nancy Titterton had been killed.

A maid in the apartment below offered an interesting

piece of information; she had been preparing lunch when she heard a woman's voice call: "Dudley, oh Dudley!" The name of the janitor was Dudley Mings, and he was unable to offer a verifiable alibi. His story was that he had been working alone in his basement throughout the morning. But a search of his apartment revealed nothing to connect him with the murder, and he seemed to be a man of good character. On the whole, it was probable that his alibi was true.

The search for the origin of the cord seemed hopeless. It was of the kind used on venetian blinds, and was therefore commonplace. And the sharp kitchen knife that had probably been used to cut it from her wrists contained no fingerprints.

Now the general picture of the crime was beginning to emerge. The killer had entered 22 Beekman Place through the front door, either ringing the bell to request the tenant to release the catch, or by manipulating its defective lock. Again, this argued that he was known to the victim. Once inside, he had clamped a hand over her mouth to prevent her from screaming, then stuffed a piece of cloth between her teeth. He had tied her hands behind her with the cord he had brought with him, then carried or dragged her (she weighed only 100 lb) into the bedroom. He had removed her blouse and skirt, then thrown her on to one of the two single beds and torn off her brassière and panties – both were torn. After raping her, he had knotted a pyjama jacket round her throat, as well as a red blouse. He had carried her into the bathroom and cut the cord from her wrist, after which he had turned on the shower. Then he had hurried out of the apartment, leaving the door open behind him.

All this suggested a crime that was deliberately planned, not one committed on the spur of the moment. He had brought the cord with him and taken it away again; he had wiped his fingerprints off the knife he had used to cut it. Yet he had also placed her in the shower – presumably in an attempt to revive her. That suggested a man who was emotionally involved with her – perhaps a rejected lover – rather than some casual rapist. But as Lyons interviewed every known friend of the couple, he became increasingly convinced that Nancy Titterton had not been the type to engage in a secret love affair.

The break came, as Lyons had hoped, from the crime laboratory. Dr. Alexander O. Gettler, the city toxicologist, discovered a puzzling clue when he was examining the bedclothes in his laboratory at the Bellevue Hospital. Studying the candlewick counterpane under a magnifying glass, he found a piece of white hair, less than half an inch long. It was stiffer than human hair, and the microscope revealed it to be horsehair, of the type used for stuffing furniture. In fact, it was of the same type used to stuff the love seat that had been returned on the day of the murder. Since it was too heavy in texture to have been blown into the bedroom on a gust of air, it must have been carried there on someone's clothing. That someone, Lyons reasoned, could only have been one of the two furniture men. Yet both claimed that they had not entered the bedroom. And since they had been together in the apartment until the police arrived, the only alternative was that one of them had come to the apartment earlier in the day.

Kruger's upholstery shop was on Second Avenue; Lyons found the proprietor there alone. Asked where he had been on the morning of Good Friday, Theodore Kruger replied that he had spent the morning working in the shop.

"And your assistant?"

"Johnny was out until after lunch – he had to report to the parole officer in the morning."

"He has a criminal record?"

"Only for taking a car. Now he's turned over a new leaf – he's a good boy."

Outside, Lyons told his assistant: "Johnny Fiorenza claims he went to see his probation officer on Friday morning. But the office is closed on Good Friday. Keep a tail on him until further notice."

Back at headquarters, Lyons checked on Johnny Fiorenza's record; he had been arrested four times for theft, and spent two years in Elmira for car stealing. A psychiatrist who had examined him at the time of his first arrest had reported that he was a highly emotional individual. Fiorenza had been up to the Tittertons' apartment on two previous occasions, each time with his employer, so Nancy Titterton would know and trust him.

Then came the evidence Lyons needed. The piece of venetian blind cord had been manufactured by the Hanover Cordage Company of York, Pennsylvania, and a New York wholesaler had sold a roll of it to Theodore Kruger's upholstery shop.

Lyons ordered Johnny Fiorenza to be brought in to the office. For four and a half hours, the suspect was questioned, and continued to insist that he had not been near the Tittertons' apartment on the morning of Good Friday. Then the detective took out the length of venetian blind cord and dangled it in front of his eyes. "This is what convinced us you were in the apartment on Friday.morning. We've traced it back to the furniture shop."

Fiorenza began to sweat; then he allowed his head to slump into his hands. "All right. I guess I may as well tell you about it." His story bore out what Lyons had already guessed. When Fiorenza first called at the apartment, two months before, he had become instantly infatuated with the attractive authoress; with her charm and social poise, she seemed to be everything he had always wanted – and could never hope to attain. And when he and Kruger called to collect the love seat, on the day before Good Friday, he had decided that he had to possess her at all costs. The next morning, he had telephoned his employer to say that he had to see his probation officer. Instead he had gone to Beekman Place. When Nancy Titterton called "Who is it?" he answered: "The man about the love seat", and she let him in. As he had grabbed her, she shouted: "Dudley, oh Dudley!", but only the maid in the downstairs apartment heard her. Fiorenza had rammed a handkerchief into her mouth, tied her hands with cord, and pushed her into the bedroom . . .

The jury took very little time to arrive at a guilty verdict; a few weeks later, Johnny Fiorenza went to the electric chair in Sing Sing.

One mystery remains: why did he carry her into the shower? His story was that he was shocked to find that she had died of suffocation, and tried to revive her. But in that case, she would have identified him as the rapist, and he would have been sentenced to a long term in prison. It seems unlikely that he was prepared to allow this to happen, and the only alternative is that he went to the apartment with every intention of killing Nancy Titterton. Then why place her in the bath? There can be only one explanation: it was intended as an insurance policy against getting caught. It would support his story that her death was an accident, and help to convince a jury that he was guilty of manslaughter rather than murder. Johnny Fiorenza was clearly an exceptionally cunning and far-sighted criminal, and there seems no doubt that if he had not been betrayed by a horsehair, he would certainly, as Sherlock Holmes might have said, have gone far in his chosen profession.

The Mona Tinsley Case

On 5 January 1937 a ten-year-old girl named Mona Tinsley failed to return home from her school in Newark, Nottinghamshire. A neighbour of the Tinsley family reported seeing the ex-lodger, a man called Frederick Nodder, loitering near the school. Two other people said they had seen Mona with a middle-aged man near the bus station. Nodder, who was living in the village of Hayton, some twenty miles from Newark, denied all knowledge of the child, but he was taken into custody on a bastardy warrant. Nodder had, in fact, been introduced to the Tinsleys by Mrs. Tinsley's sister, with whom he was having an affair. A few days after his arrest, Nodder changed his story, and admitted that he had met Mona in Newark and taken her home with him. But he insisted that he had put her on a bus to Sheffield, where his mistress lived. Nodder was charged with abducting Mona Tinsley – in the absence of a body he could not be charged with murder – and sentenced to seven years in gaol.

A few days after Mona's disappearance, Estelle Roberts, one of the most celebrated mediums in England, offered to help the police. Mona's parents agreed, and the police sent her a pink silk dress that had belonged to Mona. In her autobiography,* Estelle Roberts writes: "As . . . I held the soft material in my hands, I knew that Mona was dead."

But having obtained this information through psychometry, the medium then – according to her own account – addressed Mona Tinsley directly, through the agency of her "control", a Red Indian called Red Cloud. The child told her that she had been taken to a house and strangled, and Estelle Roberts "saw" a small house, with a water-filled ditch on one side, a field behind, a graveyard nearby, and an inn not far away. She seemed to travel across fields to a river.

When she described the house to the Newark police, they were so impressed by her accuracy that they invited her to go there, and sent a police car to fetch her from the railway station. The house looked exactly as she had "seen" it. She was allowed to wander around inside, and in the back bedroom, sensed the child's presence, particularly near a water tank. She was able to tell the police that Mona had slept in the back bedroom, and learned that they had found a child's handkerchief in the water tank. Mona was strangled in the back bedroom. She had spent much of her time in the downstairs front room, copying something out of a book. The police had found scraps of paper with the child's writing on it. She added that after killing her, Nodder

* Fifty Years a Medium.

256

had left the house with the body by the side door. The police asked "Why not the front door?", and she admitted she had no idea. They told her that the front door had been permanently closed with screws.

She then led the police past the graveyard she had "seen", over a bridge and across the fields. She told them: "Beyond these fields there is a river. You will find the child's body there."

The police had already dragged the river without success. But they now had good reason for supposing that the body would be found in the river. In her introduction to the *Trial of Frederick Nodder*, Winifred Duke states: "A clairvoyant insisted that Mona Tinsley was dead and had appeared to her. The child declared that she had been strangled, her body placed in a sack, and then conveyed on wheels to the water and thrown in." Another medium told Mr. Tinsley that Mona would be found in the River Idle. The medium had tasted mud in her mouth. A third woman informed the Newark police that Mona's body would be recovered in water at a place thirty miles in a north-westerly direction from Newark, "close to an open meadow or pasture land, with tall trees lining the bank". It is not clear which of these three references is to Estelle Roberts.

In June 1937, a boating party on the River Idle noticed an object in the water, close to the bank; it proved to be Mona Tinsley's body, the head jammed in a drain below water level; the place corresponded closely to the medium's description. A sack with an odour of decaying flesh was found nearby. Nodder was tried a second time, and although he still strenuously denied killing Mona, he was sentenced to death.

Nodder's wife had left him because of his numerous infidelities. He was a heavy drinker, who had lost jobs through drunkenness. It seems probable that, while he had been a lodger in the Tinsleys' house (he had to leave after three weeks for non-payment of rent) he had developed a sexual obsession with Mona – there is some evidence that he was a paedophile. He may have been drinking heavily at the time he impulsively decided to meet her out of school and abduct her. What happened after that is uncertain; but at midday on the following day, a child was seen standing in the back doorway of Nodder's house. By the time it was dark, Mona was dead, and Nodder hurried across the fields towards the river, which was swollen with heavy rains. By nine o'clock he was in the local pub, drinking heavily. He returned home to find the police waiting.

C.W